The IFEEL Pictures

Clinical Infant Reports
Series of ZERO TO THREE/National Center
for Clinical Infant Programs

Editorial Board

Clinical Infant Reports is a series of book length publications of ZERO TO THREE/National Center for Clinical Infant Programs designed for practitioners in the multidisciplinary field of infant health, mental health, and development. Each volume presents diagnostic and therapeutic issues and methods, as well as conceptual and research material.

The IFEEL Pictures

A New Instrument for Interpreting Emotions

Editors

Robert N. Emde, M.D.
Joy D. Osofsky, Ph.D.
Perry M. Butterfield, M.A.

International Universities Press, Inc.
Madison • Connecticut

Library of Congress Cataloging in Publication Data

The IFEEL pictures : a new instrument for interpreting emotions / editors, Robert N. Emde, Joy D. Osofsky, Perry M. Butterfield.
  p. cm. — (Clinical infant reports series of the ZERO TO THREE/National Center for Clinical Infant Programs)
  Includes bibliographical references and indexes.
  ISBN 0-8236-2453-6
  1. IFEEL Pictures (Psychological test) 2. Mother and infant. 3. Emotions in infants. 4. Facial expression—Testing. 5. Face perception—Testing. 6. Mothers—Psychological testing. I. Emde, Robert N. II. Osofsky, Joy D. III. Butterfield, Perry M. 1932– . IV. Series: Clinical infant reports.
  [DNLM: 1. Emotions—in infancy & childhood. 2. Facial Expression—in infancy & childhood. 3. Pattern Recognition, Visual—physiology. WS 105.5.E5 I23]
  RJ507.P35I44 1993
  155.42′224′0287—dc20
  DNLM/DLC
  for Library of Congress   92-49134
                                                                              CIP

Manufactured in the United States of America

ZERO TO THREE/National Center for Clinical Infant Programs is a non-profit, tax-exempt corporation. It was established in 1977 by representatives from the fields of mental health, pediatrics, child development, and related fields, as well as community leaders, in order to improve and support professional initiatives in infant health, mental health, and development.

Contents

Contributors

Mark I. Appelbaum, Ph.D. Professor of Psychology, Vanderbilt University, Nashville, Tennessee.

Lynn C. Blackwood, Jr., Ph.D. Psychologist, Family Development Institute, Norfolk, Virginia.

Perry M. Butterfield, M.A. Research Associate, Department of Psychiatry, University of Colorado Health Sciences Center, Denver, Colorado.

Pamela M. Cole, Ph.D. Psychologist, National Institute of Mental Health, Bethesda, Maryland.

Anne M. Culp, Ph.D. Human Development Specialist, Corporate Extension Services, Oklahoma State University, Stillwater, Oklahoma.

Rex E. Culp, Ph.D., J.C. Professor and Head, Department of Family Relations and Child Development, Oklahoma State University, Stillwater, Oklahoma.

Susanne Denham, Ph.D. Psychologist, George Mason University, Fairfax, Virginia.

Martin Drell, M.D. Louisiana State University Medical Center, New Orleans, Louisiana.

Robert N. Emde, M.D. Professor of Psychiatry, University of Colorado Health Sciences Center, Denver, Colorado.

Chikako Fukatsu Keio University, Tokyo, Japan.

Yoko Hamada Keio University, Tokyo, Japan.

Della M. Hann, Ph.D. Personality and Social Processes Branch, National Institute of Mental Health, Rockville, Maryland.

Kako Inoue Tokyo Metropolitan University, Tokyo, Japan.

Ellen Kveton, Psy.D. Private Practice, Tidewater, Virginia.

Ann Lodge, Ph.D. Psychologist, Family Resource Development Center, Chesapeake, Virginia.

Margaret McDowell, B.A. Family Resource Development Center, Chesapeake, Virginia.

Keigo Okonogi, M.D. Professor of Psychiatry, Keio University, Tokyo, Japan.

Joy D. Osofsky, Ph.D. Professor of Pediatrics and Psychiatry, Division of Infant, Child and Adolescent Psychiatry, Louisiana State University Medical Center, New Orleans, Louisiana.

Doreen Ridgeway, Ph.D. Psychologist, Water Mill, New York.

Alan Rountree, Psy.D. Department of Psychiatry and Behavioral Science, Eastern Virginia Medical School, Norfolk, Virginia.

Jarmila Skrinjaric, M.D. Professor of Psychiatry, "Rebro," Zegreb, Yugoslavia.

Nathan Szajnberg, M.D. Director, Child and Adolescent Psychiatry, Children's Hospital, Medical College, Milwaukee, Wisconsin.

Toshiko Takiguchi St. Margaret's Junior College, Minneapolis, Minnesota.

Barbara Usher, B.A. Researcher, National Institute of Mental Health, Bethesda, Maryland.

Elizabeth Wagner, B.A. Researcher, National Institute of Mental Health, Bethesda, Maryland.

Carolyn Zahn-Waxler, Ph.D. Laboratory of Developmental Psychology, National Institute of Mental Health, Bethesda, Maryland.

Preface

This book introduces a new research tool, Infant Facial Expressions of Emotion from Looking at Pictures (IFEEL Pictures). The initial chapters describe the basic technique, its background, and psychometric development. The subsequent chapters offer results from a variety of research studies in which investigators have used the IFEEL Pictures in different settings. The final chapters discuss the basic technique and a number of modified versions in the light of evolving methods for probing emotional processes in the infant's caregiving environment.

The IFEEL Pictures began as a by-product of work on infant facial expressions of emotion that included an interest in their development, their variations, and their communicative value for caregivers. As we assembled pictures of infants, we soon realized we had the makings of a promising procedure for exploring the ways in which parents and others "read" and interpret infant emotions. Since emotional expressions could be thought of as the language of infancy, and important for caregiving, perhaps a technique for exploring caregiver responses to standard infant pictures could be useful for researchers interested in exploring variations in caregiving. Perhaps such a technique could eventually prove useful in clinical settings, where the early identification of problems in caregiving could lead to understanding and to appropriate intervention.

A number of investigators (many of whom are represented in the current volume) became intrigued with the research potential of the IFEEL Pictures and began using them in studies. Some helped in expanding our reference sample of normal maternal responses; others helped in exploring the meaning of responses by comparing them with other measures; still others engaged in comparisons between groups of subjects. The technique had an appealing amount of face validity and all agreed that methods for measuring emotions and emotional availability of caregivers were badly needed, both for basic research and for studies of populations at risk. But caution was required from the outset. We realized that the meaning of picture interpretations needed to be explored and the technique itself needed to evolve into a manageable and convenient form. Time was required to see if the technique would be useful to more than a handful of researchers. Above all, we wished to avoid premature and unwarranted assumptions concerning the meaning of responses for normative processes, individual differences, and risk for pathology. For these reasons, although early versions of the IFEEL Pictures have been available since the late 1970s, we have refrained from prior publication and the current book contains the first reports launching the technique. Collaborators using the IFEEL Pictures became united in their resolve to delay publication so that the presentation of the technique could be as coherent and full as its current state of evolution permitted. The IFEEL Pictures represent a research instrument that is still in an early phase of development; however, the chapters in this volume document the instrument's usefulness. Adding to the timeliness of publication, we now have a bound standardized picture set and a computer-assisted scoring program available from the editors (see chapters 4 and 5 and appendix A-5 for details).

The book is organized into five sections.

Section I provides theoretical background. The reader whose primary interest is in using the IFEEL Pictures and who is familiar with recent research on emotional expressions and development, may wish to skip this section. The section arose in response to many users' requests and from our belief that in order to understand both the limitations and the potential of the technique, the reader needed to be aware of its rationale in the context of recent scientific views of emotion, infant development, and the caregiving environment.

Section II provides information relevant for understanding the methodology of the IFEEL Pictures. The collaborative history of the technique describes the evolution from earlier versions to the current version and the reasons for change. The current version is then described, along with its recommended use. A discussion of the operating characteristics and psychometric properties of the instrument, as well as a presentation of validation studies follows. An important point to be made, even in our Preface, is that although we believe results using the IFEEL Pictures offer a key to some important processes in their deviations, the technique has not yet been standardized for individual differences research.

Section III presents four studies of group comparisons. In addition to normative samples of mothers, the IFEEL Pictures have been used in the study of adolescent mothers, mothers at risk for child maltreatment, depressed mothers, and mothers of premature infants. Results, while promising, are best regarded as preliminary, and the reader will need to study the populations that are of particular interest.

Section IV deals with modifications of the IFEEL Pictures and related uses of pictures of infant emotions. Since this mode of assessment is still evolving, the section offers the reader additional ideas and incentives for gathering research and clinical information.

Finally, in Section V, we look ahead by addressing research needs in the context of clinical implications.

We wish to acknowledge the help, encouragement, and patience of many. First and foremost, the editors would like to acknowledge the goodwill of the authors, many of whom could have gained earlier publication of their separate contribution using the IFEEL Pictures. A special thanks goes to Mark Appelbaum, whose methodological contributions went well beyond the single chapter that bears his name. Shirley Speller, our able Word Processing Operator, managed all our manuscripts, providing assistance in matters of formatting, style, references, and organization, with an enthusiasm and diligence that is much appreciated. We would also like to thank Stanley Greenspan of the National Center of Clinical Infant Programs' Publication Committee and Martin Azarian and Margaret Emery of International Universities Press for their encouragement and assistance.

We are grateful for the financial support from several sources: Laurence P. McArthur for special project support, enabling us to print the IFEEL Pictures; the John D. and Catherine T. MacArthur Foundation for enabling collaborative linkages; and the National Institute of Mental Health for funding the work of two of the editor–investigators (NIMH project grant #MH22803 and Research Scientist Award #5K02MH36808 for Robert N. Emde, and NIMH project grants #MH36895 and #MH39487 for Joy D. Osofsky).

Part I:
Theoretical Background

1

A Framework for Viewing Emotions

Robert N. Emde

The IFEEL Pictures ask parents and others for their views of emotions. The technique then systematically organizes such views and provides a basis for comparison with views of others collected under similar circumstances. People tell us their views in practical everyday terms such as: "scared," "fascinated," and "cheerful." As researchers and clinicians, however, our views need to be stated in more abstract, theoretical terms. We need to orient our views by taking into account the best state of our knowledge and thinking and, to do this, we often need to state what we know in broad, general terms. This chapter offers a framework for viewing infant emotions in such terms. A good deal of recent research can be integrated in this manner and a theoretical background can be established for interpreting responses of particular individuals or groups, using the IFEEL Pictures.

A historical perspective is informative. Emotions have been viewed as central in human psychological functioning throughout recorded history. Aristotle saw emotions as comprising one of the domains in a tripartite system of cognition, emotion, and motivation. A brief but dramatic period in recent history, however, provided an alternative view to that of emotion centrality. During the first fifty years of the twentieth century, psychology was preoccupied with a stimulus-response model of the mind. Information was viewed as flowing in one direction and the processing of information took place along a line leading toward response. Emotions were not considered central or helpful but instead as disruptive states that were intermittent and reactive to certain classes of stimuli (either external or drive-related). Emotions were regarded as secondary and even as epiphenomenal. Such a model predominated in both theories of learning and psychoanalysis, as has been reviewed previously (Emde, 1989). Since mid-century, however, a different view has emerged as a result of newer cognitive and biological approaches. The new view seems closer to the ancient one in that there is now consensus that emotions are central. From an adaptational standpoint, emotions are recognized to be an important part of everyday human functioning for which our evolutionary biology has prepared us. Emotions are helpful, in other words, for individuals who are engaged in a process of communicating and "fitting in" with an environment of others. Today's model of the mind is not a linear one based on a passive stimulus–response sequence, but instead is a dynamic one based on organized interactions. Ongoing activity is considered the sine qua non of life and development. Instead of being considered disruptive, intermittent, and reactive states, emotions are thought of as adaptive, active, and ongoing processes.

Emotions in infancy are highly organized, ongoing processes, according to this view. Among their other functions, they are biologically prepared communication signals that help infants and caregivers in the process of adaptation and "fitting together." They also have a major role in facilitating development within the family environment and its particular culture. This brings us to some necessary considerations about development.

Infant Emotions within a Developmental Systems Orientation

A set of principles has emerged from recent research which can guide our thinking about emotional signals and their use in infancy. These principles underlie what we have referred to above as the newer organizational model of the mind. More specifically, they deal with what might also be called a developmental systems orientation with respect to emotions. They give us a "map" for interpreting infant emotional expressions according to what we know about emotions in mental functioning and in development; they also point to the importance of such expressions in the sharing of experience and in caregiver availability.

The first principle is, quite simply, that emotions are inseparable from other aspects of mental functioning. If we think of the ancient tripartite view of the mind, we could apply this principle by saying that no emotion is without a cognitive or motivational aspect. Different views of emotion may therefore depend upon one's "window" or angle of perspective and this will necessarily give more or less of a cognitive or motivational coloration. Today's scientists would also give emphasis to another aspect of mental functioning of major significance for emotions, namely, the expressive–communicative aspect. Indeed, one could array a continuum of functions for emotions, as Hinde (1985) has suggested, with motivational and communicative functions anchoring each end of the proposed continuum and with cognitive functions intertwining throughout. Why are these considerations important to us? In interpreting emotion communications, whether in everyday life or in using the IFEEL Pictures, one expects to encounter varying degrees of "purity" of emotions like anger, fear, or surprise. Correspondingly, one would expect to see varying degrees of cognitive understanding, mobilization for action, and communicative intent in any particular emotional expression.

A second principle is that human emotions are biologically prepared for communication at birth and undergo development. The newborn's emotions are already organized and structured for adaptive functioning as a result of our evolutionary heritage, such that experience is monitored and motivated according to what is pleasurable or not pleasurable. But, even more important, the young infant is organized to send emotional signals to caregivers that will indicate states of need, satisfaction, degree of arousal, and degree of openness to new experience. To bring this to mind, we need merely to think of the difference in our probable responses to the crying infant, the bright-eyed alert infant, and the smiling infant. We might also think of our responses to the quiet, peaceful-looking infant who is sleeping versus the whimpering, frowning infant who seemingly cannot get to sleep.

Infant emotions develop over time and provide a universal set of guides for caregiving. In earliest infancy, emotions are keyed primarily to express distress and pleasure, along with varying degrees of interest and arousal. By six postnatal months, discrete patterned emotions of joy, surprise, anger, fear, sadness, disgust, and interest develop and are used as signals in caregiving (Emde, 1980; Izard, Huebner, Risser, McGinnes, and Dougherty, 1980). These are the categorized emotions that are used in scoring the IFEEL Pictures. They are expressed in infancy and continue as a core aspect of self and signaling throughout life (Emde, 1983). With advancing development, the communication of emotions becomes increasingly more complex and subtle, with verbal as well as nonverbal signaling, and with blended, conflicting, and sequential emotions assuming more importance.

The development of emotions shows the influence of both maturational factors (wherein we can describe an expectable age-related normative progression) and social learning (wherein we can describe an increasing influence of individual experience in the family environment). Although hereditary factors continue to influence the timing and style of emotional development (Plomin, 1986), learning factors consequent upon individual caregiving relationship experiences will assume increasing importance for the child's emotional experience and communication. Again, the reader might ask: Why is this important in thinking about the techniques and results presented in this book? The answer is twofold: First, it means that in interpreting the emotional communications of infants there will be both normative regularities, presumably representing a basic core of adaptational functions, and individual variation, representing the uniqueness of the caregiving environment. Second, it means that the caregiver's individual emotional life will have developed along individual lines so as to make important contributions to the interpretive process.

This brings us to a third principle: Emotions are an abstraction that must be anchored in individual experience; moreover in infancy they must be anchored in individual, shared experience. Emotions are a construct. They cannot be reified by being thought of as isomorphic or identical with particular facial expressions, voice qualities, physiological patterns or words. In a similar vein, they cannot be thought of in static terms since they are coherent sequential experiences over time, usually occurring over a matter of seconds. At the neurophysiological level, the coherence of emotions can be thought of as organized in the central nervous system. At the psychological level the coherence of emotions can be thought of as organized in the course of individual experience. Each individual actively pulls together or freshly "constructs" the meaning of each emotion using particular memories and expectations. At the interpersonal level, the coherence of emotions is organized in the context of shared meaning with others. Interestingly, we know through empathy and emotional communications that some emotions are universal; these "Darwinian" emotions, as we have mentioned, are strongly biologically prepared and in their direct form, they are communicated clearly (Darwin, 1872). There is a universal basis, therefore, for shared meaning. But most emotions are less constrained by our common biology and are more complex. They are not universal, and are learned in the course of individual development within the context of human relationships.

According to this principle, infancy experience is special. The construction of emotional experience occurs in a shared emotional responsive environment provided by the caregiver. Early basic emotions are fine-tuned by the infant's experience with the caregiver. One might say that early infant emotions become exercised and coherent in this way and that a common sense about feelings and their regularities becomes established. The subtleties of individual experience can then come into play as these emotions are blended, compounded, and otherwise included in the stream of mental life. Emotions developing in later infancy and toddlerhood show more direct influence from internalized experiences occurring within the infant–caregiver relationship. The world of shared meaning and of "intersubjectivity" with the caregiver determines what the infant is proud of, ashamed about, shares positive emotion about, or about which he expresses hurt feelings. The implications of this principle for the reader of this book are clear. In interpreting the meaning of emotional communications in infancy, we must be concerned with their dyadic shared nature and connect them to the infant–caregiver relationship experience.

This brings us to a fourth principle. The emotional availability of the caregiver is important for the infant's development. That the caregiver must not only be physically available but also emotionally available for the child's optimal functioning has been shown by a substantial amount of research and has been included in clinically related theories of early development (Bowlby, 1969; Mahler, Pine, and Bergman, 1975; Emde, 1983). The discussion of the prior principles buttresses the fourth principle in indicating that a considerable amount of the infant's emotional life is dependent on basic emotions becoming exercised and fine-tuned with the caregiver and on more complex emotions developing from a basis of shared meaning with the caregiver and others. Again, there are implications for our interests. Significant variations in interpreting infant emotional communications on the part of caregivers may be connected to variations in emotional availability. These in turn may reflect on the kinds of emotions that are exercised and internalized by infants.

Contrasting Views of Emotions: Dimensions versus Categories; Early Development versus Later Development

Two sets of contrasting views about emotions are directly relevant to the IFEEL Pictures. These contrasting views have heretofore been manifest in different literatures, used different terms, and, in a very real sense, have represented different "truths" about emotion. The IFEEL Pictures are a mode of inquiry which seeks to tap all of these domains of truth. The summary of contrasting views presented below is offered so that the reader can make full use of the opportunities provided by the IFEEL Pictures for an integrated understanding.

The first contrast is between emotional signals viewed as dimensions versus emotional signals viewed as categories. Although the IFEEL Pictures technique focuses on emotions as categories (such as joy, sadness, and surprise), one could readily say that the most rudimentary view is a dimensional one. According to this view, emotions are seen most prominently on a dimension going from pleasure to nonpleasure. They are also seen on a dimension going from low to high arousal (or activation). Some dimensional views include a third dimension which may be labeled as going from internally oriented to externally oriented, from acceptance to rejection, or from low to high control.

The dimensional literature reflecting studies of emotion is a rich one, and there is a striking amount of consensus. Not only are the dimensions mentioned above seen in the early, more philosophical theories of psychology (Spencer, 1890; Wundt, 1896, as quoted in Izard, 1971; Freud, 1915) but they are seen in later measurement-based approaches, including factor analytic measures, semantic differential measures, and multidimensional scaling measures (Abelson and Sermat, 1962; Gladstone, 1962; Frijda and Philipszoon, 1963; Osgood, 1966; Frijda, 1970). Moreover, the empirical work in adults has now been supplemented by studies in infants (Emde, Kligman, Reich, and Wade, 1978; Emde, 1980a) and in school-aged children (Russell and Ridgeway, 1983) where a similar organization has been found for emotional expressions. At whatever age, the most prominent dimension found is that of hedonic tone, the next most prominent is that of arousal, and a third dimension is sometimes but not always seen, and is variously labeled if seen. The third dimension seems likely to be a product of one's "window" or vantage point into the emotion system rather than a central aspect of emotions per se. Thus, some investigators have seen "control" (Osgood, 1966), others "attention–rejection" (Woodworth and Schlosberg, 1954), and others internally oriented/externally oriented (Emde et al., 1978).

Categorical views of emotion deal with basic patterns, configurations or "syndromes" of behavior and experience. Charles Darwin, more than a hundred years ago, pointed to a number of basic categories of emotion that had evolved in the human in an organized patterned fashion (Darwin, 1872). Each category of emotion served a set of species-important adaptive functions; these functions included mobilizing for action and signaling others about one's state and probable or intended actions. Silvan Tomkins (1962, 1963) revived Darwin's theory, which had not received much serious attention during the first half of the century when drive-reduction and stimulus-response (S-R) models of the mind prevailed. Consistent with an emerging organizational model, Tomkins put Darwin's categories of emotion (e.g., joy, surprise, anger, fear, sadness, disgust, interest, and others) front-and-center in a theory of adaptive mental functioning and brought together an array of biological and cross-cultural propositions. Tomkins's work also gave rise to two independent teams of investigators who tested the species-wide universality for the categories of emotional expression. Cross-cultural research by Ekman and his colleagues (Ekman, Sorenson, and Friesen, 1969; Ekman, Friesen, and Ellsworth, 1972), and by Izard (1971) was dramatic in providing convergent evidence for the universality of facial patterns of emotion including the above-mentioned joy, surprise, anger, fear, sadness, disgust and, to a lesser extent, interest. The findings of universality held for both recognition and expression of these emotions. In addition, it held for nonwestern as well as western cultures and for nonliterate as well as literate cultures.

It is no exaggeration to say that this work inaugurated the contemporary era of empirical emotion study. The Ekman and Izard cross-cultural work in adults clearly implied evidence of biological patterning for the Darwinian emotion categories. Subsequent research has accumulated evidence for a coherence of patterning of these categories in channels other than facial expressions, namely, in voice (Scherer, 1982), and in the autonomic nervous system as well as the verbal expressions of feelings·(Ekman, Levenson, and Friesen, 1983). A coherence across channels of expression according to emotion category has also been documented (Ekman et al., 1983) and measurement advances have taken place in each channel (Izard, 1982; Scherer and Ekman, 1984). It is now possible to specify, for example, the muscle action unit parameters for each facial expression of an emotion category (Ekman and Friesen, 1978). Because of this specification, carefully conducted emotion manipulations can take place in experimental studies and categories of emotion signals can be analyzed for clarity and blending of multiple emotions (Izard, 1980). As was the case for the dimensions of emotion organization, research has now established that the Darwinian categories of emotion organization are present in infancy, are reliably recognized by caregivers, and are used in caregiving (Izard et al., 1980; Emde, 1980).

The dimensional and categorical views of emotion cut across all other views of emotion and they are usually thought to be measurement-dependent. Whether one view or another is taken becomes partly a matter of what one can measure, and one's style of research as well as one's theory. Typically, researchers have used one view or the other, but these different views are not competing. Indeed, the separate categories of emotion should be identifiable to a researcher as clusters represented in a generated two- or a three-dimensional theoretical space of emotions.

Earlier approaches to this kind of integrative mapping, using both emotion categories and dimensions, were set forth by Emde et al. (1978) and by Russell and Ridgeway (1983). This has led us to a significant advance in scoring that we have been able to incorporate in the IFEEL Pictures. Both categories and dimensions of emotion can be obtained from verbal responses of subjects using our method. As the reader will see in chapters 4 and 6, one of the forms of validation for emotion categories within the IFEEL Lexicon involved such a dimensional space approach. As a result of this validation study, we now have an empirically based set of dimensional values, as well as category designations for a vast set of emotion words. Ways of meaningfully displaying an individual's responses according to categories of emotion, and dimensions of emotion are discussed further in chapter 4.

A second set of contrasting views concerns early versus later development. While there could be many different developmental views of emotion according to how often one chooses to sample across the life span, two early childhood views are noteworthy because they are portrayed so often. These views distinguish between the nonverbal (or preverbal) and the verbal. The verbal domain of emotion expression, by definition, comes at the end of infancy (i.e., etymologically infancy comes from the Latin word *infans*, without language). Language adds shades and subtleties to emotion expression and many researchers believe its onset represents a sharp discontinuity in the child's experience. What is shared, jointly constructed, and communicated is somehow separated from what is privately felt and not communicated through language (Winnicott, 1965; Bowlby, 1973; Stern, 1985). Whether this is true or not, language introduces a new level of complexity to emotion organization and it will now supplement the nonverbal level, generating an abundance of culturally relevant, socialized, and idiosyncratic variations in emotion communication. The reader of this volume will come to appreciate that the IFEEL Pictures are geared to explore the rich variations of verbal free responses of caregivers and others who interact with infants. Variations amongst those who interact with infants will influence what is expressed and what is experienced.

Earlier we discussed the principles underlying a developmental systems orientation for viewing emotion. Now we will turn to this orientation to help us think about the meaning of emotional communications in infancy. Happily, we will find that it not only integrates research, but it leads us to a unified view.

Let us review what is known. Developmental theorists from a variety of traditions have described that the infant, prior to 3 months, communicates emotion according to a primary differentiation of distress and pleasure (Bridges, 1932; Spitz, 1965; Sroufe, 1979). Empirical research has provided ample confirmation of this proposition, both from the vantage point of direct measurement of infant expressions and caregiver communications. In addition, some researchers have characterized the young infant's emotional expression in terms of a differentiation of arousal states. Brazelton, Koslowski, and Main (1974) and Tronick (1980) have demonstrated that regulation of high versus low arousal states is a crucial aspect for both affective communication and the newborn's behavioral assessment (Brazelton, 1973; Brazelton, Als, Tronick, and Lester, 1979). By the time the infant is 6 to 8 months, there is general agreement that expressions of emotions include more than arousal states or distress and pleasure. The Darwinian categories are evident; these include joy, surprise, anger, fear, sadness, disgust, and interest. Researchers disagree about the age of onset for these categories of emotion, but disagreement has more to do with what is acceptable inference than what is observed. Some cite evidence for a much earlier appearance of these expressions or their elements (Oster and Ekman, 1978; Field and Walden, 1983), while others demand that to be considered theoretically significant such emotion expressions should be prominent, coherent, linked to situational events, and meaningful to caregivers (Emde, 1980; Campos, Barrett, Lamb, Goldsmith, and Stenberg, 1983). There is a consensus among researchers, however, that by the middle of the first year, each of these emotional expressions can be seen to be linked to a coherent incentive situation, a patterned action tendency, and meaningful communication. Consistent with the emotions that develop earlier, the Darwinian categories of emotion show a universality of fundamental patterning and coherence; variations are relatively minor in comparison with the more complex emotions that develop later. During the latter part of the first year and the second year of life more complex emotions are added. These grow out of the infant's experience within the caregiving relationship. Some are linked to specific relationships (e.g., love-secure attachment, avoidance-anxiety, withdrawal-depression); others are linked to the sharing of expectable situations and contexts (e.g., positive affect sharing, pride, shame, "hurt feelings expression"). During the third and fourth years still more complex emotions are added by virtue of the onset of language and the child's representations of family affective themes and role relationships (e.g., feeling left out and lonely, the beginnings of guilt, ambition, resentment, and envy). Co-construction of emotion by means of language labeling, discussion, and negotiation with others can also take place.

A Unified View Using Cognitive and Motivational Windows

Now let us return to the issue of multiple views. A developmental systems orientation makes use of multiple theoretical views in order to give meaning to the developmental data we have just summarized. Let us recall the underlying principle of inseparability of emotions from other mental functions. Cognition and motivation, the other interacting systems of the mind can, in fact, provide us with windows from which to view early emotional development. They will also give us a background for parental interpretations of infant emotions as we think about IFEEL Picture responses. What follows below is a discussion of the view from each of these windows.

First from the cognitive window. In a masterful review of emotional development, Campos et al. (1983) summarized findings under the headings of seven summarizing postulates. Two of these are not primarily cognitive, namely, that there is a core set of emotion states present throughout the life span and that emotions become socialized. But the other summarizing postulates are from the view provided by the cognitive window. These include the following: (1) that as cognitive development proceeds, new goals appear and complex intercoordinated emotions become evident; (2) that the influence of elicited circumstances changes; (3) that the relationship between emotional expression and emotional experience changes across development; (4) that coping responses to emotions change; and (5) that receptivity to others' emotional expressions change. Most theorists would agree that cognitive aspects of emotion processes include appraisal of the incentive situation, the perceived ability to cope with change, and the organization of plans. Many would also include self-monitoring and emotion labeling as significant (Arnold, 1960; Izard, 1977; Fischer, Shaver, and Carnochan, 1990). Fischer and colleagues have recently proposed a scheme in which a cognitive window accounts for the early sequential development of emotions. The problem as they see it is how the organization of emotion (and cognition) develops from an initial foundation of early basic and universal emotions to more advanced levels of sophisticated and socially constructed emotions. In their scheme they discuss a hierarchy of emotion categories with three levels. What they refer to as the "basic categories" of emotion comprise a middle level in infancy and include a set of emotions that are more or less similar to the Darwinian categories. Basic categories are ones that people agree upon most easily and they are used in everyday discourse. These emotions are universal across human cultures, present in infancy, and generally correspond to the first emotion terms learned by children as they acquire language. In thinking about emotion categories, one is helped by a prototype model elaborated by Rosch (1978). According to this model, categories in the middle of a proposed hierarchy of at least three levels are considered "basic." A superordinate category integrates across basic categories. Fischer et al. (1990) proposed that the basic category level for emotions corresponds to the Darwinian categories. The superordinate category level for early emotional development consists of the positive–negative distinction (i.e., pleasure vs. distress, possibly later becoming an evaluative distinction between good and bad). Subordinate category emotions then involve a third level; these include more specific forms of the basic category emotions and, according to Fischer et al., they develop later, making use of specific contexts and social definitions. The prototype model not only specifies a hierarchical organization of categories, but also specifies that each basic category must be defined in terms of a "best instance" or a prototype that characterizes its central aspect. People generally agree about central aspects of a prototype. This agreement is presumed to be the case with respect to the Darwinian emotions if one collects typical accounts of emotional experiences or events from adults or children. Indeed, following Tomkins (1978), the prototypes of basic categories of emotions can be described in terms of scripts. After infancy, emotion scripts involve increasingly complex cognitive processes. They contain an integration of sequences of appraisals, action tendencies, and representations of self and others, and they often occur along socially constructed modes. A strong point made by the scheme proposed by Fischer et al. is that it integrates evidence wherein certain universal fundamental emotional patterns are evident from early infancy and other more sophisticated complex emotional patterns show cultural relativity, a strong degree of experiential variation, and appear later in development.

Now we come to a motivational window. When one looks at motivations from a developmental systems orientation, one sees a strong biological preparation. The infant is born already "preprogrammed," to use our contemporary computer metaphor, by biological evolution. The infant is active, self-regulating, and has "built-in" motives and structures for social-fittedness, for affective monitoring, and for exploring and learning about the world (cognitive assimilation). These properties have been described elsewhere according to a theory of basic motives of infancy that appear early and are present throughout the life span (Emde, 1988, 1990; Emde, Biringen, Clyman, and Oppenheim, 1991). They are built upon universal, species-wide processes which have become structured through evolution. In an individual's ontogeny, they become exercised and fine-tuned in the context of experience within the early caregiver relationship. The theory of affective monitoring, one of the basic motives, provides another unified view that integrates what we described earlier as contrasting views of emotion. The active, self-regulating social human being from the start of postnatal life monitors experience according to what is pleasurable or not (i.e., according to dimensions of experience). Later, in the first year, the infant comes to monitor experience according to basic categories of emotion (e.g., anger, joy, surprise, fear) and to seek guidance for action from emotional expressions of others if confronted by situations of uncertainty. In other words, the infant increasingly uses emotional communication to resolve uncertainty and regulate behavior accordingly. During the second year, emotional communications, especially those that involve exchanges of mixed and blended expressions, are used in negotiating circumstances of prohibition and safety during exploration. Emotion exchanges during the second and third years increasingly involve an integration of meanings expressed in words, as well as face and voice.

Affective monitoring is a central integrative process in the motivational window of infant development. It becomes a basis for internalizing rules about reciprocity, standards, and empathy with caregivers and others. It continues as central in negotiations of shared meaning with others, about what is expected, what is valued, and what is desired. Indeed, there is every reason to believe that affective monitoring continues as a central mediator in new motivational structures that regulate self in relation to other and the individual's sense of "we" (Emde, 1988; Emde and Buchsbaum, 1990). Such considerations therefore fuel our interests in assessing the variations in affective monitoring and interpretation of signals.

Summary and Conclusion

The IFEEL Pictures array adult interpretations of a standard set of infant expressions. This chapter provides a theoretical background for thinking about such interpretations and for thinking about emotions in infancy.

The theory we have reviewed is based on recent research in normal development and is guided by a developmental systems orientation. A number of principles have been enumerated. First, emotions necessarily include

other interacting aspects of mental functioning, such as
cognition and motivation. Second, emotions are strongly
biologically prepared (i.e., preprogrammed for functioning by our evolutionary heritage) and also develop in law-
ful ways gaining increasing complexity as a result of both
maturation and learning. Third, emotions in general are
a construct and must be anchored in individual, shared
experience, wherein coherence and organization is provided the infant by accumulated interactions with the caregiver. Fourth, emotional availability of the caregiver is important for the infant's development.

Contrasting views of emotions previously led to different theoretical generalizations that have summarized differing kinds of research. Thus, our knowledge includes
agreed-upon research generalizations about the ways in
which infant emotions can be organized according to dimensions (pleasure–unpleasure and arousal) and according to categories or patterns (e.g., fear, joy, anger,
and surprise). Our knowledge also includes agreed-upon
research generalizations about the ways in which infant
emotions develop. Research generalizations about early infancy involve nonverbal emotional communications and
those about later development involve language.

The chapter has also reviewed how the state of our
knowledge is such that we can now integrate these views.
The developmental systems orientation enables us to
achieve a theoretical background that provides such an
integration. Cognition and motivation, other interacting
systems of mental functioning, can provide us with "windows" from which we can gain a unified view of early
emotional development.

From a cognitive "window," the schemes provided by
the Campos and Fischer groups are ones that link early
and later development and that integrate the Darwinian
approaches of emotion categories in infancy with dimensional approaches. They also provide a basis for linking

infant emotions to the later world of adult emotions, involving complex goals, scripts, and cultural variations. From a motivational "window" the scheme provided by the author and his group has also unified the contrasting views of emotion. The basic self-regulating and social-exploratory activity of the infant also includes motivational structures for affective monitoring. Emotional experience, and expressions of that experience, that are at first largely dimensional are soon supplemented by categories of patterned emotion expression and experience; these can be "mapped" on the former. Emotional development in infancy, from the motivational window, is seen as the development of shared meaning. Rules guiding reciprocity, empathy, and the internalization of prohibitions and standards result from emotional exchanges between infant and caregiver. In the course of such experiences, adult and verbal communications involving emotion are linked to nonverbal ones.

The IFEEL Pictures provide us with a practical new method that taps all four views of emotional communication (dimensional, categorical, nonverbal, and verbal). It is hoped that its use will be enhanced by the theories that integrate these views.

References

Abelson, R. P., & Sermat, V. (1962), Multidimensional scaling of facial expressions. *J. Experiment. Psychol.*, 63:546–554.

Arnold, M. (1960), *Emotion and Personality*, Vols. 1–2. New York: Columbia University Press.

Bowlby, J. (1969), *Attachment and Loss*, Vol. 1. New York: Basic Books.

——— (1973), *Attachment and Loss*, Vol. 2. New York: Basic Books.

Brazelton, T. B. (1973), *Neonatal Behavior Assessment Scale*. Philadelphia: J. B. Lippincott.

———— Als, H., Tronick, E., & Lester, B. (1979), Specific neonatal measures: The Brazelton neonatal behavior assessment scale. In: *Handbook of Infant Development*, ed. J. Osofsky. New York: John Wiley.

———— Koslowski, B., & Main, M. (1974), The origins of reciprocity: The early mother–infant interaction. In: *The Effect of the Infant on Its Caregiver*, Vol. 1, ed. M. Lewis & L. Rosenblum. New York: Wiley-Intersciences, pp. 49–76.

Bridges, K. M. B. (1932), Emotional development in early infancy. *Child Develop.*, 3:324–341.

Campos, J. J., Barrett, K. D., Lamb, M. E., Goldsmith, H. H., & Stenberg, C. (1983), Socioemotional development. In: *Handbook of Child Psychology*, Vol. 2, ed. M. Haith & J. J. Campos. New York: John Wiley, pp. 783–915.

Darwin, C. (1872), *The Expression of Emotions in Man and Animals.* Chicago: University of Chicago Press, 1965.

Ekman, P., & Friesen, W. V. (1978), *Facial Action Coding System.* Palo Alto, CA: Palo Alto Consulting Psychologists Press.

———— ———— Ellsworth, P. (1972), *Emotion in the Human Face.* New York: Pergamon Press.

———— Levenson, R. W., & Friesen, W. V. (1983), Autonomic nervous system activity distinguished among emotions. *Science*, 221:1208–1210.

———— Sorenson, E., & Friesen, W. (1969), Pan-cultural elements in facial displays of emotion. *Science*, 164:86–88.

Emde, R. N. (1980), Levels of meaning for infant emotions: A biosocial view. In: *Development of Cognition, Affect and Social Relations. Minnesota Symposia on Child Psychology*, Vol. 13, ed. W. A. Collins. Hillsdale, NJ: Lawrence Erlbaum Associates, pp. 1–37.

———— (1983), The prerepresentational self and its affective core. *The Psychoanalytic Study of the Child*, 38:165–192. New Haven, CT: Yale University Press.

———— (1988), Development terminable and interminable: I. Innate and motivational factors from infancy. *Internat. J. Psycho-Anal.*, 69:23–42.

———— (1989), Toward a psychoanalytic theory of affect: I. The organizational model and its propositions. In: *The Course of Life*, Vol. 1, rev. ed., ed. S. I. Greenspan & G. H. Pollock. Madison, CT: International Universities Press.

———— (1990), *Presidential Address*: Lessons from infancy: New beginnings in a changing world and a morality for health. *Infant Ment. Health J.*, 11/3:196–212.

———— Biringen, Z., Clyman, R. B., Oppenheim, D. (1991), The moral self of infancy: Affective core and procedural knowledge. *Develop. Rev.*, 11.

———— Buchsbaum, H. K. (1990), "Didn't you hear my mommy?" Autonomy *with* connectedness in moral self emergence. In: *Development of the Self Through the Transition*, ed. D. Cicchetti & M. Beeghly. Chicago: University of Chicago Press.

———— Kligman, D. H., Reich, J. H., & Wade, T. D. (1978), Emotional expression in infancy: I. Initial studies of social signaling and an emergent model. In: *The Development of Affect*, ed. M. Lewis & L. Rosenblum. New York: Plenum, pp. 125–148.

Field, T., & Walden, T. (1983), Perception and production of facial expressions in infancy and early childhood. In: *Advances in Child Development and Behavior*, Vol. 16, ed. H. Reese & L. Lipsitt. New York: Academic Press.

Fischer, K. W., Shaver, P., & Carnochan, P. (1990), How emotions develop and how they organize development. *Cognit. & Emot.*, 4:81–127.

Freud, S. (1915), Instincts and their vicissitudes. *Standard Edition*, 14:109–117. London: Hogarth Press, 1957.

Frijda, N. (1970), Emotion and recognition of emotion. In: *Feelings and Emotions*, ed. M. B. Arnold. New York: Academic Press.

———— Philipszoon, E. (1963), Dimensions of recognition of expression. *J. Abnorm. & Soc. Psychol.*, 66:45–51.

Gladstone, W. H. (1962), A multidimensional study of facial expression of emotion. *Austral. J. Psychol.*, 14:19–100.

Hinde, R. A. (1985), Was "The expression of the emotions" a misleading phrase? *Animal Behavior*, 33:985–992.

Izard, C. (1971), *The Face of Emotion*. New York: Meredith & Appleton-Century Crofts.

―――― (1977), *Human Emotions*. New York: Plenum.

―――― (1980), *Maximally Discriminative Facial Movement Coding*. (MAX). Newark, DE: University of Delaware Press.

―――― (1982), Measuring emotions in human development. In: *Measuring Emotions in Infants and Children*, ed. C. Izard. Cambridge, U.K.: Cambridge University Press.

―――― Huebner, R., Risser, D., McGinnes, G. C., & Dougherty, L. (1980), The young infant's ability to produce discrete emotional expressions. *Develop. Psychol.*, 16/2:132–140.

Mahler, M. S., Pine, F., & Bergman, A. (1975), *The Psychological Birth of the Human Infant: Symbiosis and Individuation*. New York: Basic Books.

Osgood, C. (1966), Dimensionality of the semantic space for communication via facial expression. *Scand. J. Psychol.*, 7:1–30.

Oster, H., & Ekman, P. (1978), Facial behavior in child development. In: *Minnesota Symposia on Child Psychology*, Vol. 2, ed. A. Collins. New York: Thomas Y. Crowell.

Plomin, R. (1986), *Development, Genetics, and Psychology*. Hillsdale, NJ: Lawrence Erlbaum.

Rosch, E. (1978), Principles of categorizations. In: *Cognition and Categorization*, ed. E. Rosch & B. B. Lloyd. Hillsdale, NJ: Lawrence Erlbaum.

Russell, J. A., & Ridgeway, D. (1983), Dimensions underlying children's emotional concepts. *Develop. Psychol.*, 19:795–804.

Scherer, K. R. (1982), Methods of research on vocal communication: Paradigms and parameters. In: *Handbook of Methods in Nonverbal Behavior Research*, ed. K. R. Scherer & P. Ekman. Cambridge, U.K.: Cambridge University Press, pp. 136–198.

―――― Ekman, P., eds. (1984), *Approaches to Emotion*. Hillsdale, NJ: Lawrence Erlbaum.

Spencer, H. (1890), *The Principles of Psychology*. New York: Appleton.

Spitz, R. A. (1965), *The First Year of Life*. New York: International Universities Press.

Sroufe, L. A. (1979), Socioemotional development. In: *Handbook of Infant Development*, ed. J. Osofsky. New York: John Wiley, pp. 462–516.

Stern, D. (1985), *The Interpersonal World of the Infant*. New York: Basic Books.

Tomkins, S. S. (1962), *Affect, Imagery, Consciousness*, Vol. 1. New York: Springer.

—— (1963), *Affect, Imagery, Consciousness*, Vol. 2. New York: Springer.

—— (1978), Script theory: Differential magnification of affects. In: *Nebraska Symposium on Motivation*, Vol. 26, ed. H. E. Howe & R. A. Dienstbier. Lincoln: University of Nebraska Press.

Tronick, E. (1980), The primacy of social skills in infancy. In: *Exceptional Infant*, Vol. 4, ed. D. B. Sawin, R. C. Hawkins, L. O. Walker, & J. H. Penticuff. New York: Brunner/Mazel, pp. 144–148.

Winnicott, D. W. (1965), Ego distortion in terms of true and false self. In: *The Maturational Processes and the Facilitating Environment*. New York: International Universities Press.

Woodworth, R. S., & Schlosberg, H. S. (1954), *Experimental Psychology*. New York: Holt.

Wundt, W. (1896), *Grundriss der Psychologie*, trans. C. H. Judd.

2

Infant Emotions and the Caregiving Environment

Robert N. Emde

The previous chapter offered a theoretical background that focused on emotions in the context of the infant's normal developmental processes, thus reviewing what is expectable from the vantage point of the infant. Most readers of this book, however, will consider using our IFEEL Pictures technique for research which explores *variations in the caregiving environment of the infant.* Ultimately, the IFEEL Pictures may find a place as an assessment tool both in normative and prevention–intervention research as well as in clinical research and practice. Variations must be seen against a background of knowing what is expectable and must be seen within the context of knowing about normal developmental processes. This includes an understanding of infant development in relation to the caregiving environment.

Normative Processes

Our developmental systems orientation is again helpful here. It is especially useful to review three principles that emerge from what we have learned. These principles represent hard-won knowledge gained over the past three decades and have been contributed through the efforts of both clinicians and researchers. As such, they can now be generalized as guidelines for our thinking about infant emotions and their interpretation by caregivers.

The first principle can be generalized by saying that development in infancy is a reciprocal and transactional process. All aspects of development, ranging from the biological to the social aspect, depend upon sequences of active engagement occurring between the infant and its caregiving environment. Reciprocal influences are iterative, continuing as the complexity of organization increases. Individuality is therefore best understood in terms of "matches" between infant and environment and continuity is best understood in terms of consistency in the production of organism–environment interactions. The transactional view has been used to explain behavioral outcomes following perinatal complications in the midst of varying child-rearing environments (Sameroff, 1975; Sameroff and Chandler, 1976), and it has also been used to explain how continuities of temperament depend on "goodness of fit" with caregiving environments (Chess and Thomas, 1984). But, as has been reviewed elsewhere (Emde, 1988), it is not just the environment in general that is crucial for infant transactions. Evidence points to the specifically experienced environment within the infant–caregiver relationship. Early experience, in fact, may be formative, not because infant behavioral patterns are set in an enduring way, but rather because infant–caregiver relationship patterns are set in an enduring way. Relationship experiences become internalized by the individual, continue as strong influences in development throughout childhood, and are activated in similar relationship contexts throughout later life (Bretherton and Waters, 1985; Stern, 1985; Sroufe and Fleeson, 1986). This kind of a formulation fits in well with current psychoanalytic perspectives. It also fits in with recent clinical research indicating the tragic continuities in disturbed patterns of mothering, that is, with "Ghosts in the Nursery" to use the Fraiberg metaphor (Fraiberg, Adelson, and Shapiro [1975]; see also Cramer and Stern [1986]) as well as with recent cross-generational developmental research showing a continuity across three generations for insecure attachment relationships (Main, Kaplan, and Cassidy, 1985; Ricks, 1985; Grossman, Fremmer-Bombik, Rudolph, and Grossman, 1987).

The British pediatrician–psychoanalyst Donald Winnicott once made a celebrated statement to the effect that there was no such thing as a baby; psychologically, he meant, there is only baby-with-mother. The profound dependence of the baby's mental functioning on that of the caregiver has profound implications for our clinical theory. If we paid more attention to the formative aspects of experience for the infant–caregiver relationship, later on we might see more continuities deriving from infancy. Indeed, the developmental research of two decades has not given much support to the idea of a "sensitive period" for infancy experience in terms of its setting fixed patterns of significant individual behavior. Continuity of the caregiving environment has been shown to be more predictive of behavioral outcome than has any particular kind of infant experience. Thus, what may appear to be a lack of continuity from the individual's point of view may be seen as continuity from the point of view of the caregiving relationship, particularly if the developmental context of that relationship is taken into account.

A second principle supplements the transactional one and also generalizes aspects of our hard-won knowledge. This concerns the fact that there are strong developmental functions in the human. Such functions reflect universal innate tendencies for species-important developmental outcomes that seem "buffered" against individual variation. These tendencies—often referred to as "self-righting" tendencies—enable the developing individual to maintain an integrity during major hazards and environmental perturbations. Thus, children who are congenitally blind (Fraiberg, 1977) or congenitally deaf (Freedman, Cannady, and Robinson, 1971), who are born without limbs (Decarie, 1969), or who have cerebral palsy (Sameroff, 1981, personal communication), all go through infancy with different sensorimotor experiences, but typically develop object permanence, representational intelligence, and self-awareness in early childhood. Other self-righting tendencies are shown by the well-documented observations of developmental resiliency wherein there is a tendency to get back on a developmental pathway after a deficit or early adversity (Waddington, 1962; Sameroff and Chandler, 1976). This kind of resiliency is illustrated by severe infant retardation due to deprivation which is later corrected by environmental change (see examples in Clarke and Clarke [1977]).

While our newer view of developmental processes, with transactions and strong developmental functions, is not as simple as our older view of sensitive periods for early experience, the newer view is more hopeful. If we discover untoward variations in the early caregiving environment and can intervene so as to be helpful, correction and resilience can occur. Development can then get back on track. There is every reason to believe that core aspects of early emotional development and emotional signaling—those that involve dimensions and categories of patterned emotional expression—are highly buffered against environmental perturbation and stress and can be considered strong developmental functions. It is a matter for clinical research, therefore, to pick up the variations in the caregiving environment in this area and to enhance resiliency. It is our hope that the IFEEL Pictures will contribute to such an effort.

A final principle that generalizes our hard-won knowledge should not surprise the reader: emotional availability is a central aspect of the adaptive caregiving environment. Let us return to our earlier discussion of basic motivations. The active, self-regulating, social and affective human infant must exercise these early motivational structures with the caregiver. We have learned, moreover, that the infant's affective monitoring must be matched in appropriate fashion by the caregiver's affective monitoring. A transactional process occurs here as well. Emotional availability is a dyadic process, with monitoring on both sides of the infant–caregiver relationship. The main burden in this process is, of course, on the caregiver, who must be emotionally available, that is, sensitive and responsive over time to the infant's emotional cues. The caregiver must also help to move things forward in development during those windows of opportunity that appear during wakefulness (Winnicott, 1957; Sander, 1985), and help to guide the child forward to greater understanding and skills (Vygotsky, 1978). Some infants have special problems in sending emotional signals, presenting particular difficulties for mothers, for example, infants who have experienced intrauterine growth retardation (Brazelton, 1975), those who are congenitally blind (Fraiberg, 1968), and those with Down's syndrome (Emde and Brown, 1978). These can be thought of as variations in emotional availability from the infant side. But variations in emotional availability from the parent's side are probably more widespread. This leads us to our next topic, namely, that of individual differences in caregiving and risk.

Individual Differences in Shared Meaning and Risk for Later Problems

We have described our hard-won knowledge about developmental transactions and social reciprocity. But the early caregiving relationship is not asymmetrical. The human infant is altricial and cannot survive without caregiving by an adult who provides basic physiological regulatory functions of nourishment, warmth, behavioral state cycling, and contingent stimulation. In addition to physiological needs, the caregiver must assume responsibility for protection and for providing the basic consistent responses for affiliation and for sensorimotor systems to develop. The caregiving relationship is also asymmetrical in another sense. The caregiver leads the child in development, providing a form of fundamental teaching by pulling the infant forward in development; what Vygotsky referred to as operating in the "zone of proximal development." The caregiver communicates a little bit beyond the infant's current developmental level in order to model more complex behavior for internalization. A mother, for example, will typically treat a 4-month-old as if he or she was capable of understanding and playing like a 6-month-old, and the infant frequently will respond with more organized play. Similarly, the 12-month-old's first words are given elaborate meanings and contexts by caregivers and this leads to the toddler appreciating those words as being imbedded in particular contexts (Bruner, 1982; Kaye, 1982).

The implications for emotional communication with this kind of asymmetry are clear. Sensitive caregivers have a much greater share of responsibility for perceiving and understanding emotional signals coming from their infants than do infants from their caregivers. Sensitive caregivers will add more complexity to the emotional signals of their infants than the latter intend or even understand. Researchers must sort out when such added complexity by caregivers is not operating in the "zone of proximal development" and may represent a risk factor, rather than a helping factor. It is to this task that the IFEEL Pictures are aimed.

SHARED MEANING

This brings us to a most profound aspect of early experience from the point of view of individual differences and risk. Caregivers operating sensitively in the zone of proximal development are emotionally available. They respond to the individuality of the infant, and shared meaning develops over time. We know that beginning around 6 to 8 months of age and continuing for the next year and a half (even prior to language as we usually think of it), the infant's world is characterized by shared meaning or what has been referred to as "intersubjectivity" (Trevarthen and Hubley, 1979; Bretherton, McKnew, and Beeghly-Smith, 1981; Stern, 1985). In the latter part of the first year, shared meaning involves repeated interactions with the caregiver with a sense of the past and expectations about what is to come, with shared intentions and with shared emotions. There is, as Bretherton has put it, a "matching of minds." The situation is dramatized by a form of emotion signaling in infancy that we and others have called social referencing (Campos and Stenberg, 1981; Feinman and Lewis, 1983; Sorce, Emde, Campos, and Klinnert, 1985; Klinnert, Emde, Butterfield, and Campos, 1986). In a typical social referencing experiment an infant explores a playroom and encounters one of several contrived situations of uncertainty (e.g., a toy robot, an apparent drop-off of a crawling surface, or an unusual toy). The infant then looks to mother. If mother signals a facial expression of fear or anger, the infant avoids the new situation; if mother signals joy or interest, the infant approaches and explores the new situation. Similar regulatory effects of emotional signals occur with mother's expressions through face or voice and most effects are clear within a minute or two. But beyond our social referencing experiments, shared meaning soon takes on particular forms depending on the caregiving relationship experience. One observes this in infant and caregiver with stylized surprise games, joint expectations of what belongs where and when, and various everyday routines of going places, feeding, and sleeping. The majority of infancy experiences that are internalized and go forward in individual development are partly or wholly of the shared meaning variety.

We have alluded to the fact that the differences in the caregiver relationship experience will yield differences in early childhood that will be manifest in social interaction contexts beyond the caregiving relationship (Sroufe, 1983). As Stern (1985) has described so well, the caregiving relationship experience in infancy becomes a basis for ongoing working models of self in relation to significant others. We would emphasize that the caregiver's emotional availability to the infant is crucial in this process and that its assessment is often useful in clinical screening. If development is going well the clinician is apt to see a range of emotional expressions in interactions between caregiver and infant, with a balance of pleasure and interest. If development is not going well, one is apt to see a restricted range of expressions and a shift toward negative emotions or withdrawal–disengagement. No matter how the situation was started, such restrictions and deviations will be manifest on both sides of the interacting dyad (Emde, Gaensbauer, and Harmon, 1981).

Forms of shared meaning in later infancy and toddlerhood are now the subject of increasing study. Not only do shared meanings form a basis for language acquisition during the so-called one-word phase, but they also form a basis for a sense of rules, a sense of "we" in addition to self and other and a sense of early morality (Emde, 1988).

Overall, this discussion leaves us with two implications. Important individual differences in infancy necessarily involve shared meaning and its origins in both caregiver and infant. Furthermore, variations in emotional availability may play a key role in such individual differences. Both implications add fuel to our rationale for assessing individual differences in caregivers' interpretations of infant emotional signals.

RISK AND DISORDER

Contemporary views of risk and disorder in infancy are based on these considerations. A usual definition of risk would focus on the likelihood of the later developmental occurrence of psychopathology (e.g., emotional or conduct disorder) in the child. Another definition of risk might focus on the likelihood of the development of enduring problems in the family. As might be inferred from our previous discussion, the two categories of risk often go together. Broad risk groups predispose to problems in both child and family. These include: poverty or low socioeconomic status; major infant difficulties which present unusual challenges or stress (e.g., prematurity, major physical handicaps, mental retardation); teenage parents and their infants; prolonged caregiver separation in the perinatal period; untoward family stress events such as a death in the immediate family or family breakup. These broad risk groups are identified because the likelihood of later disorder is greater than it is in nonrisk groups. Intervention programs can then be targeted so as to prevent later disorders occurring in the proportion of those within the risk group who would otherwise develop the problems.

Definitions of disorder in infancy have been changing. The field of infant psychiatry is an active one, as three growing organizations and an international journal illustrate, but the field has lacked an agreed-upon diagnostic scheme.[1] Discussions among infant clinicians are increasingly taking account of the developmental framework we have enumerated. Considering the developmental centrality of the infant–caregiver relationship experience, and the fact that relationship experiences are in the process of becoming internalized, some have suggested that the concept of disorder in infancy needs to be situated beyond the individual. Regulatory disorders in behavior are seen as residing not in the infant, but in the infant–caregiver relationship. Thus, a developmentally oriented nosology of relationship disorders (or short-term disturbances) has been proposed (Sameroff and Emde, 1989). Regulatory disturbances could involve *over-* or *under*regulation of the relationship and, if persistent, they could manifest themselves in the areas of feeding, sleep, or attachment disorders (Anders, 1989). At the present time this kind of nosology will be more useful to clinicians working in infancy than individual-based schemes, which tend to be adult-oriented, for example, DSM-III (American Psychiatric Association, 1980). For the purposes of this volume, we could say that any new research tool that assesses variations in the caregiver's interpretation of infant emotions would fit in well with this new thinking about early relationships and the disorders that may affect them. The identification of unusual responses could lead to further investigation and to an understanding of problems in the infant–caregiver relationship. Since relationship disturbances or disorders are likely predisposing factors for later individual disorders, their identification could set in motion targeted interventions. Since patterns of behavior are not yet fully internalized or fixed in infancy, to the extent that maladaptive

---

[1]The organizations are: The International Association for Infant Mental Health, the National Center for Clinical Infant Programs, and the World Association of Infant Psychiatry and Allied Disciplines; the Journal is the *Infant Mental Health Journal.*

caregiver relationship experiences can be altered, positive cycles of adaptation can be set in motion. These in turn can be self-reinforcing when the child later begins to apply more effective models of self and other in new contexts (e.g., with peers and teachers). Those who carry out early intervention are hopeful that, if early problems in the relationship can be identified, appropriate intervention can often have long-lasting effects.

Assessment Tools Are Needed

While there are some grounds for optimism with intervention, we are in need of assessment tools for understanding troublesome problems in early caregiving. Some assessments are available that have arisen from recent developmental research, taking account of emotional signaling and availability. Although these research assessments are time-intensive, and generally less applicable for either group studies or clinical application—they are worth reviewing as a background for the IFEEL Pictures. The existing assessments fall into two categories: observational methods and interview methods.

OBSERVATIONAL METHODS

Since it is through repeated experiences with the caregiver that the infant comes to understand the consequences and meaning of his or her emotional signals, most research assessments have aimed at direct observations of caregiving interactions (Emde and Easterbrooks, 1985). One of the most widely used assessments has been the maternal sensitivity rating scales devised by Ainsworth and colleagues (Ainsworth, Blehar, Waters, and Wall, 1978); these have been used for quantifying observations of spontaneous home interactions such as feeding, physical contact, and emotional communication. Four nine-point scales assess dimensions of sensitivity–insensitivity to the infant's signals, acceptance–rejection, cooperation–interference, and accessibility–ignoring. These scales generally require at least one hour of observation after the mother and infant feel comfortable with the observer. A recent modification of the Ainsworth scales (often referred to as "Maternal Sensitivity Scales") was created by Biringen, Robinson, and Emde (1987) and Biringen and Robinson (1991) who anchored ratings according to specific behaviors with the use of video recordings. Other rating scales of caregiver–infant interactions have been devised for use with spontaneous behavior and semistructured situations. These include a set of scales devised by Clarke, Musick, Stott, and Klehr (1980) and by Durfee, Klein, Fivel, Bennett, Morgan, and Blehar (1977).

Other observational methods that assess emotional signaling and availability between infant and caregiver require laboratory observations and control. Perhaps the best known is the "strange situation" (Ainsworth and Wittig, 1969). A laboratory situation makes use of observations of play and of maternal separations and reunions in order to assess "security of attachment" in a manner that presumably reflects the historical patterns of mother–infant interaction during the first year of life. Although this procedure was not designed to evaluate infant emotions, the patterning of emotional responses is a component of the assessment of security of infant–parent attachment bonds. The "strange situation" has yielded a rich array of research related to attachment patterns, and has also generated a number of modifications that have been employed for clinical purposes, including one introduced by Gaensbauer and Harmon (1982) and Solyum (1982). The "strange situation" assessment was designed for infants and toddlers approximately 11 to 24 months of age, and it has now become the basis for designing additional age-appropriate assessments of separations and reunions from an attachment figure during the third and fourth years of life (Greenberg, Cicchetti, and Cummings, 1990). The "strange situation" has also been used to assess the quality of the infant–father bond in the context of emotional signaling (Main and Weston, 1981; Easterbrooks and Goldberg, 1984). Other promising observational assessments that have been used less widely include Lewis and Michalson's (1983) scales of socioemotional development and Stern's (1985) systematized observations of "affect attunement."

Other laboratory-based methods have focused on assessing emotional signaling and its perturbations more directly. One method has been to ask mothers to be "stony-faced" and unresponsive to their infants for a minute or two when the young infant is in an infant-seat facing them (Tronick, Als, Adamson, Wise, and Brazelton, 1978). Infants typically attempt to engage their mothers again in interaction and then, failing that, they avert their gaze and become distressed. One might say that a perturbation had been introduced that interfered with the infant's expectations that mother would be emotionally responsive and available. Tronick and Gianino (1986) believe that this kind of perturbation may be similar to what happens to infants of depressed caregivers. Another method introduces a perturbation in mother's emotional availability during the infant's second year by having the mother read a newspaper. Fifteen-month-olds under this condition were found to explore less and be less playful than when their mother was not preoccupied (Sorce and Emde, 1982). Although individual difference assessments are not yet available for the above methods, related work of Zahn-Waxler, Cummings, McKnew, and Radke-Yarrow (1984) may point to individual differences of clinical relevance.

The latter investigators found meaningful differences in 18- and 20-month-old infant responses to depressed and nondepressed mothers who were facially unresponsive for two minutes.

Two more recent observational methods offer additional promise, especially since they are focused on emotional signaling and can be used either in home or laboratory. The first of these concerns affect exchanges between caregiver and infant or child (Osofsky, Culp, Eberhart-Wright, and Hann, 1990). This instrument systematizes ratings of videotapes using thirty-second time units for the following categories of observation: positive and negative shared affects, positive and negative nonshared affects, and shared mixed affects that are labeled either appropriate or questionable. Another rating system under development consists of an emotional availability rating scale battery (Biringen, Robinson, and Emde, 1987). The battery contains separate ratable dimensions of maternal sensitivity, lack of intrusiveness, and child responsivity.

INTERVIEW METHODS

The interview has long been recognized as the central method for obtaining information about individuals, their particular histories, and what is important to them. What is optimal is an open and free-ranging interview with a caregiver about the quality and day-to-day details of caregiving and about hopes, desires, satisfactions, and frustrations with the infant—especially if the interview can follow up on responses having to do with feelings and emotional communications. But open-ended interviews are time-intensive; moreover, they need to be supplemented by systematic interviews for research that seeks to generalize knowledge by making comparisons across individuals. Semistructured interviews have therefore been created wherein predesigned topics are queried systematically, but in a manner that is flexible so that interviewers can exercise tact, skill, and emotional sensitivity. Two such interviewing methods, stemming from the attachment line of research, are particularly promising: the Adult Attachment Interview (Main et al., 1985) and the Parent Attachment Interview (Bretherton, Biringen, Ridgeway, Maslin, and Sherman, 1989).

OTHER METHODS

Methods other than observation and interview involve the use of self-report instruments and questionnaires. Parental reports of infant temperament, although not specifically designed to sample emotional expression or experience, do provide a measure of the infant's propensity for expressing different kinds of emotions. Extensively used instruments of this sort include: the Infant Behavior Questionnaire of Rothbart (1981); the Temperament Questionnaire of Carey and McDevitt (1978); and the EAS of Buss and Plomin (1984). The excellent discussion by Goldsmith and Campos (1982) reviews these instruments from the perspective of emotional development.

Questionnaires about emotion can help in assessing the degree to which parents may demonstrate a tendency for being emotionally available to their children. Perhaps the most widely used instrument for directly surveying emotional experience is the Differential Emotion Scale, originally designed for obtaining self-perceptions from adults (Izard, 1972). This instrument was modified by our research team so as to capture parental perceptions of infant emotional experience (Johnson, Emde, Pannabecker, Stenberg, and Davis, 1982). The very fact that we found that caregivers could easily provide meaningful information about Darwinian categories of emotion encouraged us to develop a photographic approach to probing parental emotional responses (Darwin, 1872).

Summary and Conclusion

Three generalizations from recent research frame our thinking about individual differences in the caregiving relationship and about ways to assess problems in that relationship. First, development in infancy is a reciprocal and transactional process. Individuality and continuity may best be understood in terms of "matches" and dynamic exchanges between the infant and the caregiving environment. Second, emotional signaling and communication are probably strong developmental functions, with a core set of emotional expressions buffered against individual variation and environmental stress so that species-wide development is highly likely. This makes it possible to assess variation-meaningful blends of emotion and deviant features of emotional communication in particular caregiving relationships. Third, emotional availability in the infant–caregiver relationship is an important characteristic of normal development. Both infant and caregiver engage in affective monitoring of each other, but the main responsibility in this process lies with the caregiver, who must be emotionally available in terms of being sensitive and responsive over time to the infant's emotional signals.

Shared meaning between the infant and caregiver develops over time and involves a common sense of the past and expectations about what is to come. Shared intentions and shared emotions increasingly characterize observed interactions. If development is going well, the clinician is apt to see a range of emotional expressions between caregiver and infant, with a balance of shared pleasure and interest. If development is not going well, one is apt to see a restricted range of expressions and a shift toward negative emotions or withdrawal–disengagement, with problems shown on both sides of the interacting dyad.

Today's views of risk and disorder in infancy are based on the centrality of the infant–caregiver relationship in

promoting development. Broad risk factors such as poverty, prematurity, physical handicap, teenage parenting,
and prolonged separation from the caregiver predispose
to problems in both child and family. Since relationship
experiences are in the process of becoming internalized
during infancy, some have suggested that regulatory disorders in behavior reside not in the infant but in the infant–caregiver relationship. Correspondingly, since relationship disorders or disturbances are likely predisposing
factors for later individual disorder, their identification
can set in motion targeted interventions.

Assessment tools are needed for early identification
of problems and to take into account emotional signaling
and emotional availability. Several research assessments
are reviewed, including maternal sensitivity rating scales,
"strange situation" evaluations, and relationship-based
scales of socioemotional development. Other observational
methods assess emotional signaling by means of experimental perturbations, while still other methods rate affect
exchanges and emotional availability in more naturalistic
situations. Interview methods, as well as parental report
instruments, are also reviewed.

The IFEEL Pictures, presenting caregivers with a
standard series of photographs of infants with various
emotional expressions, are an assessment tool that arose
in the context described above. This picture-based instrument for assessing emotional availability is theoretically
promising, but more research remains to be done before
we can state its potential with any degree of certainty.

References

Ainsworth, M. D. S., Blehar, M., Waters, E., & Wall, S. (1978),
    *Patterns of Attachment: A Psychological Study of the Strange
    Situation*. Hillsdale, NJ: Lawrence Erlbaum.

44   ROBERT N. EMDE

—— Wittig, B. A. (1969), Attachment and the exploratory behavior of one-year-olds in a strange situation. In: *Determinants of Infant Behavior*, Vol. 4, ed. B. M. Foss. London: Methuen, pp. 113–136.
Anders, T. F. (1989), Clinical syndromes, relationship disturbances, and their assessment. In: *Relationship Disturbances in Early Childhood*, ed. A. J. Sameroff & R. N. Emde. New York: Basic Books, pp. 125–144.
Biringen, Z., & Robinson, J. (1991), Emotional availability in mother child interactions: A reconcept for research. *Amer. J. Orthopsychiatry*, 6:258–271.
—— —— Emde, R. N. (1987), *Emotional Availability Scales*. Typescript. University of Colorado Health Sciences Center.
Brazelton, T. B. (1975), Anticipatory guidance. *Pediat. Clin. N. Amer.*, 22/3:533–544.
Bretherton, I., Biringen, Z., Ridgeway, D., Maslin, C., & Sherman, M. (1989), Attachment: The parental perspective. In: *Infant Ment. Health J.*, Special Issue, ed. C. H. Zeanah & M. L. Barton. 10/3:203–221.
—— McKnew, S., & Beeghly-Smith, M. (1981), Early person knowledge as expressed in verbal and gestural communication: When do infants acquire a "theory of mind?" In: *Infant Social Cognition*, ed. M. E. Lamb & L. R. Sherrod. Hillsdale, NJ: Lawrence Erlbaum, pp. 333–373.
—— Waters, E., eds. (1985), Growing Points in Attachment Theory and Research. *Monographs of the Society for Research in Child Development*, 50(1–2, Serial No. 209).
Bruner, J. (1982), *Child's Talk: Learning to Use Language*. New York: W. W. Norton.
Buss, A. H., & Plomin, R. (1984), *Temperament: Early Developing Personality Traits*. Hillsdale, NJ: Lawrence Erlbaum.
Campos, J. J., & Stenberg, C. (1981), Perception, appraisal, and emotion: The onset of social referencing. In: *Infant Social Cognition*, ed. M. Lamb & L. R. Sherrod. Hillsdale, NJ: Lawrence Erlbaum, pp. 273–314.
Carey, W., & McDevitt, S. (1978), Revision of the infant temperament questionnaire. *Pediatrics*, 61:735–739.

Chess, S., & Thomas, A. (1984), *Origins and Evolution of Behavior Disorders: From Infancy to Early Adult Life.* New York: Brunner/Mazel.

Clarke, A. M., & Clarke, A. D. B. (1977), *Early Experience: Myth and Evidence.* New York: The Free Press.

Clarke, R., Musick, J., Stott, F., & Klehr, K. (1980), *The Mother's Project: Rating Scales of Mother–Child Interaction,* typecript.

Cramer, B., & Stern, D. (1986), Mother–infant psychotherapy: Objective and subjective changes. Paper presented at the Third World Congress of Infant Psychiatry and Allied Disciplines, Stockholm, Sweden, August.

Darwin, C. (1872), *The Expression of Emotions in Man and Animals.* Chicago: University of Chicago Press, 1965.

Decarie, T. G. (1969), A study of the mental and emotional development of the thalidomide child. In: *Determinants of Infant Behavior,* Vol. 4, ed. B. M. Foss. London: Methuen, pp. 167–287.

Durfee, J. T., Klein, R. P., Fivel, M. W., Bennett, C. A., Morgan, G. A., & Blehar, M. D. (1977), *Infant Social Behavior Manual. JSAS Catalogue of Selected Documents in Psychology,* 7, 38, MS 1467 (typescript).

Easterbrooks, M. A., & Goldberg, W. A. (1984), Toddler development in the family: Impact of father involvement and parenting characteristics. *Child Develop.,* 55:740–752.

Emde, R. N. (1988), Development terminable and interminable: I. Innate and motivational factors from infancy. *Internat. J. Psycho-Anal.,* 69:23–42.

———— Brown, C. (1978), Adaptation to the birth of a Down's syndrome infant: Grieving and maternal attachment. *J. Amer. Acad. Child Psychiatry,* 17:299–323.

———— Easterbrooks, M. A. (1985), Assessing emotional availability in early development. In: *Early Identification of Children at Risk: An International Perspective,* ed. W. K. Frankenburg, R. N. Emde, & J. W. Sullivan. New York: Plenum, pp. 79–101.

———— Gaensbauer, T. J., & Harmon, R. J. (1981), Using our emotions: Some principles for appraising emotional development and intervention. In: *Developmental Disabilities in*

Preschool Children, ed. M. Lewis & L. Taft. New York: S. P. Medical & Scientific Books, pp. 409–424.

Feinman, S., & Lewis, M. (1983), Social referencing at ten months: A second-order effect on infants' responses to strangers. *Child Develop.*, 54/4:878–887.

Fraiberg, S. (1968), Parallel and divergent patterns in blind and sighted infants. *The Psychoanalytic Study of the Child*, 23:264–300. New York: International Universities Press.

——— (1977), *Insights from the Blind*. New York: Basic Books.

——— Adelson, E., & Shapiro, V. (1975), Ghosts in the nursery. *J. Child Psychiatry*, 14/3:387–421.

Freedman, D. A., Cannady, C., & Robinson, J. S. (1971), Speech and psychic structure. *J. Amer. Psychoanal. Assn.*, 19:765–779.

Gaensbauer, T. J., & Harmon, R. J. (1982), Attachment behavior in abused/neglected and premature infants: Implications for the concept of attachment. In: *The Development of Attachment and Affiliative Systems*, ed. R. N. Emde & R. J. Harmon. New York: Plenum, pp. 263–279.

Goldsmith, H., & Campos, J. (1982), Toward a theory of infant temperament. In: *The Development of Attachment and Affiliative Systems*, ed. R. N. Emde & R. J. Harmon. New York: Plenum, pp. 161–193.

Greenberg, M. T., Cicchetti, D., & Cummings, E. M., eds. (1990), *Attachment in the Preschool Years—Theory, Research, and Intervention*. Chicago: University of Chicago Press.

Grossman, K., Fremmer-Bombik, E., Rudolph, J., & Grossman, K. E. (1987), Maternal attachment representations as related to child–mother attachment patterns and maternal sensitivity and acceptance of her infant. In: *Relations Between Relationships Within Families*, ed. R. A. Hinde & J. Stevenson-Hinde. Oxford: Oxford University Press.

Izard, C. (1972), *Patterns of Emotion: A New Analysis of Anxiety and Depression*. New York: Academic Press.

Johnson, W. F., Emde, R. N., Pannabecker, B. J., Stenberg, C., & Davis, M. (1982), Maternal perception of infant emotion from birth through 18 months. *Infant Behav. & Develop.*, 5:313–322.

Kaye, K. (1982), *The Mental and Social Life of Babies: How Parents Create Persons.* Chicago: University of Chicago Press.

Klinnert, M. D., Emde, R. N., Butterfield, P., & Campos, J. J. (1986), Social referencing: The infant's use of emotional signals from a friendly adult with mother present. *Development. Psychol.,* 22/4:427–432.

Lewis, M., & Michalson, L. (1983), *Children's Emotions and Moods.* New York: Plenum.

Main, M., Kaplan, N., & Cassidy, J. (1985), Security in infancy, childhood and adulthood: A move to the level of representation. In: Growing Points of Attachment Theory and Research. *Monographs of the Society for Research in Child Development,* 50(1–2, Serial No. 209), pp. 66–104.

———— Weston, R. (1981), The quality of the toddler's relationship to mother and father: Related to conflict behavior and the readiness to establish new relationships. *Child Develop.,* 52/2:932–940.

Osofsky, J. D., Culp, A. M., Eberhart-Wright, A., & Hann, D. M. (1990), *Emotional Availability Observation Scales.* Typescript. Louisiana State University Medical Center, New Orleans.

Ricks, M. H. (1985), The social transition of parental behavior: Attachment across generations. In: Growing Points in Attachment Theory and Research. *Monographs of the Society for Research in Child Development,* ed. I. Bretherton & E. Waters. 50(1–2, Serial No. 209), pp. 211–227.

Rothbart, M. K. (1981), Measurement of temperament in infancy. *Child Develop.,* 52:569–578.

Sameroff, A. J. (1975), Transactional models in early relations. *Hum. Develop.,* 18:65–79.

———— Chandler, M. (1976), Reproductive risk and the continuum of caretaking casualty. In: *Review of the Child Development Research: Vol. 4,* ed. F. D. Horowitz. Chicago: University of Chicago Press, pp. 187–244.

———— Emde, R. N., eds. (1989), *Relationship Disturbances in Early Childhood: A Developmental Approach.* New York: Basic Books.

Sander, L. (1985), Toward a logic of organization in psychobiological development. In: *Biologic Response Styles: Clinical Implications,* ed. K. Klar & L. Siever. Monograph Series. Washington, DC: American Psychiatric Press.

Solyum, A. E. (1982), Affect development and its assessment in infancy. *Infant Mental Health J.*, 3:276–277.

Sorce, J. F., & Emde, R. N. (1982), The meaning of infant emotional expressions: Regularities in caregiving responses in normal and Down's syndrome infants. *J. Child Psychol. & Psychiatry*, 23/2:145–158.

———— ———— Campos, J. J., & Klinnert, M. D. (1985), Maternal emotional signaling: Its effect on the visual cliff behavior of 1-year-olds. *Develop. Psychol.*, 21/1:195–200.

Sroufe, L. A. (1983), Infant-caregiver attachment and patterns of adaptation in preschool: The roots of maladaptation and competence. In: *Minnesota Symposium in Child Psychology*, ed. M. Perlmutter. Hillsdale, NJ: Lawrence Erlbaum, pp. 41–81.

———— Fleeson, J. (1986), Attachment and the construction of relationships. In: *The Nature and Development of Relationships*, ed. W. Hartup & Z. Rubin. Hillsdale, NJ: Lawrence Erlbaum.

Stern, D. (1985), *The Interpersonal World of the Infant*. New York: Basic Books.

Trevarthen, C., & Hubley, P. (1979), Secondary intersubjectivity: Confidence, confiding, and acts of meaning in the first year. In: *Action, Gesture and Symbol*, ed. A. Lock. New York: Academic Press, pp. 183–229.

Tronick, E., Als, H., Adamson, L., Wise, S., & Brazelton, T. B. (1978), The infant's response to entrapment between contradictory messages in face-to-face interaction. *J. Amer. Acad. Child Psychiatry*, 17:1–13.

———— Gianino, A. (1986), The transmission of maternal disturbance to the infant. In: *Maternal Depression and Infant Disturbance*, ed. E. Z. Tronick & T. Field. San Francisco: Jossey-Bass.

Vygotsky, L. S. (1978), *Mind in Society: The Development of Higher Psychological Processes*. Cambridge, MA: Harvard University Press.

Waddington, C. H. (1962), *New Patterns in Genetics and Development*, Vol. 21, Columbia Biological Series. New York: Columbia University Press.

Winnicott, D. W. (1957), *Mother and Child*. New York: Basic Books.

Zahn-Waxler, C., Cummings, E. M., McKnew, D. H., & Radke-Yarrow, M. (1984), Altruism, aggression, and social interactions in young children with a manic-depressive parent. *Child Develop.*, 55:112–122.

Part II:

Development of a New Methodology

3

The Collaborative History of the IFEEL Pictures

Robert N. Emde

The previous chapters offered a general theoretical background for the IFEEL Pictures. This chapter will review the story of our Colorado research that led up to the current multiregional collaborative effort.

The IFEEL Pictures present infant facial expressions sampled over the years from our studies of normal development. All pictures are of one-year-olds and most emotional expressions are typical of everyday life, rather than being selected as ideal or prototypic examples of particular emotions. When we ask parents and others to interpret these pictures, we encourage them to give simple, unrestrained verbal responses. These responses are then coded in a straightforward way and a comparison is made with expectable responses from others. We consider the IFEEL Pictures to be part of an assessment technique that is still evolving. Although most of the pictures were originally taken for a variety of research purposes during 1974 through 1976, a unifying goal has guided us in the years since; namely, that we could eventually use these pictures for studying differences in parents' (and possibly children's) perceptions or interpretations of infant emotions.

Many have worked with me over the years on the development of picture sets which might be used in this way. As I tell the story of preliminary and basic studies leading up to the standard assessment technique, I will mention collaborators separately only when describing unpublished work. Published work is identified in specific citations. The present volume marks the first accounting of studies using the IFEEL Pictures.

Early Studies of Infant Facial Expressions of Emotion Using Judgments from Pictures

Our early studies on emotional development in the infant were focused on emotional expressions in relation to physiological and maturational events (Polak, Emde, and Spitz, 1964a,b; Emde and Koenig, 1969a,b; Emde and Harmon, 1972). Subsequent longitudinal investigations were motivated by basic concerns related to mental health and psychiatry (Emde, Gaensbauer, and Harmon, 1976; Sorce and Emde, 1982; Emde and Brown, 1978; Campos, Emde, Gaensbauer, and Henderson, 1975; Emde, Kligman, Reich, and Wade, 1978). But after a time we became bothered by a nagging question: How did we know that what we were calling emotional expression in babies was related to the later emotional experience that our patients talked about and that we found so central in our clinical work? The preverbal infant could not tell us how he or she felt. In using a variety of viewpoints, we learned that defining or "indexing" emotions by physiological or situational correlates alone was unreliable and made little sense. Our continuing longitudinal studies, viewing emotions as naturalistic expressions or as nonverbal communications, both in the home and in the laboratory, reassured us, however, with one recurring viewpoint. We found that facial expressions and other behaviors that we had presumed to call emotional regularly communicated both feelings and meaningful messages for parents who used them in caregiving. We were therefore encouraged to devote more systematic efforts to the sampling and measurement of these expressions.

Such a venture was also encouraged from another source. The volumes of Izard (1971) and of Ekman, Friesen, and Ellsworth (1972), critically reviewed previous work on the accuracy of judgments of adult facial expressions of emotion and found strong consistencies in findings from experimental studies. Ekman and his group found that most adult judges could agree on at least seven categories of emotion. These included: happiness, surprise, fear, anger, sadness, disgust–contempt and interest. Izard developed a similar list which, in effect, also included distress and shame. The previous chapter reviewed how these two separate investigative teams found cross-cultural evidence of universality for both the existence and recognition of these same categories of emotion.

We began to sample infant facial expressions with still photographs taken during home visits. We included spontaneous infant expressions as well as responses to standard social and nonsocial stimuli. Two studies found that adult women judges could not easily reach substantial agreement about infant emotional expressions when we used a forced choice procedure among the seven emotion categories as had been used in adult studies. Judges expressed, however, that they could tell a lot more from the infant pictures than was allowed by the forced-choice categorizing task we had presented them with. In other words, we learned that for our pictures (initially sampled from 3-month-old infants) a procedure demanding forced-choice judgments was inappropriate. Upon reconsideration, when we compared our procedure with that used in cross-cultural studies of Ekman and of Izard, we realized why this was so. The cross-cultural studies used a sampling of pictures of actors who posed peak emotional expressions; naturally the infants in our study did not dramatize their facial expressions or "pose" for our pictures. Moreover, in the everyday life of the infants we sampled, "blends" or more neutral expressions were more common than expressions of peak states. Realizing that we wanted to investigate what was typical, we therefore moved to adopt methods which would allow us to capture more of the infant's usual repertoire and its meaning. We continued systematically to sample facial expressions of normal infants during home visit sessions by means of 35 mm color photographs. The details of our sampling procedure are specified in an earlier publication (Emde, Katz, and Thorpe, 1978). Twenty photographs were systematically taken of the face and upper torso of a group of infants studied at $2\frac{1}{2}$, $3\frac{1}{2}$, $4\frac{1}{2}$, and 12 months of age. One week after taking the photographs, a return visit was made and a maternal interview was tape recorded for later transcription. Each mother viewed her baby's pictures, which were randomized (to eliminate sequence cues) and she told us in the interview what, if anything, was captured about her baby's expression in each picture.

Our next set of studies involved a modification of a free-response labeling technique that had been devised for use with judges of adult expressions by Izard (1972). Using an array of photos of actor-posed peak emotional expressions, Izard had found that the number of words that adults used to label emotions was limited. When words used by only one subject were omitted, 268 subjects used less than that number of words (224) in responding to thirty-two photographs. When a pool of judges was asked to categorize these words in accordance with his scheme of eight fundamental emotions, Izard was able to construct a lexicon of words, grouped according to each of the eight emotional categories. In three different studies, using photographs of infants of 3 to 4 months of age, we found remarkably similar findings using this approach. Using the Izard adult-derived lexicon, 86 percent of the responses from infant pictures could easily be classified. When we added two categories to Izard's scheme of eight (with clear-cut descriptive words as determined by three judges), we were able to classify 96 percent of the responses with only 4 percent falling into "other." The two new categories we added for infant responses were passive-bored and sleepy. Thus, our free response categorizing instrument for infants grew to have ten categories, plus an eleventh of "no emotion" (Emde, 1980). This infancy lexicon from our early studies continued to be used, with only minor modifications, in the preliminary studies leading up to the IFEEL Pictures technique. In 1987 an empirically based significant change in categories was introduced for our current version (see chapter 4).

Another approach to investigating the expression and recognition of emotions in infancy involved application of a multidimensional scaling technique devised by Shepard (1962a,b, 1974). In our application of this technique, a large number of judges were asked to sort stimulus cards (either infant pictures or mothers' verbal responses to their own infant pictures) into one or more piles, putting those cards that seemed to belong together in the same pile. After completing the task with twenty-five cards, judges were asked to label each pile. A computer analysis then took the data from the raters and gave an output which included: (1) a frequency count of labels applied to each card; (2) a similarity matrix which gave a numerical value to the number of times each pair was placed together; and (3) the multidimensional scaling output itself. In our

studies, all raters were adult women who were experienced
with children. The computer program generated a special
model of data points so that pictures judged as relatively
similar were represented as relatively close together in the
model, and pictures judged as relatively dissimilar were
relatively far apart. In nearly twenty such analyses involving separate sampling of pictures and of mothers' verbal
interpretations of their own infant pictures, similar results
were obtained. Two-dimensional solutions were characteristic before 3 months of age and three-dimensional solutions were characteristic afterwards, as noted in chapter 1.
Two-dimensional portrayals included hedonic tone and
activation while three-dimensional organizations added a
third dimension of lesser prominence which we designated
as internally oriented/externally oriented (Emde et al.,
1978).

     An early cross-validation study explored the extent to
which our dimensional scaling technique, which was not
dependent on judges' verbal mediation, might validate or
even help refine our free response categorizing technique.
Would the categories of messages from free verbal responses appear together in the similarity sorting of pictures? The answer appeared to be yes. In a study in which
fifty raters were randomly assigned to either a similarity
sorting task or a free response labeling task, we found a
strong tendency for seventy-five infant pictures similarly
labeled in the free response paradigm to be close together
in the three-dimensional space generated from multidimensional scaling. Results showed strong statistical significance for three different sets of pictures. Early studies
were also encouraging with respect to reliability of facial
judgments from infant pictures. In studies using the same
infant pictures sampled at 3½ months of age but with different groups of raters obtained at different times, results
were striking. Of pictures categorized as a single emotion

in a first judgment study, 80 percent were judged beyond criterion level for the same category in a second study. Similar results occurred for facial expressions sampled at 12 months. Agreement was even more dramatic when correlations were done between the extent to which groups of judges agreed that a given emotion category was present. For all studies at both ages, judgment study correlations ranged from .84 to .96.

We then asked other questions about picture sampling. After all, we had sampled infants' facial expression under somewhat arbitrary conditions and represented them in still photographs. To what extent was "usual performance" at some distance from our arbitrary conditions? To what extent was the still photograph a meaningful unit when we know that emotional life is embedded in temporal patterns of activity? A study was therefore designed to compare still photographs with movies. The movies contained thirty-second sequences of the infant's face and upper torso which led up to each still photograph that was sampled. In three separate experimental sessions it was found that more than 75 percent of our photographs that met criteria for stability were judged to be in the same category as the movie sequences using our free response categorizing technique. Disagreements with judgments from photographs were explained by the addition of new information occurring during the 30-second movie segment; these included events such as a yawn, eye closure, or smile. Thus, within the thirty seconds and under the conditions of our sampling, discrete events of emotional expression seemed reasonably well portrayed by our still photographs. Another way of thinking about this is that our photographs captured expressions that were communicated in small time units; such expressions may or may not depend upon sequential coding for their interpretation.

Another question about "usual performance" had to do with the infant's "behavioral day." In order to gain an estimate as to what expressions were over- or underrepresented by our somewhat arbitrary sampling, we did a continuous, time-lapse video recording of a single infant's face and upper torso during a twelve-hour period from 8:00 A.M. to 8:00 P.M. The infant was 3½ months of age and filming was done at home with mother instructed to carry on a "typical" day with the infant. (We subsequently established that the day of filming was indeed typical for the baby in terms of sleep, wakefulness, and feeding, when compared with records of the previous week and with normative data previously collected from longitudinal studies.) After completion of filming, we sampled still photographs of the videotape at ten-minute intervals throughout the twelve-hour period. Photos were then judged by twenty-five women as in our previous free response categorizing studies. Results indicated that our previous picture sampling had overrepresented joy and underrepresented sleep, and that blends of emotion were prominent in both methods of sampling. It should also be mentioned that 77 percent of the remaining twelve unfilmed hours of the infant's twenty-four-hour day consisted of sleep (Emde, 1980).

Other studies of this period focused on infant facial expressions of emotion in conditions of clinical deviance. Would methods that involved judgments of still photographs lead to more understanding of deviant emotional signals? A study of pictures sampled from Down's syndrome infants was enlightening (Emde et al., 1978). A multidimensional scaling approach was applied to pictures sampled from Down's infants at 3½ months. The technique was also applied to the mothers' verbal responses of these infants' pictures with such responses obtained through interviews one week after the initial sampling.

Mothers' responses were transcribed, placed on 3 × 5 cards, and subjected to similarity sorting procedures as were the photographs. Separate sorting studies for the photographs and for verbal responses gave similar results. The goodness of fit on dimensional outcomes was lower for these infants, fewer dimensions were obtained, and the dimensions were difficult to interpret or label. In other words, there was more "noise" in the signaling system of the Down's infants than for a comparison group of non-handicapped, normal infants. Since the same results were obtained from the pictures by independent judges, as well as from the biological mothers' verbal interpretations of their own infants' pictures, the findings could be interpreted as characteristic of the Down's infants and not their mothers, even though the latter were undergoing some difficulties in adaptation. Another study was more clinically oriented (Emde and Brown, 1978). It documented that not only is there more uncertainty in the Down's syndrome infant's emotional signaling, but the social smile is deviant by its dampened intensity, poor eye-to-eye contact, and lack of "crescendoing" activation. Instead of rewarding a social interaction and being engaging and "fun," the smile of the 3-month-old Down's child tends to disappoint. It is different from what is expected. In many families, the disappointing smile initiates a second wave of grieving for the normal child who was not born.

Further Validity Studies on Judgments of Infant Emotions from Pictures

To jump ahead a bit chronologically, a large collaborative study was carried out with the Izard laboratory to ascertain to what extent different teams of untrained judges in different laboratories in Delaware and Colorado could agree about facial expressions of emotions from infant pictures. Free response labeling and subsequent categorizing were used as a procedure in both laboratories. The modified lexicon for infancy with ten emotion categories was used for the categorizing. Agreement was assessed in replication studies, both within and across laboratories, using common sets of stimulus pictures generated in each laboratory. The idea was that although neither laboratory's stimulus sets of pictures could be considered representative of infant facial behavior in general, the two sets together offered more heterogeneity. The Colorado set was of 12-month-old infants sampled for "usual expressions." The Delaware set was of 2- to 10-month-old infants who were videotaped during an immunization visit to a public health clinic with still photographs subsequently selected for clear examples of emotion categories. All pictures consisted of a display of the face and upper torso. Each laboratory generated two picture sets according to the conditions described above and then exchanged them with the other laboratory. This resulted in four shared picture sets in each laboratory that could be used for judgment studies. Collaborative research could then proceed with replication studies within each of the two laboratory settings, as well as across laboratory settings, and using four different infant picture sets. A total of sixteen groups of untrained adult judges were used, eight in each laboratory.

The results of the study were striking. Agreements, assessed by correlating one group's judgments of the emotions present in a picture set with a second group's judgments, were high for joy, interest, distress–sadness, and surprise and somewhat less high for bored–sleepy, anger, and fear. Across-lab replications showed even higher agreement. Mean correlational values for all of the emotions mentioned ranged from .71 to .96. Interestingly, an analysis of the characteristics of the judges indicated that those who had more experience with children saw significantly more interest in the pictures, while those less experienced with children saw more fear. In summary, these results gave strong evidence that untrained judges can agree about the emotion-related social signal value of an infant's facial expressions and that groups of judges within each geographic region produce similar replication results (Emde, Izard, Huebner, Sorce, and Klinnert, 1985).

The above studies involved normal infants. Thus we could say that everyday emotional expressions and selected clear emotional expressions from normal infants could convey reliable messages to adults. But what about infants who were not normal? We pursued our studies with Down's syndrome facial expressions in an attempt to further understand the social meaning of infant emotional expressions. In comparison studies involving pictures sampled from normal infants and from Down's syndrome infants, we sought to see if there was a systematic relationship between the recognition of infant emotional expressions and the consequences of such recognition for caregiving. We assumed that effective communication requires contributions from both participants. The infant must be capable of presenting clear displays for each discrete emotion experienced so that the caregiver can monitor changes. The caregiver, in turn, must be sensitive to the infant's emotional signals and react with strategies that are matched to their meaning.

Two judgment studies involving pictures sampled from Down's syndrome and normal infants provided evidence that the above assumptions were correct (Sorce and Emde, 1981). In a first study, biological mothers served as respondents to their own infants' pictures taken on an earlier visit. Mothers' responses to a structured interview were recorded and transcribed. For each picture, a mother was asked what her infant was feeling and how she would typically respond, if at all. Her verbatim typed descriptions were later placed onto index cards for categorization by independent and naive judges. Results indicated that although categories of emotional expression did not differ between the Down's infant pictures and the normal infant pictures, the normals had a significantly higher proportion of judged high-intensity expressions and a lower proportion of low-intensity expressions. Categories of caregiving response were linked to emotion categories in both groups, but mothers of Down's infants were more stimulating in their stated caregiving interventions, especially during low emotional intensity. Since there were more low-intensity signals in Down's syndrome infant expressions, we considered that this tendency might be a form of compensation wherein the mothers of Down's infants recalibrated their responsiveness in line with the realities of a dampened expressive system found in their own infants.

This conclusion was confirmed in a second study in which the same sets of photos were judged by a larger sample of mothers who had normal infants of the same age as those in the first study but who were unfamiliar with the particular infants portrayed in the photos. These mothers sorted categories of emotional expression from the pictures and then gave their caregiving responses connected with each picture on a separate sorting procedure. As predicted, a second group of mothers (who had normal infants) saw more low-intensity emotional expressions in the Down's syndrome set of pictures than in the normal set; they also replicated the emotional expression categories seen in both sets by the biological mothers of the first study. Also in replication, they produced striking regularities in caregiving patterns for both normal and Down's syndrome pictures. Moreover, the regularities in caregiving judgments elicited in this independent group of mothers were related to recognized emotional expression signals, irrespective of whether they occurred from normal or Down's syndrome infants; in other words, there was no recalibration based on experience with a handicapped infant.

Our overall conclusion gave encouragement to the hypothesis that infant emotional signaling is a "natural language" for caregiving. Mothers who were unfamiliar with the photographed infants, like the biological mothers of these same infants, recognized emotional signal categories and responded to them with similar statements about probable caregiving activities. In both studies, the intensity of emotional signaling seemed a meaningful factor in guiding caregiving reactions and the particular emotion category seemed to guide which caregiving behavior would be selected as being appropriate. Even in a population of infants with deviant expressions, the associations appeared to hold between recognized facial patterns and caregiving activity. Finally, our attention was drawn to the importance of the caregiver's adaptation in this process. The biological mothers of the Down's syndrome infants made an adaptation in which they recalibrated their response threshold downwards for their deviant infants who had dampened expressions. They increased their tendency to intervene when their infants were not highly aroused. Mothers who were unfamiliar with both groups of infants did not evidence this compensatory adjustment.

The questions explored by the above studies dealt with the meaning of sampled infant photographs in judgments which were free of contextual cues. In judgment studies, we established that our pictures were evocative stimuli which elicited regular responses of emotion categories and that these responses could also be linked to regular or expectable caregiving interventions. The Down's syndrome studies also drew our attention to the importance of caregiver "fine tuning" to these expressions. Fine tuning, based on repeated interactions with an individual infant, seemed to involve adjustments in the level of stimulation but not the pattern of response. This finding pushed us more in the direction of what we had imagined earlier.

Could our pictures be used to type individual and group differences among those caregivers at risk for having problems with reading emotional signals? Could we identify caregivers who had problems reading the "language of infancy" in this way?

We used one of our standard picture sets of infant facial expressions to collect data concerning parental responses from those at high risk for child abuse and neglect. Data from ninety-eight mothers of infants in this risk population were obtained using our method of free response judgments and subsequent categorizing. Results of this study will be described in detail in chapter 8, but the preliminary results were contrary to our expectations. Our original idea was that responses to infant pictures would yield information about *parental perceptions* and that we might generate a technique which would ultimately prove useful in identifying individual differences in abilities for reading emotion signals. Correspondingly, we might be able to identify deviant parental perception needing rectification. Because of this line of thinking, we applied signal detection strategies borrowed from the field of perception in order to look at our risk population and compare that population with our group data obtained from low-risk, normal, mothers. We devised techniques to "weight" each of the pictures in our set according to the clarity of its emotion signal; we then assigned a factor to that picture according to which clear emotion signal pictures (usually agreed upon) carried more weight than unclear, blended, or low-intensity emotion pictures. Our expectation was that there would be substantial differences between high- and low-risk mothers. To our great surprise, we obtained no such differences!

We then shifted our line of thinking. It occurred to us that we should look at the distribution of emotion categories across the entire picture set, rather than looking for accuracy on a picture-by-picture basis. In other words, we should treat our picture set more like a projective technique such as a Rorschach or a Thematic Apperception Test (TAT). The picture set, treated as a whole, would present an opportunity for respondents to reflect any bias they might have about infant emotional expressions. When we shifted our analysis to one of content according to emotion categories across the picture set, we found major differences. Nearly one half of our high-risk group was identified as being two standard deviations or more from our low-risk group. The identified individuals in the high-risk group were also deviant in other ways, as determined from separately collected data in the high-risk study (see chapter 8).

The surprising results of our high-risk mother study produced a turnaround in both our thinking and our approach. We realized that since emotion signals are highly adaptive and strongly biologically prepared in our species, we should not expect clear emotional signals to be misinterpreted. Hence, the signal detection approach showed no differences between troubled and nontroubled mothers. On the other hand, when all emotion responses were considered and when low-intensity signals and blended emotional signals were given emphasis, troubled mothers could express a bias toward less interest and more sadness or disgust, for example. Practically speaking, we decided to continue our development of a potential assessment tool for studying caregivers and others' responses to these pictures. We would drop signal detection approaches, however, and use content analysis of responses. We would think in terms of respondents' interpretations instead of perceptions.

Recent Collaborative Efforts Leading Up to This Volume

Collaborative interest in what soon became known as the IFEEL Pictures became more intense in the 1980s. Early in the decade, as a result of work with Carroll Izard and

Joy Osofsky and their respective laboratories in Delaware and Kansas, we again made conservative modifications in the lexicon used for categorizing free responses of those looking at pictures. This was done in order to make categorizing more appropriate for infancy. As a consequence, we subdivided two emotion categories and tailored some word meanings to be more appropriate to usage by mothers of babies (see chapter 4). One category, formerly designated as "distress" was subdivided into "sadness" and "distress" (discomfort or pain). Another category, formerly designated as "shame–shyness" was subdivided into "shame–guilt" and "shyness." During this time Perry Butterfield, in our Colorado laboratory, began to focus her considerable skills on organizing our expanding collaborative efforts and on developing a standardized common data base. Since 1982, there has been considerable development of our picture set for purposes of standardization and validation. This work was a collaboration between the Colorado (Emde and Butterfield) and Kansas (Osofsky and Culp) groups.

Others who actively encouraged our efforts and joined in collaborative activities in the early 1980s included Carolyn Zahn-Waxler of the NIMH Laboratory of Developmental Psychology, Daniel Stern of New York Hospital/Cornell University Medical Center and, a bit later, Doreen Ridgeway, who became a MacArthur postdoctoral fellow at Colorado State University. The latter brought considerable skills and experience in emotion expression measurement and scaling to our collaborative work and this is reflected in the volume. Finally, the story of our being able to launch the IFEEL Pictures in this volume was made possible by a further addition to our collaborative team. Joy Osofsky, with her persistent interests in furthering the psychometric aspects of our developing method, interested Mark Appelbaum with some of our problems. Mark was persuaded to join us, first as a statistical consultant, and then as a collaborator who has guided our methods and their evolution.

A particularly happy development was our being able to design a dimensional approach to scoring our IFEEL Pictures to supplement our free response categorizing approach. The dimensional approach is described in chapter 6 by Ridgeway who also documents how it provides additional validation for the emotion categories; categories, as predicted, cluster together in a two-dimensional space when judgments studies, using her techniques, are carried out. As a result of additional studies carried out by Ridgeway and by Butterfield, a final version of the lexicon was prepared (see chapter 4, appendix A-5) in which both categorical and dimensional values can be assigned to emotion words. A computer program developed by Appelbaum and Kean is now available to assist in the scoring of words into both empirically based categories and dimensional values (see chapter 5).

Many others are currently doing exploratory research using the current version of our IFEEL Pictures. In addition to research in the United States, ongoing work is being carried out in Sweden, France, Argentina, and Japan. Some studies will be included as chapters in this volume (see section IV on Related Techniques). Others will be summarized in chapter 15 and a preliminary report concerning the use of a Japanese IFEEL Picture Set is presented in appendix C.

References

Campos, J., Emde, R. N., Gaensbauer, T. J., & Henderson, C. (1975), Cardiac and behavioral interrelationships in the reactions of infants to strangers. *Develop. Psychol.*, 11/5:589–601.

Ekman, P., Friesen, W., & Ellsworth, P. (1972), *Emotion in the Human Face*. New York: Pergamon Press.

Emde, R. N. (1980), Levels of meaning for infant emotions: A biosocial view. In: *Development of Cognition, Affect and Social Relations. Minnesota Symposia on Child Psychology*, Vol. 13, ed. W. A. Collins. Hillsdale, NJ: Lawrence Erlbaum Associates, pp. 1–37.

——— Brown, C. (1978), Adaptation to the birth of a Down's syndrome infant: Grieving and maternal attachment. *J. Amer. Acad. Child Psychiatry*, 17:299–323.

——— Gaensbauer, T. J., & Harmon, R. J. (1976), Emotional Expression in Infancy: A Biobehavioral Study. *Psychological Issues*, Monogr. 10/37. New York: International Universities Press.

——— Harmon, R. J. (1972), Endogenous and exogenous smiling systems in early infancy. *J. Amer. Acad. Child Psychiatry*, 11:177–200.

——— Izard, C., Huebner, R., Sorce, J. F., & Klinnert, M. D. (1985), Adult judgments of infant emotions: Replication studies within and across laboratories. *Infant Behav. & Develop.*, 8/1:79–88.

——— Katz, E. L., & Thorpe, J. K. (1978), Emotional expression in infancy. II. Early deviations in Down's syndrome. In: *The Development of Affect*, ed. M. Lewis & L. Rosenblum. New York: Plenum, pp. 351–360.

——— Kligman, D. H., Reich, J. H., & Wade, T. D. (1978), Emotional expression in infancy: I. Initial studies of social signaling and an emergent model. In: *The Development of Affect*, ed. M. Lewis & L. Rosenblum. New York: Plenum, pp. 125–148.

——— Koenig, K. L. (1969a), Neonatal smiling and rapid eye movement states. *J. Amer. Acad. Child Psychiatry*, 8:57–67.

——— ——— (1969b), Neonatal smiling, frowning, and rapid eye movement states. II. Sleep-cycle study. *J. Amer. Acad. Child Psychiatry*, 8:637–656.

Izard, C. (1971), *The Face of Emotion*. New York: Meredith & Appleton-Century-Crofts.

——— (1972), *Patterns of Emotion: A New Analysis of Anxiety and Depression*. New York: Academic Press.

Polak, P. R., Emde, R. N., & Spitz, R. A. (1964a), The smiling response. I. Methodology, quantification and natural history. *J. Nerv. & Ment. Dis.*, 139:103–109.

—————— —————— —————— (1964b), The smiling response. II. Visual discrimination and the onset of depth perception. *J. Nerv. & Ment. Disease*, 139:407–415.

Shepard, R. (1962a), The analysis of proximities: Multidimensional scaling with an unknown distance function. I. *Psychometrika*, 27:125–140.

—————— (1962b), The analysis of proximities: Multidimensional scaling with an unknown distance function. II. *Psychometrika*, 27:219–246.

—————— (1974), Representation of structure in similarity data: Problems and prospects. *Psychometrika*, 38/4:373–421.

Sorce, J. F., & Emde, R. N. (1981), Mother's presence is not enough: The effect of emotional availability on infant exploration. *Develop. Psychol.*, 17/6:737–745.

—————— —————— (1982), The meaning of infant emotional expressions: Regularities in caregiving responses in normal and Down's syndrome infants. *J. Child Psychol. & Psychiatry*, 23/2:145–158.

4

The IFEEL Pictures: Description, Administration, and Lexicon

Perry M. Butterfield and Doreen Ridgeway

Selection and Description

The current standard set of IFEEL Pictures (IFP) consists
of thirty photographs that are published in booklet form
for purposes of convenience in administration (The
IFEEL Picture Set).[1] Previous standard sets of IFEEL Pictures contained a larger number of photographs and are
indexed in appendix A-1. Information about the reference
sample is available for all of the subsets of pictures, particularly the current IFEEL Picture set (see chapter 5) and its
immediate precursor, the IFEEL-40 Picture set. The latter
contains the forty photographs initially selected for standardization; thirty of these make up the current standard
set. In this section, we will review the history of how we
chose our pictures and describe the current set, along with
some of its variations. The IFEEL Pictures constitute a

---

[1]The IFEEL Pictures booklet, R. N. Emde, P. M. Butterfield, and J. D.
Osofsky (1987), is available at cost from the authors. Address requests to: IFEEL
Pictures Booklet, % Dr. R. N. Emde, University of Colorado Health Sciences
Center, 4200 East Ninth Avenue, Box C268-69, Denver, Colorado 80262.

stimulus set that offers incentives for research and assessment. As such, the pictures can be adapted for multiple uses and we would expect work with them to continue evolving.

The Choice of Pictures in the Standard Set

We assembled a large pool of 35 mm color photographs of one-year-old infants—head and shoulder views. Photographs were taken during home visits as previously described. Early versions of picture sets were used to obtain mothers' judgments of emotions, using seventy pictures that were chosen to represent a range of emotions from five different children. Subsets of the seventy pictures were then assembled for ease of administration and usually consisted of either thirty-five or forty pictures. In selecting our pictures, photographic quality was taken into account. Some pictures were enlarged and cropped to emphasize the facial expression or to delete contextual cues.

In the evolution of our picture set from a pool of seventy pictures to a standard set of forty pictures (the immediate precursor to the IFP) we made further modifications. We selected a new picture that contained elements of fear and we chose five additional pictures of a black baby to add ethnic balance. The resulting IFEEL-40 Picture set has been used in a number of studies reported in the present volume.

During work with these early versions of the pictures, nine emotion categories were represented. The nine emotion categories included: (1) enjoyment–joy; (2) interest–excitement; (3) distress–anguish; (4) passive–bored; (5) surprise–startle; (6) anger–rage; (7) fear–terror; (8) disgust–contempt; (9) shame–humiliation (Lexicon, July 25, 1979). Most pictures were selected for their blends of emotion in order to allow for variability of interpretation.

Still, a few clear signals or what might be considered "prototypes" of emotion categories were retained.

The distribution of emotional content across picture sets was assessed for each new sample of subjects as well as for each new version of the sets themselves. A reference table of emotional content according to data from earlier samples of subjects and from earlier versions of picture sets is available from the authors on request. As the IFEEL Pictures continued to evolve, we paid attention to having blends of multiple emotions represented so that a typical picture would have response tendencies for more than one emotion (see chapter 6, Figure 6.4). Chapter 5 describes the distribution of numbers of responses within each emotion category for our current standard IFEEL Pictures set.

Our coding of maternal emotion words (the lexicon) also continued to evolve. For purposes of the present discussion, it is important to point out that the analysis of the lexicon led us to separate the emotion category of sad from distress–anguish, shy from shame–humiliation, and content from passive-bored and from joy. These changes in the lexicon increased the number of emotion categories represented to twelve instead of nine. The number of pictures that would then be expected to represent each emotion category would, correspondingly, be fewer than before.

Our final IFEEL Picture set containing thirty pictures resulted from our testing experience, suggesting that a smaller number of pictures would be more manageable and would still yield rich information from individual respondents (Butterfield, 1986).

As already mentioned, earlier versions of the IFEEL Pictures were used in some of the studies reported in this volume. They were subsets of the original seventy pictures and reference information is available concerning them, along with the expectable categories of emotion. Such information can be reviewed as part of the relevant studies and by referring to appendix A-2. Some earlier studies used a random order of presentation of pictures instead of the current fixed order that is now recommended. Analyses showed no differences in results from random or fixed order presentations—a fact that made us more comfortable in binding the pictures in the IFEEL Pictures booklet.

How to Use the IFEEL Pictures

The published booklet of IFEEL Pictures contains numbered color photographs in a bound form for easy administration. As described in the previous section, the pictures were chosen primarily for their blends of emotion, and some for their ambiguity. The variety of coloring, shadowing, and clarity of the photographs is designed to model daily occurrences rather than to re-create clear prototypes of emotional expressions. With this approach, there are, typically, a number of different emotions that can be used to characterize any given picture. Thus, the overall profile of a respondent is what might yield an extreme projection of emotionality. For example, if a mother records ten pictures as "angry," which constitutes one-third of the set, or seven pictures as "guilty" (one-fourth of the set), her profile would be remarkably different from the broad range of usual maternal responses.

ADMINISTRATION

To administer the IFEEL Pictures, the mother or other respondent is given the booklet along with a corresponding numbered response sheet (see appendixes A-3, A-4). The directions given are as follows: "Here are some pictures of babies' facial expressions. Please tell us, in one word if possible, the strongest and clearest feeling that

125

129

106

110

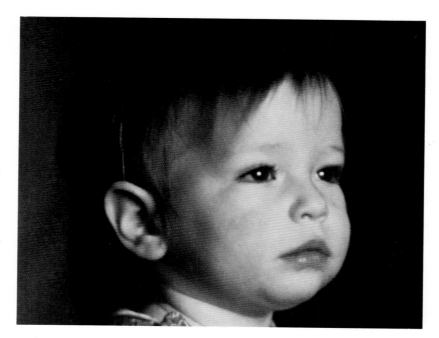

116

108

119

113

each baby is expressing. There are no right or wrong answers. Please respond with what first comes to your mind.
We would like to have you turn the pages of the Picture
Booklet one at a time and in the space on this sheet which
has the same number as the picture you are thinking
about, write down what each baby is feeling." *Note*: There
are some special circumstances where prompts may be necessary. If the tester is asked "What do you mean by feelings?" or "I can't think of any feeling words," and if the
tester believes that instruction through example is necessary for an individual or group of individuals, the following procedure is recommended. The tester explains by
saying "Let me give you a list of words that we think of as
feeling words. Such words are joy, sadness, distress, fear,
surprise, disgust, shame, shy, withdrawn, interest, con-
tented." It is important that a tester uses all of the emotion
categories which will be coded when giving such a prompt
and it is crucial to note that the supplemental explanation
was given.

A visual check of the finished score sheet while the
mother is still present is helpful in order to catch any ambiguous or nonfeeling words such as "cute," "grunting,"
"wired," "overcome." Occasionally a description of actions
rather than feelings is given such as "hungry" or "where's
Mom?". When a first response is unclear the tester can ask
the respondent, "What feeling do you mean by that?" or
"Tell me more about what you mean." In this way, a more
complete set of data can be obtained.

If a respondent has trouble with expressing her
thoughts due to language or writing limitations, the responses to the IFEEL Pictures may be given verbally with
the tester recording on the response sheet. In this case,
caution must be taken not to direct the respondent. It is
common to be asked such questions as these: "This is a
hard one, what do you think she looks like?"; "Would you

call this sadness?"; "I just can't think of the word for this look. Can you?" The tester should be encouraging in such circumstances but should not give directed answers to such questions. The verbal administration method may have advantages in speeding up responses, but it also carries a risk of a different kind of tester–respondent interaction. For this reason, we recommend this modification of procedure be used conservatively. It should always be noted and if used for group data, the modified procedure should be consistent for the entire sample.

SCORING RESPONSES

There are two methods for scoring the word responses from IFEEL Pictures. These are: (1) a categorical method, which classifies a subject's response as belonging to a specific emotion category such as joy, sad, etc., and (2) a dimensional method which classifies a subject's response by coordinates of emotional intensity and hedonic tone.

With the first method, responses are scored according to twelve categories of emotion. These categories are made up of words that tend to cluster together when rated for their dimension of positive versus negative hedonic tone and high versus low arousal (see chapter 6). These clusters of words are grouped or categorized in the Lexicon under an emotional label and code number. The categories are: (1) surprise, (2) interest, (3) joy, (4) contentment, (5) passive, (6) sad, (7) cautious–shy, (8) shame–guilt, (9) disgust, (10) anger, (11) distress, (12) fear. The category "Other" is used for words which are unclear and do not fit into a designated emotion category, such as *charming, evasive, jerked around, hungry, moody.*

With the second method, responses are scored according to their location on two dimensions. The coordinates on these dimensions for each word can then be summed by emotion or by quadrant on a dimensional scoring map giving a separate value of hedonic tone and arousal for each subject or for a subject pool. The quadrants represent high arousal/positive, low arousal/positive, low arousal/negative, and high arousal/negative. The quadrant system may be useful in describing a subject who may have both positive and negative emotions represented as expected but who shows an unusual distribution of responses, such as using primarily low arousal/positive and low arousal/negative words or subjects who have both high arousal/positive and high arousal/negative responses. Finally, the quadrant system may provide a useful array when one considers that there is increasing evidence to support the view that positive and negative emotions are organized independently (Emde and Easterbrooks, Typescript).

A computer-assisted program is available for scoring responses to the IFEEL Pictures (appendix A-5). The program allows the coder to enter the word given for each picture directly from the subjects' numbered response sheet. The program then scores the data according to categories and dimensions. Words have been assigned into categories based on previous research as already described. Words are given dimensional values based on two studies that are described in chapter 5. Following the automatic assignment of values for each word, the computer program will generate a descriptive analysis for each subject and summarize any requested group analyses, along with comparative profiles using the reference sample. The nature of the latter comparisons will become clear when reading the next section of this chapter.

IFEEL Pictures Booklet users may also score responses without the computer-assisted program. For manual scoring, each response word for a subject is located in the IFEEL Pictures Lexicon in order to find the emotion category to which it belongs (appendix A-5). The word response is then assigned the relevant code number for that category. Code numbers are summarized for each individual, and may be used for group analyses and for comparisons with the IFEEL Reference Sample (as described in the next chapter). For dimensional scoring, without the computer-assisted program, each response must also be located in the Lexicon where the coordinates for the hedonic and arousal dimensions (derived from our earlier studies) are listed. A separate score can then be computed for hedonic tone and emotional arousal, both with respect to individual subjects and groups of subjects.

A profile display of categorized responses may be useful for interpreting responses of individuals or groups, particularly when manual (non-computer-assisted) scoring is carried out. An example of a profile is presented in Figure 4.1. The profile gives a background of reference sample mean scores by emotion category and allows for the display of an individual subject's (or group's) values against this background. Thus, individuals might be identified who are three or more standard deviations above or below the mean on one or more emotions; such individuals might then be considered extreme and targeted for further inquiry. In the example presented in Figure 4.1, one sees extremely high fear. The variation in emotion content within the Reference Sample and within other control samples reported in this volume is consistently narrow. Therefore a subject profile with two or more emotions which are two standard deviations beyond the mean is worthy of inquiry.

A second useful approach in looking at individual subjects' scored responses may be to consult the table that reflects the content of each emotion for each picture in our Reference Sample (see chapter 5 and Table 5.9). Thus, seeing an anger response to a picture for which the typical

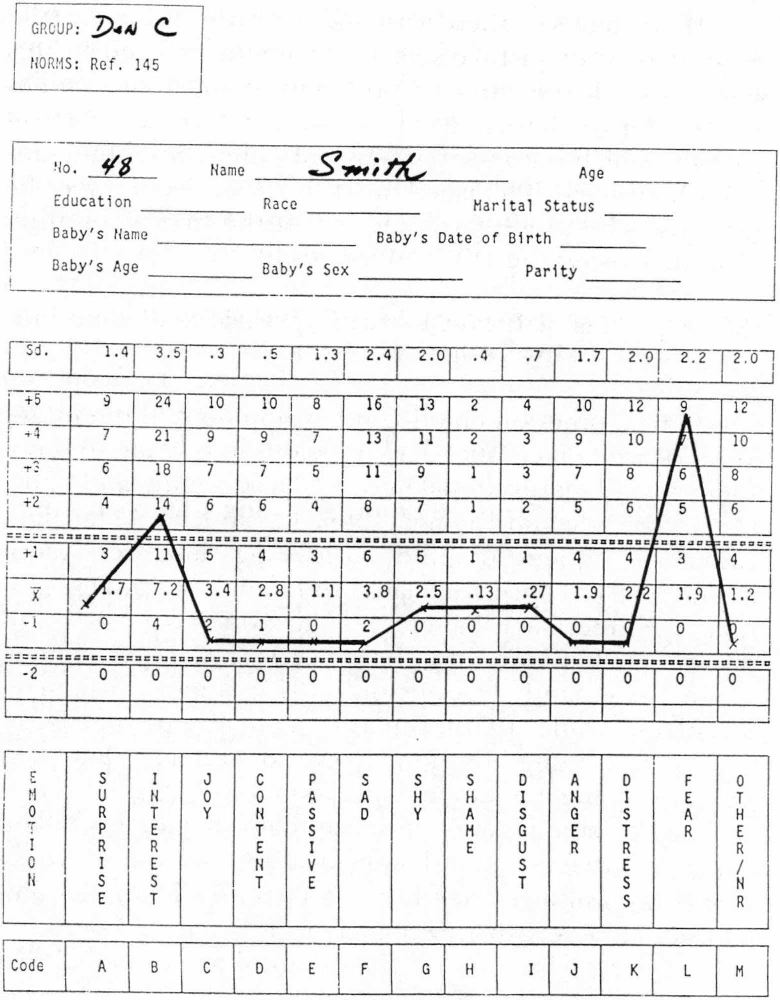

GROUP: *Dan C*

NORMS: Ref. 145

No. _48_ Name _Smith_ Age _____

Education _____ Race _____ Marital Status _____

Baby's Name _____ Baby's Date of Birth _____

Baby's Age _____ Baby's Sex _____ Parity _____

Sd.	1.4	3.5	.3	.5	1.3	2.4	2.0	.4	.7	1.7	2.0	2.2	2.0
+5	9	24	10	10	8	16	13	2	4	10	12	9	12
+4	7	21	9	9	7	13	11	2	3	9	10		10
+3	6	18	7	7	5	11	9	1	3	7	8	6	8
+2	4	14	6	6	4	8	7	1	2	5	6	5	6
+1	3	11	5	4	3	6	5	1	1	4	4	3	4
X̄	1.7	7.2	3.4	2.8	1.1	3.8	2.5	.13	.27	1.9	2.2	1.9	1.2
-1	0	4	2	1	0	2	0	0	0	0	0	0	0
-2	0	0	0	0	0	0	0	0	0	0	0	0	0

EMOTION	SURPRISE	INTEREST	JOY	CONTENTMENT	PASSIVE	SAD	SHY	SHAME	DISGUST	ANGER	DISTRESS	FEAR	OTHER/NR
Code	A	B	C	D	E	F	G	H	I	J	K	L	M

FIGURE 4.1
Subject Profile/IFEEL Pictures.

response is rarely anger and frequently joy may result in incentives for further inquiry.

In summary, we find that the IFEEL Pictures are easy to administer with minimal training required for testers. Respondents typically say that they enjoy the experience, and testing can be done in a variety of settings such as pediatric offices, day care centers, or during home visits. We recommend the use of our computer-assisted scoring program since it automatically categorizes and assigns dimensional values to words; the program adds efficiency and minimizes coding errors. Manual scoring, however, can also be done quite readily and our Reference Sample can provide useful initial comparisons (see chapter 14). We will next consider the IFEEL Pictures Lexicon and describe the process by which we have refined our categories of emotion words and added their dimensional values.

The IFEEL Pictures Lexicon: Refining Categories and Adding Dimensions

A lexicon of emotion labels accompanies the IFEEL Pictures (see appendix A-5). This lexicon provides a scoring system through which the subject's recorded response to each photo is assigned to one of twelve discrete emotion categories. The subject's response is also assigned two-dimensional values of hedonic tone and arousal. Both the categorical and dimensional approaches to scoring are possible because of previous research with respect to individual lexicon words. The remainder of this chapter will describe the process by which we have refined categories and added dimensions for the Lexicon.

REFINING CATEGORIES

The Lexicon used for the IFP was initially adapted from the one used to study adults who responded to photos of adult faces (Izard, 1972). The original adult picture-based lexicon was rated according to nine categories that included: happiness, surprise, fear, anger, passive–bored, disgust–contempt, interest, distress–anguish, and shame –humiliation. In coding responses to photos of infant facial expressions, it soon became apparent that a substantial number of words used to describe babies were not included in the original lexicon (Emde, Izard, Huebner, Sorce, and Klinnert, 1985). Examples of such words included *fussy, naughty, secure*. Many of these words were added to the lexicon, thus creating the need to collect normative or "reference" information. As we continued to use the lexicon, we encountered more words which were uncodable and we thus found it necessary to create an "other" category. Some words falling into the "other" category were specific to babies but did not meet the criteria of denoting "feeling or emotion." Such responses might describe physiological–behavioral states like "nursing," "hungry," and "nauseated." Other words seemed to describe expressions such as *fixated, innocent,* and *needs protection.*[2]

As we began to use the IFP Lexicon for women identified as being at risk for parenting (see chapters 7, 8, and 9), we encountered further variability in responses. We expanded the words in our "Other" category due to the large number of uncodable words and, at the same time, we also decided to increase the specificity of emotion categories within the lexicon. Two of the original nine emotion categories mentioned above were subdivided. These categories were the original ones of distress–anguish and shame–humiliation. "Distress" now became reserved for words which conveyed physical discomfort such as *pain, upset, hurting, fussy,* and *distress*. A new category, "sad," was

---

[2]An extensive list of "other" words is now included as part of the IFEEL Pictures Lexicon.

created for such words as *broken-hearted, despairing, hopeless, rejected, depressed,* and *unloved.* The original category shame–humiliation was also split into a category "shy"—which included words such as *bashful, timid, embarrassed,* and a category shame–guilt—which included judgmental words such as *blameworthy, remorseful, naughty,* and *guilty* (Emde, Butterfield, Osofsky, Gaddis, Ridgeway, Stern, Kaplan, and Zahn-Waxler, 1986).

ADDING A DIMENSIONAL APPROACH

As research continued, we became more aware of the value of including a dimensional approach in our work (Butterfield, Ridgeway, Appelbaum, Emde, and Osofsky, 1989). Not only would such an approach allow us to obtain information relevant for dimensional theories of emotion (see chapter 2), but also it would provide, in one assessment tool, a comparison of both categorical and dimensional views. From another perspective, the dimensional comparison could be thought of as an aspect of cross-validation for the IFEEL Pictures categorization method. Obtaining dimensional information could document the extent to which the "categories" of emotion in the Lexicon "map on" to expectable areas of a two-dimensional space for hedonic tone and arousal (see chapters 5 and 6).

Figure 4.2 illustrates a graphic arrangement of how the categories relate to the dimensional space. It represents the words in the current Lexicon as they were placed by mothers asked to reflect a baby's feelings. Interrelationships are striking when placing the categories within a spatial configuration, forming, in effect, a "map of emotions" in which closeness in space represents similarity of feelings. The center of the space on such a map represents a neutral feeling. Around the periphery, in roughly a circular order, fall the commonly encountered emotion-denoting words. Thus, underlying this arrangement can be seen

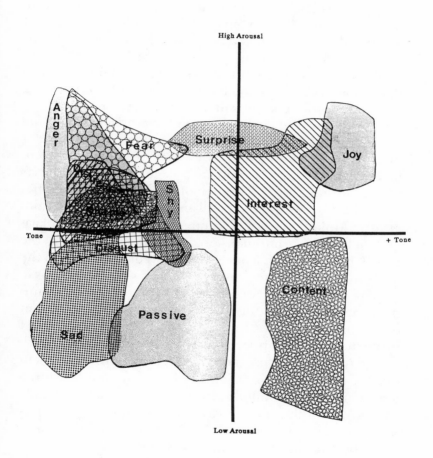

FIGURE 4.2
Dimensional coding map.

two bipolar dimensions: hedonic tone (positive–negative) along the horizontal axis and degree of arousal (activation–sleepiness) along the vertical axis. As mentioned in chapter 2, this model relates to a long line of theorizing that has emphasized dimensions on a circular structure of emotions (Woodworth and Schlosberg, 1954; Abelson and Sermat, 1962; Russell and Weiss, 1983; Emde, Kligman, Reich, and Wade, 1978; Plutchik, 1980). Empirical evidence for the circular model originally involved a scaling of twenty-eight emotion words (Russell, 1980).

Ridgeway (see chapter 6) conducted studies with the IFEEL Pictures using a dimensional model. Dimensions of meaning attributed to the IFEEL Pictures were studied in mothers of 2-year-olds and in college students. Subjects indicated similarity between emotions by placing the photographs of the infants' facial expressions together into groups. Multidimensional scaling of the pair-wise similarities yielded a two-dimensional structure in which the IFEEL expressions fell in roughly a circular order with the dimensions of pleasure–displeasure and degree of arousal. Similar results were found for mothers and college students which was not the case with free labeling of infant emotions (see chapter 6). The form and the meaning of this structure was supported through unidimensional scaling on the hedonic tone and the degree of arousal dimensions. Cross-validation using the free response categorizing technique and multidimensional scaling yielded highly significant results. There was a strong tendency for pictures similarly labeled in the free response paradigm to be close together in the two-dimensional space.

The early lexicons had grouped words into emotion categories by consensus of the experimenters. It was intriguing to contemplate an empirically based lexicon with word location defined by mothers contemplating how their infants would feel if defined as "miserable."

Ridgeway began this task with another sample of college females who were asked to indicate the positions of words on a graphic space for two basic dimensions of hedonic tone and arousal. Using the resulting scaling, homogeneity within each discrete category was then examined. The technique is taken from Russell and Weiss's Affect Grid (Russell and Weiss, 1983) in which scores for each dimension can range from one to nine. Each subject was given a set of instructions on how to use the Affect Grid and was then told: "We want you to describe what it is like when you feel ———— (the target word). Pause to think just what the feeling is like. Then use the grid below to describe this feeling. Remember that each position in the grid refers to how you might feel" (see appendix A-4). Each subject rated thirty-two different emotion-related terms. The set of terms rated by each subject was randomly selected from the total list of early lexicon words. All members of each group of fifty rated the same thirty-two items to provide reliability data. For each emotion-related word, mean positive–negative tone and mean high–low arousal scores were computed across all subjects who rated that word.

The clustering of words mapped by the college students about their feelings closely parallel the original lexicon. These results were heartening and led us to pursue a sample of mothers who would be asked to map each word from their infant's point of view. That is, "If your baby (all babies were 12 to 24 months old) feels 'excited' where would you place his or her feeling on the Affect Grid?" In the mother-respondent study, we encompassed the total of 162 words used by the Reference Sample mothers by virtue of having three different questionnaires administered to different samples of mothers, each questionnaire contained 54 different words. Seventy-eight middle-class mothers completed the forms (26 mothers per 54-word set).

In general, the results from the mothers agreed with the results from the college students, with some notable exceptions. Group means for 85 percent of the words rated by the two groups of subjects were within .23 to .30 of a rating point from one another on our 9-point scale. However, 15 percent of the words fell into different categories. For example, "studying" was viewed by mothers as interest and by college students as passive–bored.

As illustrated in Figure 4.2, the circular order of emotion categories around the perimeter of the two-dimensional space validated previous research. The emotion word placement by mothers was adopted for the IFEEL Lexicon, each word was given a dimensional coordinate score which identified it on the dimensional map. Words such as *thoughtful, delighted,* and *joyous* fell into the combination of positive hedonic tone and high arousal. The bottom right quadrant contains calm, relaxed, and peaceful and is a combination of positive tone and low arousal. Moving on around the circumplex, the bottom left quadrant contains sad, lonely, and depressed and is the combination of negative tone and low arousal. The top left quadrant contains angry, afraid, and tense and is a combination of positive tone and high arousal. At the positive end of the pleasure axis are feelings such as "caring," "energetic," "loving," "assured," and "playful"; feelings such as "pain," "hate," and "humiliation" are at the low end. At the high end of the arousal axis are feelings such as "surprised," "excited," "horrified," whereas "sleeping," "depressed," and "tired" are at the low end. Clearly defined emotion words fall at the edge of the two-dimensional space, whereas more ambivalent emotion descriptors such as "concentrating," "undecided," or "indifferent" fall closer to the center of the space.

The results led to some notable changes in the original lexicon. A new category, Content, was added. This cluster includes words pulled from both joy and passive that were defined by the mothers to be high on hedonic tone, but low on arousal ("peaceful," "relaxed," and "tranquil"). The category passive now contains only words which cluster together in the low tone and low arousal quadrant (*bored, disturbed, withdrawn,* and *exhausted*). Some words did not cluster with the presumed category of the early lexicon. Readjustments were made to place all words in the current lexicon within the clusters or categories selected by the mothers. An example is "miserable" which was formerly in the category sad but was mapped by mothers considering their infant's feeling state as negative tone, high arousal, clustering with distress. In this context, "miserable" is read more as teething or hungry, rather than depressed. These studies of dimensional representation allowed us to have our subjects map many of the words from earlier studies that had been collected in the category Other. These words are now included as available data in the scoring lexicon.

The Current Lexicon

The current IFEEL Pictures Lexicon includes twelve emotion categories and two additional categories, Other and No Response, for use for uncodable responses. Emotion categories include: surprise, interest, joy, content, passive, sad, cautious–shy, shame–guilt, disgust–dislike, anger, distress, and fear. Entries within a category are based on clusters defined by dimensional scaling in terms of hedonic tone and degree of arousal.

Most of the studies in this volume report results that are coded using the current lexicon. Some studies, however, were completed prior to the current lexicon and used an earlier version (chapters 8 and 9). The lexicon which now accompanies the IFP is based on the mother's judgments and provides a dimensional coordinate score of hedonic tone and arousal for each word as well as a categorical placement code (see appendix A-5). The result is that a subject's response to a picture can be scored and compared to a reference norm using either the categorical or the dimensional rating system.

The reader now has the background and current information needed to use the IFEEL Pictures in research. The next chapter describes the operating characteristics and psychometric properties of the IFEEL Pictures and will provide a more detailed anchoring for the descriptions we had given.

References

Abelson, R. P., & Sermat, V. (1962), Multidimensional scaling of facial expressions. *J. Experiment. Psychol.*, 63:546–554.

Butterfield, P. M. (1986), Women "at risk" for parenting disorders perceive emotions in infant pictures differently. Poster presentation to Third World Congress of the World Association of Infant Psychiatry and Allied Disciplines, Stockholm, Sweden.

———— Ridgeway, D., Appelbaum, M. I., Emde, R. N., & Osofsky, J. D. (1989), A new methodology for scoring the IFEEL pictures. Paper presented at Fourth World Congress of the World Association of Infancy Psychiatry and Allied Disciplines. Lugano, Switzerland.

Emde, R. N., & Easterbrooks, M. A. (1991) Positive emotions and the toddler, UCHSC (Typescript).

———— Butterfield, P. M., Osofsky, J. D., Gaddis, E., Ridgeway, D., Stern, D. N., Kaplan, T., & Zahn-Waxler, C. (1986), Parental perceptions of infant emotions: A new instrument. Paper presented at the International Conference on Infant Studies, Los Angeles.

———— Izard, C., Huebner, R., Sorce, J. F., & Klinnert, M. D. (1985), Adult judgments of infant emotions: Replication studies within and across laboratories. *Infant Behav. & Develop.*, 8/11:79–88.

———— Kligman, D. H., Reich, J. H., & Wade, T. D. (1978), Emotional expression in infancy: I. Initial studies of social signaling and an emergent model. In: *The Development of Affect*, ed. M. Lewis & L. Taft. New York: Plenum, pp. 409–424.

Izard, C. (1972), *Patterns of Emotion: A New Analysis of Anxiety*. New York: Academic Press.

Plutchik, R. (1980), *The Emotions: A Psychoevolutionary Synthesis*. New York: Harper & Row.

Russell, J. A. (1980), A circumplex model of affect. *J. Pers. & Soc. Psychol.*, 39:1161–1178.

———— Weiss, A. (1983), *The Affect Grid: A Single-Item Mood Scale* (Typescript). University of British Columbia, Vancouver.

Weiss, P. (1938), *Principles of Development*. New York: Holt.

Woodworth, R. S., & Schlosberg, H. S. (1954), *Experimental Psychology*. New York: Holt.

5

Operating Characteristics and Psychometric Properties of the IFEEL Pictures

Mark I. Appelbaum, Perry M. Butterfield, Rex E. Culp

The operating characteristics and psychometric properties of the IFEEL Pictures (IFP) were derived from a 145-member reference population described below, as well as from data collected in two additional samples (a short-term test–retest sample, and a sample examining long-term stability) which will be described as they are introduced. The characteristics of the IFP are described both in terms of an Emotion Category scoring approach and an Emotion Dimensional scoring approach. In all cases, the raw protocols were rescored using the computerized IFEEL Pictures scoring program (Kean and Appelbaum, 1990) and, as a consequence, the data correspond to the Lexicon provided in the scoring program (see appendix A-5 for examples of the Lexicon). The data were scored following the conventions described in chapter 4.

The Reference Sample

The Reference Sample is made up of 145 mothers of infants between the ages of 3 and 12 months when the data were collected. The Reference Sample was developed by combining data from five subsamples in order to assure a broad representation of age and economic status. Three of the subsamples were collected in Denver, one from a pediatric clinic in a county hospital ($n = 21$), and two subsamples of mothers who had volunteered to participate in two different studies of child development ($n = 30$, $n = 37$, respectively). Two additional subsamples were recruited from a range of pediatric office-based practices in Topeka, Kansas ($n = 32$, $n = 25$, respectively).[1] Demographic characteristics of the 145-member Reference Sample are presented in Table 5.1. While the five subsamples differ along a number of demographic characteristics, there were virtually no differences among the subsamples in terms of their responses to the IFP stimuli.

The Reference Sample is, essentially, a white (93.7%) middle-class sample (mean maternal education of 14.53 years) of nonadolescent mothers (mean maternal age 28.61) with, on average, 1.81 children.

Basic Descriptive Data Obtained from the Reference Sample

EMOTION CODES

The basic descriptive data obtained from the responses of the Reference Sample are presented in Tables 5.2, 5.3, and 5.4. Table 5.2 contains the raw frequencies of responses within each of the fourteen emotion categories provided by the members of the Reference Sample. These vary from a very wide range of responses (0–16) within the interest category (category B), to rather constricted ranges (0–3) for the Shame–Guilt (category H) and (0–4)

---

[1] The early version of the Reference Sample involved three of the five groups ($n = 83$) and is used in chapters 8 and 9.

TABLE 5.1
Demographic Characteristics of the Reference Sample (N = 145)

Age		
Mean	28.64	
Standard Deviation	4.83	
Skewness	−0.06	
Kurtosis	−0.24	
75th Percentile	32	
50th Percentile	29	
25th Percentile	26	
Race		
White	135	(93.7%)
Black	7	(4.9%)
Hispanic	2	(1.4%)
Number of Children		
Mean	1.81	
Standard Deviation	1.00	
Skewness	1.68	
Kurtosis	3.71	
Marital Status		
Not Married	16	(11.1%)
Married	128	(88.9%)
Maternal Education (in years)		
Mean	14.53	
Standard Deviation	2.31	
Skewness	0.19	
Kurtosis	−0.99	
75th Percentile	16	
50th Percentile	14	
25th Percentile	12	
Target Child's Gender		
Male	77	(53.5%)
Female	67	(46.5%)
Missing	1	

TABLE 5.1
(continued)

Target Child's Age (in months)	
Mean	12.46
Standard Deviation	6.48
Skewness	0.77
Kurtosis	1.49
75th Percentile	14
50th Percentile	13
25th Percentile	7.5

Disgust–Dislike category (category I). The same data, converted to percentages, are presented in Table 5.3. Table 5.4 contains the summary statistics for emotion category usage by the subjects in the reference sample.

OTHER AND NO RESPONSE CATEGORIES

As can be seen in Tables 5.2, 5.3, and 5.4, relatively few responses of the members of the Reference Sample fell into the nonscorable categories of "Other" and "No Response." Of the 145 members of the Reference Sample, 121 (or 83.4%) responded to all thirty of the IFEEL Pictures. Of the total 4350 responses in this sample only 51 (1.17%) were refusals or failures to respond. The maximum number of "No Response" responses from any subject was four. One may conclude from these data that the task and stimuli are reasonable for subjects of the type included in the Reference Sample.

Of the 4417 actual responses collected, 4299 (or 98.8%) fell into codable emotion categories. Only 118 (2.67%) of the responses were responses which fell into the "Other" category; 53.7 percent of all respondents had no responses which fell into the "Other" category, and

TABLE 5.2

Distribution of Responses of the Reference Sample by Emotion Category

Number of Responses Scored in This Category	A	B	C	D	E	F	G
0	38	2	1	1	66	8	31
1	27	1	6	34	35	17	25
2	45	6	26	28	18	25	21
3	21	12	58	40	18	26	24
4	9	14	30	23	4	15	24
5	4	15	16	11	3	20	8
6	1	14	6	6	1	13	7
7	–	18	1	1	–	11	2
8	–	11	–	–	–	7	2
9	–	14	1	1	–	2	1
10	–	12	–	–	–	1	–
11	–	8	–	–	–	–	–
12	–	7	–	–	–	–	–
13	–	6	–	–	–	–	–
14	–	2	–	–	–	–	–
15	–	1	–	–	–	–	–
16	–	2	–	–	–	–	–

	H	I	J	K	L	M	N
0	129	120	32	37	52	77	121
1	14	19	41	20	28	40	10
2	1	1	31	30	23	18	5
3	1	2	15	26	10	5	6
4	–	3	10	13	12	2	2
5	–	–	12	9	6	–	1
6	–	–	3	4	6	2	–
7	–	–	1	5	4	1	–
8	–	–	–	1	1	–	–
9	–	–	–	–	2	–	–
10	–	–	–	–	1	–	–

Categories:

A	—	Surprise	H	—	Shame–Guilt
B	—	Interest	I	—	Disgust–Dislike
C	—	Joy	J	—	Anger
D	—	Content	K	—	Distress
E	—	Passive	L	—	Fear
F	—	Sad	M	—	Other
G	—	Cautious–Shy	N	—	No Response

TABLE 5.3
Distribution of Numbers of Responses (in Percentage) within
Each Emotion Category

Number of Responses Scored in This Category	A	B	C	D	E	F	G
0	26.2	1.4	0.7	0.7	45.5	5.5	21.4
1	18.6	0.7	4.1	23.4	24.1	11.7	17.2
2	31.0	4.1	17.9	19.3	12.4	17.2	14.5
3	14.5	8.3	40.0	27.6	12.4	17.9	16.6
4	6.2	9.7	20.7	15.9	2.6	10.3	16.6
5	2.8	10.3	11.0	7.6	2.1	13.8	5.5
6	0.7	9.7	4.1	4.1	0.7	9.0	4.8
7	—	12.4	0.7	0.7	—	7.6	1.4
8	—	7.6	—	—	—	4.8	1.7
9	—	9.7	0.7	0.7	—	1.4	0.7
10	—	8.3	—	—	—	0.7	—
11	—	5.5	—	—	—	—	—
12	—	4.8	—	—	—	—	—
13	—	4.1	—	—	—	—	—
14	—	1.4	—	—	—	—	—
15	—	0.7	—	—	—	—	—
16	—	1.4	—	—	—	—	—

	H	I	J	K	L	M	N
0	89.0	82.8	22.1	25.5	35.9	53.1	83.4
1	9.7	13.1	28.3	13.8	19.3	27.6	6.9
2	0.7	0.7	21.4	20.7	17.9	12.4	3.4
3	0.7	1.4	10.3	17.9	6.9	3.4	4.1
4	—	2.1	6.9	9.0	8.3	1.4	1.4
5	—	—	8.3	6.2	4.1	—	0.7
6	—	—	2.1	2.8	4.1	1.4	—
7	—	—	0.7	3.4	2.8	0.7	—
8	—	—	—	0.7	0.7	—	—
9	—	—	—	—	1.4	—	—
10	—	—	—	—	0.7	—	—

Categories:

A	—	Surprise	H	—	Shame–Guilt
B	—	Interest	I	—	Disgust–Dislike
C	—	Joy	J	—	Anger
D	—	Content	K	—	Distress
E	—	Passive	L	—	Fear
F	—	Sad	M	—	Other
G	—	Cautious–Shy	N	—	No Response

TABLE 5.4
Summary Statistics—Emotion Category Use by Reference Subjects

Code	Emotion Category	% of Total Responses	Mean	Standard Deviation	Skewness	Kurtosis
A	Surprise	5.56	1.67	1.37	.57	2.93
B	Interest	24.11	7.23	3.42	.29	2.56
C	Joy	11.13	3.36	1.30	.80	5.11
D	Content	9.40	2.82	1.54	.79	3.95
E	Passive	3.72	1.12	1.35	1.22	3.99
F	Sad	12.51	3.75	2.31	.41	2.42
G	Cautious–Shy	8.18	2.46	2.03	.68	3.08
H	Shame–Guilt	.44	.13	.41	3.91	21.92
I	Disgust–Dislike	.90	.27	.74	3.62	17.17
J	Anger	6.28	1.88	1.67	.87	3.02
K	Distress	7.40	2.22	1.94	.76	3.05
L	Fear	6.48	1.94	1.35	1.35	4.37
M	Other	2.71	.81	1.21	2.41	10.76
N	No Response	1.17	.35	.92	2.93	11.40

93.1 percent had two or fewer such responses. The rather heavy "tailedness" of both the "Other' and "No Response" categories are indexed by the very high levels of kurtosis seen in these two categories.

HIGH FREQUENCY CATEGORIES

Three of the emotion categories (interest, joy, and sad) constitute the high-frequency categories, that is, those in which the mean number of responses is three or greater. These three categories account for nearly one-half (47.75%) of all of the responses of the Reference Sample. These three categories are not only frequently used, they are used at least somewhat by nearly all respondents. Only 1.4 percent of the subjects never gave responses in the interest category, only 0.7 percent never gave responses in the joy category, and only 5.5 percent never gave responses in the sad category. Clearly, responses in the Interest category were by far the more often used (mean rate being 7.23 such responses per subject) with three to ten such responses being very typical of a subject in the Reference Sample, and 24.11 percent of all responses being in this category. Sad responses (mean rate being 3.75) and joy responses (mean rate being 3.36) were the next most frequently used categories, but were together used slightly less often than the interest response category. All three categories show distributions which are not heavily skewed and whose kurtosis is not terribly deviant from that seen in the normal distribution.

MEDIUM FREQUENCY CATEGORIES

Seven of the fourteen emotion categories fall into the medium use range—average usage of one to nearly three responses per subject. These categories (surprise, content, passive, cautious–shy, anger, distress, and fear) together account for 47.02 percent of the total responses of the Reference Sample (just slightly less than the three most frequent categories). Subjects will typically use one or two responses in each of these categories, but it is not uncommon to find subjects who do not use responses in one or more of these categories at all—although words in the content category are used at least once by almost all subjects. These categories are quite homogeneous in regard to their means, standard deviations, skewness, and kurtosis. They do not seem to deviate greatly from normally distributed variates.

RARE CATEGORIES

Two of the categories (shame–guilt and disgust–dislike) can be described as rarely used categories—mean usage less than one per subject. Their means of 0.13 and 0.27 respectively indicate that words in these emotion categories are very rarely used in this task. Eighty-nine percent of the subjects never used a word in the shame–guilt category and 82.8 percent never used a word in the disgust–dislike category. The distribution of responses within these two categories, together with the "No Response" and "Other" categories, are very badly skewed and have decidedly non-normal kurtosis. It would be unwise to use these categories in any analysis which is based upon the assumption of an underlying normal distribution.

DIMENSIONAL SCALING

The responses of the 145 members of the Reference Sample were also scored using the dimensional scoring options provided in the computerized scoring system. The summary statistics resulting from this scoring system are given in Table 5.5. It should be noted that while the mean score of the second dimension (arousal) is a full point greater than on the first dimension (hedonic tone), 5.93 versus 4.90, the other summary statistics scores for the two dimensions are nearly identical. In addition, these values are consistent with a normal distribution model. Finally, it should be noted that in the Reference Sample, the two dimensions are very nearly independent (i.e., uncorrelated), $r = -0.057$.

DIMENSIONS WITH EMOTION CATEGORIES

The dimensional scores of the 145 members of the Reference Sample were also examined separately within each emotion category. For this summarization of the data, presented in Table 5.6 and graphically in Figure 5.1, the two-dimensional scores (hedonic tone and arousal) were examined separately for words within each emotion category;

TABLE 5.5
Summary Statistics—Dimensional Scaling

	Dimension I: Tone	Dimension II: Arousal
N	145	145
Mean	4.90	5.93
Standard Deviation	0.39	0.40
Skewness	0.28	−0.27
Kurtosis	3.57	3.27
Selected Percentile Points		
100 (Max)	6.3	6.8
95	5.6	6.6
90	5.4	6.5
75	5.1	6.2
50	4.9	6.0
25	4.6	5.7
10	4.5	5.4
5	4.3	5.3
0 (Min)	3.9	4.7

Correlation: $r = -0.057$.

that is, for each subject the mean dimensional scores were calculated for words in the surprise, interest, joy, etc., categories. The results presented in Table 5.6 and Figure 5.1 are the means and standard deviations over subjects of the individual mean dimensional score for each category. The varying N's in Table 5.6 are indications of the number of subjects who had at least one word in the category; thus 107 subjects had at least one word in the surprise category, 143 subjects had at least one word in the interest category. It should be stressed that the individual mean scores which are then averaged over subjects to produce the mean scores and standard deviations given in Table 5.6 are based upon differing numbers of words used in the specific category by each subject.

TABLE 5.6
Summary Statistics—Emotion Dimensions with Emotion
Categories

Category	Dimension I: Pleasure			Dimension II: Arousal		r
	N	Mean	Standard Deviation	Mean	Standard Deviation	
A	107	5.94	0.49	7.73	0.13	−0.26
B	143	6.22	0.45	6.58	0.45	0.53
C	144	8.23	0.21	7.42	0.23	0.28
D	144	7.35	0.43	3.40	0.87	−0.07
E	79	4.50	0.52	2.57	0.63	0.08
F	137	2.84	0.24	3.99	0.36	0.16
G	114	3.69	0.24	5.57	0.37	0.21
H	16	3.07	0.40	5.63	0.50	−0.24
I	25	2.46	0.34	5.96	0.26	0.28
J	113	2.52	0.38	7.42	0.49	−0.78
K	108	2.30	0.34	6.22	0.57	−0.43
L	93	2.43	0.45	7.41	0.45	−0.60

Categories:

A	—	Surprise	H	—	Shame–Guilt
B	—	Interest	I	—	Disgust–Dislike
C	—	Joy	J	—	Anger
D	—	Content	K	—	Distress
E	—	Passive	L	—	Fear
F	—	Sad	M	—	Other
G	—	Cautious–Shy	N	—	No Response

The positioning of the emotion categories within the dimensional space, as indicated by the means of responses with categories, shows the same general counterclockwise arrangement of the emotion categories (beginning with surprise in the 12 o'clock position) as was seen in the data set used to develop the dimensional system. It should be noted that while the correlation of the dimensions was effectively zero over the entire data set, the correlations of the two dimensions when disaggregated by emotion category show considerable variation. There is a high negative correlation between hedonic tone and arousal within the

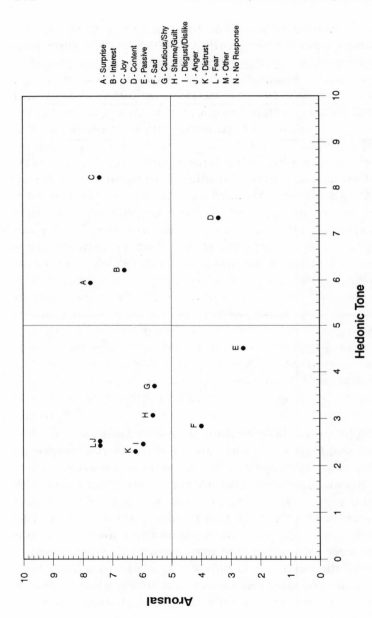

FIGURE 5.1

Location of emotion category means within dimensional space.

anger, fear, distress, surprise, and shame–guilt categories, while there is a high positive correlation between these two dimensions within the interest, joy, and disgust–dislike categories.

INDIVIDUAL PICTURE DATA

The data provided by the Reference Sample are also arrayed individually for each of the thirty cards which make up the IFP in Tables 5.7, 5.8, 5.9, and 5.10 as well as in Figure 5.2. Table 5.7 provides the distribution of the 4350 responses to emotion categories for each of the thirty pictures. For instance, in response to picture 101, forty-four subjects responded with words which were assigned to emotion category C (joy), fifty-one responded with words which were assigned to emotion category B (interest). Table 5.8 provides the percentage of responses within an emotion category which came from responses to a particular picture. For example, of the emotion category C (joy) responses (of which there were a total of 489), 9 percent came in response to picture 101, none came in response to picture 102, none from picture 103, 22.9 percent came in response to picture 104. Table 5.9 gives the distribution of category responses to each card. Thus, of the responses to card 101, 2.76 percent were emotion category A (surprise) responses, 35.2 percent were emotion category B (interest) responses, 30.3 percent were emotion category C (joy) responses, 26.2 percent were emotion category D (content) responses.

From the data provided in Table 5.8 one can see that, in general, responses in most of the emotional categories were evoked by many of the stimuli. However, in a few cases, for example, emotion categories A, C, D, and H (surprise, joy, content, and shy–cautious) the majority of the responses within that category were evoked by three

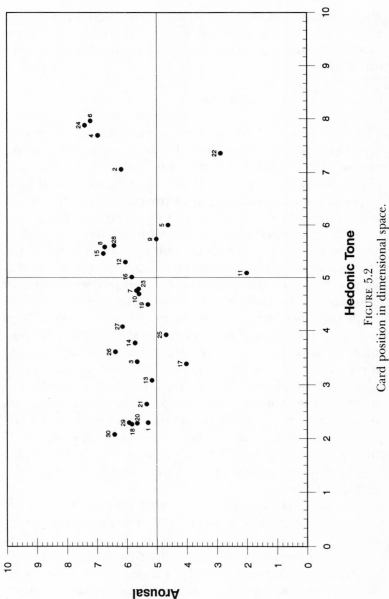

FIGURE 5.2
Card position in dimensional space.

TABLE 5.7

Frequencies of Emotion Category Usage Reference Sample By Card

Card Number	Emotion Category						
	A	B	C	D	E	F	G
101	4	51	44	38	1	1	1
102	0	0	0	0	8	43	0
103	7	22	0	1	5	24	38
104	0	19	112	5	2	1	1
105	3	43	7	63	11	0	6
106	2	9	127	3	0	0	1
107	5	67	2	4	9	8	25
108	73	41	2	4	4	1	11
109	1	64	6	33	17	3	11
110	1	41	3	41	8	4	16
111	3	90	5	2	3	4	22
112	0	12	1	3	7	66	5
113	0	38	0	2	4	10	41
114	71	42	1	2	2	0	12
115	7	67	9	3	7	8	19
116	0	14	2	10	26	69	2
117	0	0	0	0	1	53	0
118	0	46	4	14	10	30	8
119	0	0	0	1	2	50	0
120	0	2	0	0	4	63	7
121	1	65	3	11	3	6	28
122	0	0	0	137	7	0	0
123	0	66	1	7	11	8	29
124	9	6	127	1	0	0	0
125	2	22	12	14	4	36	18
126	4	19	15	0	2	7	10
127	27	41	0	0	2	7	13
128	18	91	4	3	3	0	12
129	1	1	0	0	0	42	2
130	0	70	2	2	0	5	20
Total	239	1049	489	404	163	549	358

Categories:

A	—	Surprise	H	—	Shame–Guilt
B	—	Interest	I	—	Disgust–Dislike
C	—	Joy	J	—	Anger
D	—	Content	K	—	Distress
E	—	Passive	L	—	Fear
F	—	Sad	M	—	Other
G	—	Cautious–Shy	N	—	No Response

TABLE 5.7
(Continued)
Frequencies of Emotion Category Usage Reference Sample By Card

Card Number	H	I	J	K	L	M	N	Total
101	1	0	0	4	0	0	0	145
102	0	0	22	62	4	6	0	145
103	1	5	3	10	25	3	1	145
104	0	0	2	0	0	2	1	145
105	1	0	0	1	1	9	0	145
106	0	0	1	0	0	2	0	145
107	0	1	2	1	15	4	2	145
108	0	0	0	1	3	1	4	145
109	0	0	1	2	1	1	5	145
110	0	0	1	3	17	10	0	145
111	0	0	1	0	8	1	6	145
112	1	6	32	8	1	2	1	145
113	5	4	12	4	18	3	4	145
114	2	0	0	1	5	4	3	145
115	0	0	2	2	11	5	5	145
116	1	2	3	12	2	1	1	145
117	0	3	47	37	4	0	0	145
118	0	1	25	2	0	3	2	145
119	0	1	36	51	3	1	0	145
120	2	5	12	25	23	1	1	145
121	6	2	0	0	13	1	6	145
122	0	0	0	0	0	1	0	145
123	1	1	4	1	14	2	0	145
124	0	0	1	0	0	0	1	145
125	1	0	1	16	5	6	8	145
126	0	2	12	34	34	5	1	145
127	0	1	12	13	17	10	2	145
128	0	0	1	0	7	5	1	145
129	0	3	23	33	35	5	0	145
130	0	3	19	3	17	3	1	145
	22	40	275	326	283	97	56	

Categories:

A	—	Surprise	H	—	Shame–Guilt
B	—	Interest	I	—	Disgust–Dislike
C	—	Joy	J	—	Anger
D	—	Content	K	—	Distress
E	—	Passive	L	—	Fear
F	—	Sad	M	—	Other
G	—	Cautious–Shy	N	—	No Response

TABLE 5.8
IFEEL Pictures: Frequency Distribution of Pictures by Emotion (in percentages)

Picture Number	A Surprise	B Interest	C Joy	D Content	E Passive	F Sad	G Shy	H Shame	I Disgust	J Anger	K Distress	L Fear	M Other	N N/R
101	1.67	4.86	9.00	9.41	0.61	0.18	0.28	4.55	0.00	0.00	1.23	0.00	0.00	0.00
102	0.00	0.00	0.00	0.00	4.91	7.83	0.00	0.00	0.00	8.00	19.02	1.41	6.19	0.00
103	2.93	2.10	0.00	0.25	3.07	4.37	10.61	4.55	12.50	1.09	3.07	8.83	3.09	1.79
104	0.00	1.81	22.90	1.24	1.23	0.18	0.28	0.00	0.00	0.73	0.00	0.00	2.06	1.79
105	1.26	4.10	1.43	15.59	6.75	0.00	1.68	4.55	0.00	0.00	0.31	0.35	9.28	0.00
106	0.84	0.86	25.97	0.74	0.00	0.00	0.28	0.00	0.00	0.36	0.00	0.00	2.06	0.00
107	2.09	6.39	0.41	0.99	5.52	1.46	6.98	0.00	2.50	0.73	0.31	5.30	4.12	3.57
108	30.54	3.91	0.41	0.99	2.45	0.18	3.07	0.00	0.00	0.00	0.31	1.06	1.03	7.14
109	0.42	6.10	1.23	8.17	10.43	0.55	3.07	0.00	0.00	0.36	0.61	0.35	1.03	8.93
110	0.42	3.91	0.61	10.15	4.91	0.73	4.47	0.00	0.00	0.36	0.92	6.01	10.31	0.00
111	1.26	8.58	1.02	0.50	1.84	0.73	6.15	0.00	0.00	0.36	0.00	2.83	1.03	10.71
112	0.00	1.14	0.20	0.74	4.29	12.02	1.40	4.55	15.00	11.64	2.45	0.35	2.06	1.79
113	0.00	3.62	0.00	0.50	2.45	1.82	11.45	22.73	10.00	4.36	1.23	6.36	3.09	7.14

TABLE 5.8 *(Continued)*

IFEEL Pictures: Frequency Distribution of Pictures by Emotion (in percentages)

Picture Number	A Surprise	B Interest	C Joy	D Content	E Passive	F Sad	G Shy	H Shame	I Disgust	J Anger	K Distress	L Fear	M Other	N N/R
114	29.71	4.00	0.20	0.50	1.23	0.00	3.35	9.09	0.00	0.00	0.31	1.77	4.12	5.36
115	2.93	6.39	1.84	0.74	4.29	1.46	5.31	0.00	0.00	0.73	0.61	3.89	5.15	8.93
116	0.00	1.33	0.41	2.48	15.95	12.57	0.56	4.55	5.00	1.09	3.68	0.71	1.03	1.79
117	0.00	0.00	0.00	0.00	0.61	9.65	0.00	0.00	7.50	17.09	11.35	1.41	0.00	0.00
118	0.00	4.39	0.82	3.47	6.13	5.46	2.23	0.00	2.50	9.09	0.61	0.00	3.09	3.57
119	0.00	0.00	0.00	0.25	1.23	9.11	0.00	0.00	2.50	13.09	15.64	1.06	1.03	0.00
120	0.00	0.19	0.00	0.00	2.45	11.48	1.96	9.09	12.50	4.36	7.67	8.13	1.03	1.79
121	0.42	6.20	0.61	2.72	1.84	1.09	7.82	27.27	5.00	0.00	0.00	4.59	1.03	10.71
122	0.00	0.00	0.00	33.91	4.29	0.00	0.00	0.00	0.00	0.00	0.00	0.00	1.03	0.00
123	0.00	6.29	0.20	1.73	6.75	1.46	8.10	4.55	2.50	1.45	0.31	4.95	2.06	0.00
124	3.77	0.57	25.97	0.25	0.00	0.00	0.00	0.00	0.00	0.36	0.00	0.00	0.00	1.79
125	0.84	2.10	2.45	3.47	2.45	6.56	5.03	4.55	0.00	0.36	4.91	1.77	6.19	14.29
126	1.67	1.81	3.07	0.00	1.23	1.28	2.79	0.00	5.00	4.36	10.43	12.01	5.15	1.79
127	11.30	3.91	0.00	0.00	1.23	1.28	3.63	0.00	2.50	4.36	3.99	6.01	10.31	3.57
128	7.53	8.67	0.82	0.74	1.84	0.00	3.35	0.00	0.00	0.36	0.00	2.47	5.15	1.79
129	0.42	0.10	0.00	0.00	0.00	7.65	0.56	0.00	7.50	8.36	10.12	12.37	5.15	0.00
130	0.00	6.67	0.41	0.50	0.00	0.91	5.59	0.00	7.50	6.91	0.92	6.01	3.09	1.79
	100.00	100.00	100.00	100.00	100.00	100.00	100.00	100.00	100.00	100.00	100.00	100.00	100.00	100.00

TABLE 5.9

IFEEL Pictures: Frequency Distribution of Emotions by Picture (in percentages)

Picture Number	A Surprise	B Interest	C Joy	D Content	E Passive	F Sad	G Shy	H Shame	I Disgust	J Anger	K Distress	L Fear	M Other	N N/R	
101	2.76	35.17	30.34	26.21	0.69	0.69	0.69	0.69	0.00	0.00	2.76	0.00	0.00	0.00	100.00
102	0.00	0.00	0.00	0.00	5.52	29.66	0.00	0.00	0.00	15.17	42.76	2.76	4.14	0.00	100.00
103	4.83	15.17	0.00	0.69	3.45	16.55	26.21	0.69	3.45	2.07	6.90	17.24	2.07	0.60	100.00
104	0.00	13.10	77.24	3.45	1.38	0.69	0.69	0.00	0.00	1.38	0.00	0.00	1.38	0.69	100.00
105	2.07	29.66	4.83	43.45	7.59	0.00	4.14	0.69	0.00	0.00	0.69	0.69	6.21	0.00	100.00
106	1.38	6.21	87.59	2.07	0.00	0.00	0.69	0.00	0.00	0.69	0.00	0.00	1.38	0.00	100.00
107	3.45	46.21	1.38	2.76	6.21	5.52	17.24	0.00	0.69	1.38	0.69	0.00	2.76	1.38	100.00
108	50.34	28.28	1.38	2.76	2.76	0.69	7.59	0.00	0.00	0.00	0.69	10.34	0.69	2.76	100.00
109	0.69	44.14	4.14	22.76	11.72	2.07	7.59	0.00	0.00	0.69	0.69	2.07	0.69	3.45	100.00
110	0.69	28.28	2.07	28.28	5.52	2.76	11.03	0.00	0.00	0.69	1.38	0.69	6.90	0.00	100.00
111	2.07	62.07	3.45	1.38	2.07	2.76	15.17	0.00	0.00	0.69	2.07	11.72	0.69	0.00	100.00
112	0.00	8.28	0.69	2.07	4.83	45.52	3.45	0.69	4.14	22.07	0.00	5.52	1.38	4.14	100.00
113	0.00	26.21	0.00	1.38	2.76	6.90	28.28	3.45	2.76	8.28	2.76	12.41	2.07	2.76	100.00

TABLE 5.9 (*Continued*)

IFEEL Pictures: Frequency Distribution of Emotions by Picture (in percentages)

Picture Number	A Surprise	B Interest	C Joy	D Content	E Passive	F Sad	G Shy	H Shame	I Disgust	J Anger	K Distress	L Fear	M Other	N N/R	
114	48.97	28.97	0.69	1.38	1.38	0.00	8.28	1.38	0.00	0.00	0.69	3.45	2.76	2.07	100.00
115	4.83	46.21	6.21	2.07	4.83	5.52	13.10	0.00	0.00	1.38	1.38	7.59	3.45	3.45	100.00
116	0.00	9.66	1.38	6.90	17.93	47.59	1.38	0.69	1.38	2.07	8.28	1.38	0.69	0.69	100.00
117	0.00	0.00	0.00	0.00	0.69	36.55	0.00	0.00	2.07	32.41	25.52	2.76	0.00	0.00	100.00
118	0.00	31.72	2.76	9.66	6.90	20.69	5.52	0.00	0.69	17.24	1.38	0.00	2.07	1.38	100.00
119	0.00	0.00	0.00	0.69	1.38	34.48	0.00	0.00	0.69	24.83	35.17	2.07	0.69	0.00	100.00
120	0.00	1.38	0.00	0.00	2.76	43.45	4.83	1.38	3.45	8.28	17.24	15.86	0.69	0.69	100.00
121	0.69	44.83	2.07	7.59	2.07	4.14	19.31	4.14	1.38	0.00	0.00	8.97	0.69	4.14	100.00
122	0.00	0.00	0.00	94.48	4.83	0.00	0.00	0.00	0.00	0.00	0.00	0.00	0.69	0.00	100.00
123	0.00	45.52	0.69	4.83	7.59	5.52	20.00	0.69	0.69	2.76	0.60	9.66	1.38	0.69	100.00
124	6.21	4.14	87.59	0.69	0.00	0.00	0.00	0.00	0.00	0.69	0.00	0.00	0.00	5.52	100.00
125	1.38	15.17	8.28	9.66	2.76	24.83	12.41	0.69	0.00	0.69	11.03	3.45	4.14	0.69	100.00
126	2.76	13.10	10.34	0.00	1.38	4.83	6.90	0.00	1.38	8.28	23.45	23.45	3.45	1.38	100.00
127	18.62	28.28	0.00	0.00	2.07	0.00	8.97	0.00	0.69	8.28	8.97	11.72	6.90	0.69	100.00
128	12.41	62.76	2.76	2.07	2.07	28.97	1.38	0.00	0.00	0.69	0.00	4.83	3.45	0.00	100.00
129	0.69	0.69	0.00	0.00	0.00	28.97	1.38	0.00	2.07	15.86	22.76	24.14	3.45	0.69	100.00
130	0.00	48.28	1.38	1.38	0.00	3.45	13.79	0.00	2.07	13.10	2.07	11.72	2.07	0.69	100.00

TABLE 5.10
Dimension Means

Card Number	Dimension I Pleasure	Dimension II Arousal
1	2.29	5.30
2	7.06	6.19
3	3.43	5.66
4	7.69	6.97
5	6.00	4.62
6	7.96	7.22
7	4.75	5.68
8	5.58	6.74
9	5.73	5.02
10	4.69	5.60
11	5.09	2.01
12	5.30	6.05
13	3.08	5.17
14	3.77	5.73
15	5.46	6.79
16	5.01	5.84
17	3.39	4.02
18	2.26	5.84
19	4.49	5.30
20	2.28	5.66
21	2.46	5.35
22	7.36	2.88
23	4.78	5.61
24	7.88	7.41
25	3.92	4.69
26	3.61	6.39
27	4.07	6.15
28	5.61	6.43
29	2.29	5.93
30	2.07	6.42

or fewer stimuli. The general pattern, however, is that each emotion category is "prompted" by a multiplicity of stimuli (i.e., pictures). It is important to note that the source of "Other" (category M) responses is from virtually all of the pictures, as is also the case for "No Response" (category N) responses. Similarly, the data in Table 5.8 suggest that in the majority of cases, an individual stimulus is able to "pull" responses which are categorized into several different emotion categories. There are, however, several notable exceptions to this generalization. In particular, 94.5 percent of all responses to picture 122 were D (content) category responses, 87.6 percent of all responses to pictures 106 and 124 were C (joy) category responses, 77.2 percent of the responses to picture 104 were category C (joy) responses, 62.8 percent of responses to picture 28 fell into category B (interest) as did 62.1 percent of the responses to picture 111, and 50.3 percent of the responses to card 108 fell into category A (surprise). In all other cases, fewer than 50 percent of the responses to a card fell into a single emotion category. It should also be noted that in the Reference Sample no more than 7 percent of the responses to any card were category M (Other) responses, and no more than 6 percent of the responses to any card were category N (No Response) responses.

Table 5.10 provides the dimensional means for the responses to each picture (i.e., the mean score on the hedonic tone and arousal dimensions for each response to a particular card). These values are plotted in Figure 5.2 and indicate that the stimuli are reasonably separated and cover fairly well the entire "emotion space."

Relationships Between Demographic Variables and Emotions in the Reference Sample

In order to determine whether responses to the IFEEL Picture stimuli were related to the demographic characteristics of the Reference Sample, correlations between the dimensional scores and emotion category scores and the continuous demographic variables (maternal age, number of children, maternal education, and target child age) were computed. No pattern of significant correlations was detectable, and overall just under 5 percent of those correlations were significant, as would be expected by chance. In a similar vein, one-way ANOVAs were computed in order to examine differences on the dimensional scores and emotion category scores among subgroups of the Reference Sample formed on the basis of the discrete demographic variables (race, marital status, target child's gender, and subsample of the reference sample). Again, no systematic pattern of significant differences could be detected and only 10 of the 75 F's were significant (about the number expected by chance given the correlated nature of the response variables).

It, therefore, appears safe to conclude that, with respect to the Reference Sample, there are no systematic differences or relationships between the demographic characteristics of the Reference Sample and their responses (either dimensional or categorical) to the IFEEL Picture stimuli. It should be noted, however, that the number of nonwhite members of the Reference Sample is very small and therefore the power for the comparisons based upon race cited above is very small.

Reliability

In order to determine the reliability of the IFP, a separate study involving the test-retest paradigm was conducted. To this end an additional sample of forty subjects (18 at site A and 22 at site B) matching the demographic characteristics of the Reference Sample were recruited. The IFP were administered twice to these subjects with an average interadministration time of six weeks.

DIMENSIONAL SCORING

The reliability analysis for the dimensional scaling is a standard test–retest analysis, focusing mainly on the correlation of the two dimensional scales at the two time points.

TABLE 5.11
Reliability Analysis
Dimensional Scoring

Dimension	Reference Sample (N = 145)		Reliability Sample (N = 40)			
			Time 1		Time 2	
	Mean	Standard Deviation	Mean	Standard Deviation	Mean	Standard Deviation
Tone	4.90	0.39	5.10	0.49	5.97	0.38
Arousal	5.93	0.40	5.07	0.40	5.96	0.45

Correlations Dimension	Time 1–Time 2 Correlation
Tone	0.660
Arousal	0.636

The key data for this analysis are presented in Table 5.11. As can be seen in this table the test–retest correlations for both dimensions are well within the acceptable range (0.66 and 0.64); some caution is necessary, however. If one examines the means presented in Table 5.11, one will note that there is an appreciable increase in the means on both dimensions over repeated administrations, indicating that upon short-term retesting subjects are responding with more positive and "stronger" emotion words than on the first administration; that is, there is a shift to more "positive" words and words scaled as having higher arousal within an emotion category. (An examination of Table 5.12 indicates that this shift is due to the use of more

TABLE 5.12
Frequency of Category Usage Reliability Sample

Category	Time 1		Time 2	
	Mean	Standard Deviation	Mean	Standard Deviation
A	1.90	1.53	2.00	1.71
B	8.45	3.92	8.20	3.50
C	2.93	1.49	2.88	1.59
D	3.63	2.49	3.80	2.72
E	0.80	1.24	0.73	1.11
F	3.05	1.78	3.42	2.25
G	2.33	2.21	2.00	2.25
H	0.10	0.37	0.13	0.40
I	0.25	0.59	0.15	0.48
J	1.55	1.56	1.58	1.44
K	2.38	1.67	2.55	2.08
L	2.18	2.41	1.93	2.07
M	0.48	0.71	0.65	1.64
N	0		0	

Categories:

A	—	Surprise	H	—	Shame–Guilt
B	—	Interest	I	—	Disgust–Dislike
C	—	Joy	J	—	Anger
D	—	Content	K	—	Distress
E	—	Passive	L	—	Fear
F	—	Sad	M	—	Other
G	—	Cautious–Shy	N	—	No Response

positive and "stronger" words within a category, not due to a shift in the category of words used. That is, the mean number of words assigned to any given category remains virtually unchanged over time so that the changes in the dimensional scores must result from changes in the location in emotion space of the words used.) The picture is also somewhat clouded by the fact that the time 1 mean of the reliability sample on dimension 2 (arousal) is substantially below that of the Reference Sample, while the time

2 mean on dimension 1 (hedonic tone) is substantially greater than the Reference Sample mean.

EMOTION CATEGORY SCORING

Techniques for assessing the reliability of categories are less well established than for the assessment of reliability of continuously scored variables. Given that the usual use of the emotion category scoring system is the number of endorsements in each category, the two most direct ways of approaching the issue of reliability are (1) a direct comparison of the mean number of endorsements (mean frequency of endorsement) within each category at the two time periods and (2) the contingency coefficient, P, which relates the distribution of endorsements within each category at the two time points. The contingency coefficient, P, is one of the chi-square related coefficients which index the degree of association between the rows and columns of a twofold table (see, for instance, Kendall and Stuart, [1979, p. 588]). In this particular application the tables are the number of endorsements by occasion ($n \times 2$) tables which result from the test–retest experiment. A separate P is calculated for each emotion category. Values of the contingency coefficient may range from 0 to 1, but the upper limit may not be obtainable conditional on the marginal distributions. If Qp is the ordinary τ^2 statistic for the twofold table,

$$P = [Qp/(Qp + n)]^{1/2}$$

High values of P indicate strong association.

Table 5.12 contains the mean frequency of endorsements at the two time points and Table 5.13 contains the contingency coefficients.

Both ways of looking at the reliability of the categorical system indicate reasonably good "reliability" of this scoring system, with the possible exception of the category

TABLE 5.13
Contingency Coefficients Reliability Sample

Category	Contingency Coefficient
A	0.708
B	0.905
C	0.791
D	0.865
E	0.566
F	0.771
G	0.836
H	0.708
I	0.307
J	0.659
K	0.735
L	0.868
M	0.429
N	–

Categories:

A	—	Surprise	H	—	Shame–Guilt
B	—	Interest	I	—	Disgust–Dislike
C	—	Joy	J	—	Anger
D	—	Content	K	—	Distress
E	—	Passive	L	—	Fear
F	—	Sad	M	—	Other
G	—	Cautious–Shy	N	—	No Response

disgust–dislike which is a very rarely utilized category. The mean number of endorsements remains very stable over the two time periods and the contingency coefficients are quite high except for the somewhat depressed scores for the rarely used categories (passive, shame, disgust, and other).

Long-Term Stability

Since the IFP was designed to tap the mother's "emotional understanding" of infants, one may anticipate that changes over time will occur, particularly for first-time mothers who may have had little or no experience with infants and their emotions. In order to gain some insight into the degree to which one might expect such changes over developmental experience, data from a long-term longitudinal study of first-time mothers who were selected as being at low to medium risk (Osofsky and Culp, 1989) were obtained. On a small subset ($n = 27$) of the total number of first-time mothers in this study, IFP responses were obtained at 3, 6, and 13 months. The resulting summary statistics are presented in Tables 5.14, 5.15, 5.16, and 5.17.

Emotion Category Scoring

Table 5.14 contains the means and standard deviations of the number of pictures assigned to each of the fourteen emotion categories by these twenty-seven mothers at each of the three time points. Somewhat surprisingly, these means and standard deviations remain fairly stable over time and no apparent trends can be seen in these data. In virtually all of the cases the values are also quite close to those seen in the Reference Sample even though the sampling frame for this study was quite different from the one which generated the Reference Sample (cf. Table 5.4). The data in Table 5.14 give some indication of the long-term stability of the mean number of endorsements, but do not indicate the degree to which individual subjects are consistent. The contingency coefficients presented in Table 5.15 provide some indication of the degree to which subjects are consistent from time to time. While the number of subjects in this study is small, the data presented in Table 5.15 indicate a remarkable degree of consistency in terms of the numbers of items individuals cast into each category over the three time periods. The values of the contingency coefficients for this twenty-seven-member sample of subjects tested at three time periods is of the

TABLE 5.14
Longitudinal Stability–Emotional Category Scoring
(Kansas City Longitudinal Sample, n = 27)

Category	3-Month		6-Month		13-Month	
	Mean	SD	Mean	SD	Mean	SD
A	1.52	1.93	1.96	1.76	2.04	2.56
B	6.59	3.03	6.67	3.53	6.70	3.31
C	4.63	2.29	3.77	2.58	3.89	1.94
D	3.96	2.77	3.30	2.49	4.07	2.78
E	1.19	1.39	1.52	1.50	1.26	1.45
F	3.96	1.89	4.04	2.34	3.11	2.49
G	1.15	1.99	1.22	1.52	1.37	1.36
H	0.11	0.32	0.15	0.45	0.77	0.27
I	0.07	0.27	0.30	0.54	0.11	0.32
J	1.56	1.62	1.52	1.76	1.89	1.82
K	2.41	1.57	2.26	1.97	2.78	0.32
L	1.15	1.23	1.59	2.11	1.55	1.84
M	1.41	1.69	1.44	1.78	1.11	1.60
N	0.30	0.72	0.26	0.71	0.04	0.19

Categories:

A	—	Surprise	H	—	Shame–Guilt
B	—	Interest	I	—	Disgust–Dislike
C	—	Joy	J	—	Anger
D	—	Content	K	—	Distress
E	—	Passive	L	—	Fear
F	—	Sad	M	—	Other
G	—	Cautious–Shy	N	—	No Response

same order of magnitude as those derived from the forty-subject sample tested twice at an intertesting interval of no more than six weeks. Thus, with regard to the emotion categories there does appear to be a considerable, if somewhat unexpected, stability over a ten-month period. Of course, it should be cautioned that these results are based on a rather small sample.

A somewhat larger sample of subjects ($n = 64$) was available from the same study; those subjects who completed the IFP at 3 and 13 months (but not necessarily at 6 months). This sample contains, of course, the twenty-seven subjects who were seen at all three time points and,

TABLE 5.15
Long-Term Stability—Contingency Coefficients
(Kansas City Sample, n = 27)

Category	3 Month–6 Month	3 Month–13 Month	6 Month–13 Month
A	0.794	0.855	0.810
B	0.904	0.888	0.863
C	0.798	0.767	0.781
D	0.857	0.869	0.857
E	0.705	0.738	0.812
F	0.825	0.816	0.876
G	0.737	0.644	0.707
H	0.333	0.330	0.650
I	0.189	0.350	0.111
J	0.753	0.799	0.796
K	0.792	0.750	0.803
L	0.683	0.708	0.782
M	0.747	0.802	0.748
N	0.711	0.093	0.082

Categories:

A	—	Surprise	H	—	Shame–Guilt
B	—	Interest	I	—	Disgust–Dislike
C	—	Joy	J	—	Anger
D	—	Content	K	—	Distress
E	—	Passive	L	—	Fear
F	—	Sad	M	—	Other
G	—	Cautious–Shy	N	—	No Response

as a result, is not independent of the sample just discussed. The means, standard deviations, and contingency coefficients for this larger group are presented in Table 5.16. As can be easily seen the results from this larger sample are consistent with the results from the smaller subset contained within it and, if anything, give a picture of slightly greater stability than is seen in the smaller sample.

Dimensional Scoring

Results for the dimensional scoring approach for the same two samples are given in Table 5.17. With regard to the

TABLE 5.16
Long Term Stability: 3–13 Months Only
(Kansas City Sample, n = 64)

Category	3 Month		13 Month		Contingency
	Mean	SD	Mean	SD	Coeffient
A	1.45	1.66	1.96	2.13	0.840
B	7.27	3.82	7.08	3.62	0.897
C	4.27	2.21	3.83	1.91	0.813
D	3.88	2.57	3.81	2.71	0.832
E	1.16	1.42	1.13	1.43	0.697
F	3.77	2.21	3.63	2.44	0.830
G	1.08	1.28	1.27	1.46	0.517
H	0.17	0.45	0.09	0.34	0.579
I	0.13	0.42	0.13	0.49	0.666
J	1.52	1.54	1.97	1.76	0.705
K	2.70	2.10	2.78	2.15	0.729
L	0.91	1.12	1.14	1.56	0.590
M	1.44	1.53	1.00	1.83	0.609
N	0.28	0.70	0.19	0.81	0.145

Categories:
A	—	Surprise	H	—	Shame–Guilt
B	—	Interest	I	—	Disgust–Dislike
C	—	Joy	J	—	Anger
D	—	Content	K	—	Distress
E	—	Passive	L	—	Fear
F	—	Sad	M	—	Other
G	—	Cautious–Shy	N	—	No Response

mean scores one again gets a picture of unexpectedly high consistency in both the twenty-seven- and sixty-four-member sample, with surprisingly small mean differences appearing over the repeated testing. The picture of stability is, however, considerably less clear when one considers the intercorrelations of the subjects' scores over time. In the smaller twenty-seven-member sample the intercorrelations over time on dimension I (hedonic tone) are reasonably high (0.49, 0.59, and 0.70 for the time 3–6, 3–13, and 6–13 periods respectively); those for dimension II (arousal) are substantially lower (0.20, 0.36, and 0.35 respectively). The

TABLE 5.17
Long-Term Stability Dimensional Scoring

Sample I (n = 27)

	3 Month		6 Month		13 Month	
	Mean	Standard Deviation	Mean	Standard Deviation	Mean	Standard Deviation
Dimension I (Pleasure)	5.19	0.45	5.01	0.52	5.14	0.46
Dimension II (Arousal)	5.88	0.26	5.88	0.40	5.91	0.37

		Intercorrelations		
Dimension I (Pleasure)		3	6	13
	3	–	0.49	0.58
	6		–	0.70
Dimension II (Arousal)		3	6	13
	3	–	0.20	0.36
	6		–	0.35

Sample II (n = 64)

	3 Month		13 Month	
	Mean	Standard Deviation	Mean	Standard Deviation
Dimension I (Pleasure)	5.22	0.47	5.13	0.44
Dimension II (Arousal)	5.86	0.33	5.89	0.35

	Intercorrelations
	3–13 Months
Dimension I (Pleasure)	0.45
Dimension II (Arousal)	0.36

intercorrelations in the larger sample, where only time 3 and time 13 measures are available, are quite similar, 0.45 for dimension I and 0.36 for dimension II. It may be worth noting that the stability of the mean dimensional scores in these two samples is substantially greater than that seen in the short-term reliability sample.

These results, taken together, leave a somewhat murky picture of the stability of the IFP over the period of a mother's early experience with her infant. While the number of endorsements in any given emotion category seems to be rather stable both within a mother and across mothers, and while the mean dimensional ratings of the groups of mothers seem stable, there is less of an indication of stability of the dimensional scores (particularly dimension II) within mothers over time.

Conclusion

Considerable data are available on the operating characteristics and psychometric properties of the IFP, at least when it is employed with middle-class white females. The instrument does not seem to be particularly sensitive to gross demographic characteristics of the sample, seems to have substantial reliability (as assessed by short-term test–retest methods), and seems in many regards to provide a rather stable long-term measurement. It is further worth noting that the dimensional scales and the emotion category scores for the more frequently occurring categories seem to be near enough to the normal distribution to permit the cautious use of normal statistics. The availability of two scoring systems, emotion categories and dimensional scoring, allows the instrument to be used in a flexible manner.

References

Kean, G., & Appelbaum, M. (1990), *Using the IFEEL: A Scoring and Statistical Analysis Program.* Quantitative Systems Laboratory Report, No. 1, Vanderbilt University, Nashville, TN.

Kendall, M., & Stuart, A. (1979), *The Advanced Theory of Statistics,* Vol. 2. New York: Macmillan.

Osofsky, H. J., & Culp, R. E. (1989), Risk factors in the transition to fatherhood. In: *Fathers and Their Families,* ed. S. H. Cath, A. Gurwitt, & L. Gunsberg. New York: Analytic Press, pp. 145–165.

6

The Meaning of Infant Emotional Expressions in the IFEEL Pictures—Validation Studies

Doreen Ridgeway

The focus of this chapter is on the meaning that individuals attach to the emotional expressions of infants as reflected in the IFEEL Pictures (IFP). Not only should the content of the picture set be diverse, but also the methodology should reflect the nature of our perception of emotions. Hence, a number of validation studies were undertaken. These studies provided both a systematic description of content and a basis for dimensional scoring that came to supplement our categorical scoring of emotions as described in chapters 4 and 5. Before summarizing these validation studies, a brief review of relevant previous work seems appropriate.

Two ideas about the nature of our perception and interpretation of emotions have been predominant in the

Partial support for this research was provided by the Social Sciences and Humanities Research Council of Canada and the John D. and Catherine T. MacArthur Foundation Network on the Transition from Infancy to Early Childhood.

131

literature, with each capturing aspects of the meaning individuals give to the emotions of others. Chapter 1 described the research, indicating that human nonverbal affective expressions communicate emotions. Subjects looking at pictures of emotion faces were able to discern such basic emotions as happiness, surprise, fear, anger, sadness, disgust–contempt, interest, distress, and shame (Izard, 1971; Ekman, Friesen, and Ellsworth, 1972). Although each of the basic emotion categories listed above carries rather discrete information, in everyday situations, they have been found to occur as blends or combinations that are rarely at peak intensity (Emde, 1979). Low intensity and blended emotions have undoubtedly contributed to a controversy that has plagued the research literature (for a review see Russell and Bullock [1986a]). Some studies have found inconsistencies in subjects' ability to label facial expressions when situational cues were eliminated (Hunt, 1941; Spignesi and Shor, 1981; Wagner, Manstead, and MacDonald, 1983). Other studies, however, have found more consistency in subjects' labeling ability (Izard, 1971; Ekman et al., 1972; Ekman and Friesen, 1976). Part of the problem can be accounted for by the nature of the stimuli used within the various studies. Specifically, Ekman and Friesen (1976) selected facial expressions that best represented each emotion category; but other researchers have used realistic or spontaneous emotional expressions, consisting of blends and more neutral expressions which are more common in everyday interaction.

Another idea predominant in the literature is that human verbal and nonverbal affective expressions are communicated in such a way that one can discern at least two dimensions—hedonic tone and degree of arousal. Figure 6.1 illustrates that emotion categories labeled by words such as *happy, sad,* and *angry* may be interrelated in a systematic fashion—an organization that can be characterized by the two dimensions mentioned above. As the reader will notice, familiar words such as *excited, happy, sad, angry*, and *scared* fall at the outer edge of two-dimensional space whereas more atypical emotion descriptors, such as cautious, mild, and hungry, fall closer to the center of the space—in a more neutral area. Figure 6.1 has been generated by study 1, to be described below. The model it represents relates to a long line of theorizing that emphasized a circular structure of emotions (Woodworth and Schlosberg, 1954; Russell, 1980). Previous empirical evidence from which this model is derived has involved scaling of emotion-related words, in both Caucasian (Russell, 1980; Russell and Ridgeway, 1983) and cross-cultural (Russell, 1983) samples as well as scaling of facial expressions of emotions (Russell and Bullock, 1986a).

Study 1

The purpose of the first study was to assess the meaning of each IFEEL expression in the IFP along the dimensions of hedonic tone and arousal and to establish its position within the two-dimensional space. Ratings on these dimensions were obtained using Russell and Weiss's (1983) Affect Grid for a sample of fifty-eight female college undergraduates; all were single and had no children. Subjects were shown one picture at a time and asked to use a dimensional map to rate the strongest and clearest feeling that the baby was expressing.

Mean ratings of these subjects' responses on hedonic tone and arousal are presented in Table 6.1. As illustrated in Figure 6.2, some expressions fall around the perimeter of the two-dimensional space whereas others fall close to the center. The top right quadrant of Figure 6.1 shows the combination of hedonic tone and arousal, containing expressions which would be labeled by emotion descriptions such as excited, delighted, or pleased. The bottom

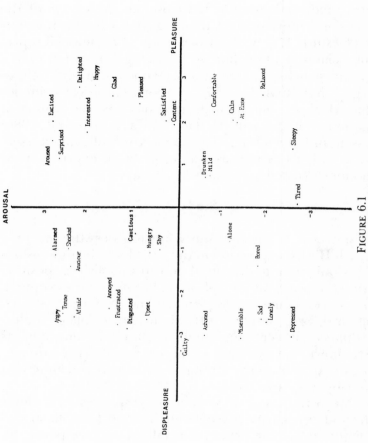

FIGURE 6.1

A circumplex model of emotions: Dimensional ratings for 38 emotion-related words

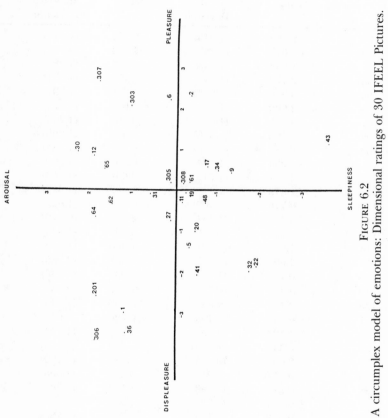

FIGURE 6.2

A circumplex model of emotions: Dimensional ratings of 30 IFEEL Pictures.

TABLE 6.1
Hedonic Tone and Arousal Ratings on 30 Facial Expressions by
Female College Undergraduates

Picture Number	Hedonic Tone		Arousal	
	Mean	Standard Deviation	Mean	Standard Deviation
101	2.293	(1.043)	− 0.362	(1.210)
102	− 3.017	(0.783)	1.241	(2.163)
103	− 1.448	(1.245)	− 0.293	(1.284)
104	2.172	(1.313)	0.155	(1.361)
105	0.379	(1.374)	− 1.259	(1.897)
106	2.000	(1.076)	1.069	(1.122)
107	− 0.259	(1.101)	− 0.069	(1.746)
108	0.793	(1.386)	1.931	(1.296)
109	0.483	(1.536)	− 0.741	(1.384)
110	− 1.034	(1.414)	− 0.466	(1.809)
111	0.121	(1.215)	0.034	(1.363)
112	− 1.879	(1.499)	− 1.983	(1.017)
113	− 0.776	(1.200)	0.121	(1.623)
114	0.914	(1.354)	2.276	(0.970)
115	− 0.069	(1.509)	0.569	(1.546)
116	− 1.603	(1.297)	− 1.966	(1.139)
117	− 3.690	(0.467)	1.948	(2.585)
118	0.448	(1.404)	− 0.931	(1.336)
119	− 3.448	(0.730)	1.259	(2.887)
120	− 2.155	(0.854)	− 0.483	(1.646)
121	− 0.034	(1.498)	− 0.224	(1.601)
122	1.103	(2.206)	− 3.603	(1.544)
123	− 0.345	(1.319)	− 0.759	(1.548)
124	2.603	(0.815)	1.810	(1.162)
125	0.017	(1.942)	− 0.276	(1.508)
126	− 0.345	(1.943)	1.534	(1.581)
127	− 0.741	(1.292)	1.879	(0.957)
128	0.500	(1.188)	1.759	(1.288)
129	− 2.552	(0.882)	1.862	(1.594)
130	0.017	(1.207)	− 0.224	(1.451)

right quadrant shows the combination of pleasure and low arousal, containing expressions that would be labeled calm, relaxed, or sleepy. As we move around the 2-D space, the bottom left quadrant shows the combination of displeasure and low arousal, containing such words as *sad, lonely,* or *depression.* Finally, the top left quadrant shows the combination of displeasure and arousal, containing expressions that are labeled by emotion descriptors such as angry, afraid, or tense. According to an earlier categorization of emotion in the photographs by the Reference Sample, using the original Lexicon, the outlying expressions appear to be the clearest examples of the Lexicon emotion categories. As can be seen, there are also those that fall closer to the center of the space and as the dimensional ratings indicate, these appear to be the more ambiguous expressions.

Moreover, the dimensional ratings illustrate that there is a good range of emotions represented in the IFP as well as a range of clarity of the cues being conveyed.

Study 2

Dimensions of meaning attributed to the IFP were examined in a second study with thirty-six mothers of 18- to 25-month-olds and thirty female college students, using a different method, one free of labels or rating scales. This approach was used to assure that the robustness of the signaling value of the pictures was not dependent on semantic mediation. A similar circular ordering in a tone-arousal space would suggest a similarity in judgments between the two methods of describing nonverbal emotion cues, and we can be confident that our basic results are not limited to semantics. A secondary concern was whether or not experience with children would influence the perception and interpretation of the messages being conveyed.

Ward's (1977) multiple sorting procedure and measure of similarity was used. Subjects were tested individually as they looked over the separated 30 IFEEL Pictures and then divided them into two piles. They were instructed to group together those babies who "feel pretty much the same—not babies who look alike, but babies who are in the same mood, who feel alike." This task was repeated with divisions into 3, 4, 7, 10, and 13 piles. Multidimensional scaling of the pair-wise similarities yielded a two-dimensional space very similar to that found in study 1. The similarity matrix was analyzed by the Gutman-Lingoes Smallest-Space Analysis (SSA-1). The two-dimensional solution yielded an acceptable value of 0.10, which failed to improve with additional dimensions (stress for the five-dimensional solution was 0.05). To test the interpretation of the first two dimensions, dimensional ratings obtained in study 1 were correlated with the multidimensional scaling coordinates. As can be seen in Table 6.2, the correlations indicated that hedonic tone and arousal are indeed a proper interpretation of the multidimensional space.

The results of both of these studies are encouraging not only because they are internally consistent but also because they are consistent with previous studies of adult facial expressions (Russell and Bullock, 1986b), verbal expressions of emotion (Russell, 1980), and response characteristics of emotional behavior (Ridgeway and Waters, 1987). In particular, with an earlier version of the IFP, Emde, Kligman, Reich, and Wade (1978) examined similar sorting done for infants' expressions at 2, 3, 4, and 12 months and found that hedonic tone emerged as the dimension carrying the most variance with arousal being the next most prominent. After two months, a third dimension emerged but was difficult to interpret. In addition, they found a strong tendency for pictures similarly labeled in the free response paradigm to be close together in the

TABLE 6.2
Intercorrelations of Unidimensional Ratings on Hedonic Tone
and Arousal and Multidimensional Scaling Coordinates for
College Students and Mothers

	Arousal	College MDS Hedonic Tone	College MDS Arousal	Mothers MDS Hedonic Tone	Mothers MDS Arousal
Hedonic Tone	−0.0826	0.9462**	0.0061	0.9270**	0.1270
Arousal		0.1022	0.7253**	0.2325	0.4432*
College MDS Hedonic Tone			0.0005	0.9743**	0.1667
College MDS Arousal				0.1796	0.8808**
Mothers MDS Hedonic Tone					0.002

*$p < 0.05$.
**$p < 0.01$.

multidimensional space. A somewhat surprising implication of these results is that groups of judges seemed to
agree about low-signal-value emotional expressions as well
as high-signal-value expressions.

With regard to the second concern, that experience
with infants may influence perception; correlations between solutions for the mothers and college students are
also presented in Table 6.2. Similar solutions were produced by the mothers and the college students, regardless
of experience with infants, and demonstrate the robustness of the emotional messages being conveyed by the
infant facial expressions.

Although there appeared to be no group differences
based on experience with infants in terms of the dimensions perceived, the question still remained whether distribution across categories would reveal any differences due
to experience. A different sample of mothers and college

students were given the IFP using the standard free response categorization procedure. Group comparisons using t-tests revealed that college students gave significantly
more responses denoting surprise (2.78 vs. 1.72), shame
(0.05 vs. 0.00), disgust (0.28 vs. 0.08), and less distress
(3.24 vs. 4.14), and interest (7.76 vs. 9.17). Analyses of
covariance revealed that demographic differences of age
of mother (20.84 vs. 28.64 years) and marital status (single
vs. married) did not take away the difference on the surprise category but did wipe out the significant differences
on interest, disgust, and distress. No responses in the
shame category for the mothers made the ANOVA non-
significant.

Study 3

In a third study, we focused on a validation of the free
response categorizing procedure used in the standard presentation of the IFP technique. This study was based on
the idea that membership within a category is graded
rather than all-or-none. Fifty-eight female college students
were asked to examine each photograph and to rate, on
an eight-point scale, how much each emotion category described the feeling shown. Thus, for each picture a respondent made twelve separate ratings (for the emotions of joy,
surprise, interest, anger, fear, sad, shame, disgust–dislike,
distress, content, passive, cautious–shy).

Overall, subjects produced reliably graded responses
when rating the degree to which the category labels applied to the expressions. Varying degree of membership
is seen clearly in Figure 6.3 which plots the mean rating of
seventeen picture expressions in the category of surprised.
(We presented seventeen pictures selected as the clearest
examples of the emotion in each category based on study
1; it was deemed trivial to demonstrate graded membership in emotion categories with pictures of ambiguous expressions or blends of several emotions.) The pictures are

ordered along the abscissa according to their position in the two-dimensional space as determined from dimensional ratings in study 1. Four points should be noted: (1) the peak or best example of the category "surprised" is the highest rated surprise expression picture 114; (2) another surprise expression picture 108 was also an excellent example; (3) some other expressions were poorer examples of surprise—ratings between 1 and 3; (4) there were also in between cases—ratings between 3 and 5. These findings suggest that the category of surprise includes not only its prototypical expressions as in 108 but others as well such as 128, 127, and 129. This systematic order within an emotion category would not be discernible if the facial expressions were ordered along the abscissa randomly rather than locating their position within the two-dimensional space.

To further illustrate, we can focus on one facial expression rather than looking at an emotion category. Consider photograph 108 (see p. 79). Based on normative ratings this expression best represents surprise and indeed its highest rating was for that category. When subjects were asked to pick one label for 108, words falling in the surprise category predominated. Still others chose descriptors including interest, joy, passive, and shy (see Figure 6.4). The meaning of this expression as revealed by looking over the full range of ratings is not captured by one category but more adequately by its varying membership in many categories.

To summarize, these findings provide support looking at the distribution of emotion across the entire picture set rather than accuracy on a picture-by-picture basis. They also account for the earlier subjective discomfort expressed by raters in the forced choice paradigm. In fact, the intercorrelations in Table 6.2 suggest a close correspondence with the present free response categorization.

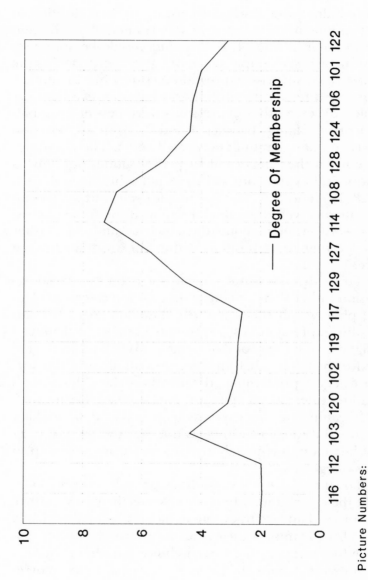

FIGURE 6.3
Surprise: Degree of membership by picture.

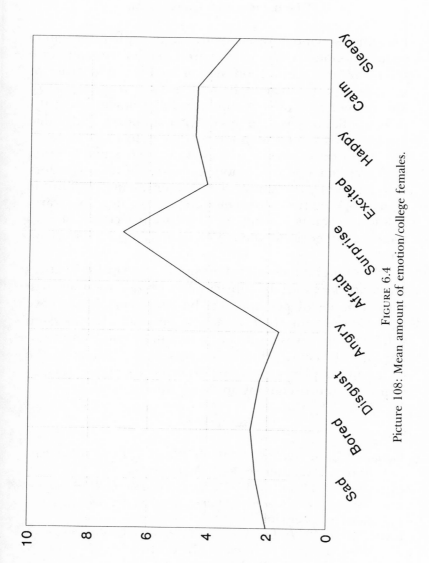

FIGURE 6.4

Picture 108: Mean amount of emotion/college females.

Discussion and Conclusion

Everyday situations often confront us with information about emotions. A person interprets that information, with some sort of classification system whether deliberate or unconscious. We believe that the system may be one of interrelated categories within the dimensional space; the three studies reported in this chapter support the idea that a circumplex model summarizes that system.

All of these studies are based on the original Lexicon where membership of emotion words within a category was derived by consensus of the experimenter within the framework of the adult emotion lexicon used by Izard. Additional studies using the dimensional circumplex to redefine categories in the IFP Lexicon is reported in chapter 4.

We reiterate an important point: the IFEEL Pictures are concerned with the subject's interpretation rather than with accuracy of perception. The emotional signals have been selected for their blends of emotion. Membership within a category is graded; it is not all or none. Our findings of different distributions across the categories for the different samples suggest that experience with infants may influence interpretations about infant emotions.

References

Ekman, P., & Friesen, W. V. (1976), *Pictures of Facial Affect*. Palo Alto, CA: Consulting Psychologists Press.

———— ———— Ellsworth, P. (1972), *Emotion in the Human Face: Guidelines for Research and an Integration of Findings*. Elmsford, NY: Pergamon Press.

Emde, R. N. (1979), Levels of meaning for infant emotions: A biosocial view. In: *Minnesota Symposium on Child Psychology*, Vol. 13, ed. W. A. Collins. Hillsdale, NJ: Lawrence Erlbaum Associates.

———— Kligman, D. H., Reich, J. H., & Wade, T. D. (1978), Emotional expression in infancy: I. Initial studies of social signaling and an emergent model. In: *The Development of Affect*, ed. M. Lewis & L. Rosenblum. New York: Plenum.

Hunt, W. A. (1941), Recent developments in the field of emotion. *Psychological Bulletin*, 38:249–276.

Izard, C. E. (1971), *The Face of Emotion*. New York: Appleton-Century-Crofts.

Ridgeway, D., & Waters, E. (1987), Induced mood and preschoolers' behavior: Isolating the effects of hedonic tone and degree of arousal. *J. Pers. & Soc. Psychol.*, 52:620–625.

Russell, J. A. (1980), A circumplex model of affect. *J. Pers. & Soc. Psychol.*, 39:1161–1178.

———— (1983), Pancultural aspects of the human conceptual organization of emotions. *J. Pers. & Soc. Psychol.*, 45:1281–1288.

———— Bullock, M. (1986a), Fuzzy concepts and the perception of emotion in facial expressions. *Soc. Cognit.*, 4:109–341.

———— ———— (1986b), On the dimensions preschoolers use to interpret facial expressions of emotion. *Develop. Psychol.*, 22:97–102.

———— Ridgeway, D. (1983), Dimensions underlying children's emotion concepts. *Develop. Psychol.*, 19:795–804.

———— Weiss, A. (1983), *The Affect Grid: A Single-Item Mood Scale* (Typescript). University of British Columbia, Vancouver.

Spignesi, A., & Shor, R. (1981), The judgment of emotion from facial expressions, contexts and their combination. *J. Gen. Psychol.*, 104:41–58.

Wagner, H. L., Manstead, A. S. R., & MacDonald, C. J. (1983), Spontaneous facial expressions and the communication of emotions. Paper presented at the 91st annual convention of the American Psychological Association, Anaheim, California.

Ward, L. M. (1977), Multidimensional scaling of the molar physical environment. *Multivar. Behav. Res.*, 12:23–42.

Woodworth, R. S., & Schlosberg, H. (1954), *Experimental Psychology*, rev. ed. New York: Holt, Rinehart & Winston.

Part III:

Group Comparisons with High-Risk Mothers

7

Perceptions of Infant Emotions in Adolescent Mothers

Joy D. Osofsky and Anne M. Culp

Introduction

Adolescent mothers have difficulty parenting their infants due to their immaturity, greater family instability, socio-economic disadvantage, limited resources, and increased evidence of depression (Osofsky, Eberhart-Wright, Ware, and Hann, 1991). Based on these factors, it would be expected that adolescent mothers' perceptions of infant emotions might be different from those of a low-risk group of parents. Early comparison studies with the IFEEL Pictures (IFP) involved collecting data from parents at risk for child abuse and neglect (Butterfield and Emde, 1986; see chapters 3 and 8). Out of these studies of risk groups came a more clearly differentiating strategy for understanding responses in terms of the distribution of emotion categories across the picture set. When the content was analyzed

This project was supported by Grant MH 36895 from the Center for Prevention Research, Division of Special Clinical Programs, National Institute of Mental Health and the John D. and Catherine T. MacArthur Foundation Network on Early Childhood Transitions.

according to emotion categories, significant differences were found between high- and low-risk groups (see chapter 8).

To evaluate whether adolescent mothers, a group at high psychosocial risk, would show a similar pattern of responses to the IFP, the measure was administered to eighty pregnant adolescents (ages 17 and under) who were participating in an ongoing longitudinal study. Their responses were compared to those of seventy-five nonpregnant adolescents sampled from a local high school and 145 low-risk mothers. It was hypothesized that adolescent mothers, similar to other high-risk mothers, would show a different pattern of responses that might be a reflection of the mother's conflictual internal state in relation to her pregnancy and baby.

Method

SUBJECTS

Three groups of subjects were studied: eighty pregnant adolescents (mean age 16 years; range 12–17 years) enrolled in the Menninger Infant Project; seventy-five nonpregnant adolescents sampled from a high school in the same city (mean age 16 years; range 15–17 years); and a reference group of 145 low-risk mothers (mean age 24 years; range 20–32 years) sampled from pediatric offices in metropolitan and rural areas of the midwestern United States.

PROCEDURES

Two studies are reported in this chapter. In the first study, the responses to the IFP were compared among the three groups of subjects. The second study focused only on the adolescent mothers and the relationship between their responses to the IFP, a prenatal interview, a newborn feeding behavioral observation, six-month feeding and play observations, and maternal depression and self-esteem scores at six months.

The standard set of IFP was used which included thirty photographs that show infants' facial expression of discrete emotions or emotion blends (see chapter 4 for a detailed description). Twelve emotions were scored from the pictures: joy, interest, content, passive, surprise, anger, fear, disgust, distress, sad, cautious–shy, and shame–guilt. The IFEEL Pictures Lexicon was used (see appendix A-5).

STUDY 1

The pregnant adolescents were administered the IFP in their last trimester of pregnancy. The subjects were clients of the city–county health department program for pregnant adolescents, as well as participants in the Menninger Infant Project, a longitudinal study of adolescent mothers and their infants.

The nonpregnant adolescents were female students in their junior or senior year at a local high school who were administered the IFP during one of their classes.

The reference group mothers were asked to respond to the IFP while waiting for a well-baby pediatric visit. The sample included both first-time mothers and those with more than one child, one of whom was currently an infant.

STUDY 2

In the second study, the pregnant adolescents' responses were related to a prenatal interview, observations of feeding interactions between the adolescent mothers and their newborn infants, and six-month feeding and play observations, as well as maternal depression and self-esteem scores. These measures were included as part of an ongoing longitudinal study of pregnant adolescents, during which they were interviewed extensively prior to the birth of their baby and followed until that child was 3 years old.

Before responding to the IFP, the adolescents were interviewed by a social worker and asked about their acceptance of the pregnancy, their personal experiences, their emotional support systems, their childhood and family dynamics, the father of their child, their education and financial resources, and their self-impressions. Based on this interview, they were given an overall risk score by the social worker.

The adolescent mothers were visited in the hospital twenty-four hours following the delivery of their child and were observed feeding their infants. Observations were rated with the Osofsky and Danzger (1974) feeding scales that included the following maternal behaviors: attentiveness, visual regard, auditory stimulation, and tactile frequency and quality.

When the infants were 6 months of age, they and their mothers visited the infant research laboratory, which was designed like a playroom, for a one-hour evaluation during which feeding and play interactions were filmed and rated. Using a revised version of the Osofsky and Danzger (1974) feeding scales (Osofsky, Culp, and Eberhart-Wright, 1984), the maternal behaviors of visual regard, auditory frequency, quality of speech, the amount of touching, affection, expressiveness, sensitivity, synchrony, and delight shown toward the infant were rated during the feeding. Play behaviors were rated with the play scales developed by Vaughn, Taraldson, Crichton, and Egeland (1980) and included maternal inventiveness, appropriateness, supportiveness, patience, the amount of reciprocal play, as well as the degree of baby satisfaction.

An interview was administered at six months postpartum to evaluate changes in life circumstances and amount of support and stress. At this time, mothers also were asked to complete self-report scales measuring self-esteem, the ISE scale (Hudson, 1982) and depression, the CES-D scale (Radloff, 1977). The twelve emotions scored from the IFP were studied in relation to the prenatal, newborn, and six-month variables.

Results

STUDY 1

The Kolmogorov-Smirov 2 Sample Test (KS) was used to test for overall differences between the groups. The groups were found to be significantly different at the .001 level for all of the comparisons (1 vs. 2; 2 vs. 3; 1 vs. 3). For each of the twelve emotions, t-test analyses were then used to determine differences between the groups on individual emotions. The means and standard deviations are reported in Table 7.1.

The responses of the pregnant adolescents differed from the reference group on seven of the twelve emotions. The pregnant adolescents showed more joy ($t = 5.5$, $p < 0.0001$), surprise ($t = 2.8$, $p < 0.001$), anger ($t = 3.4$, $p < 0.001$), and sad responses ($t = 4.9$, $p < 0.01$), and less interest ($t = 4.2$, $p < 0.0001$), content ($t = 4.9$, $p < 0.001$), and cautious–shy ($t = 6.3$, $p < 0.0001$) responses than the reference group.

The pregnant adolescents differed from their non-pregnant peers on five emotions. The pregnant adolescents were higher on joy ($t = 2.8$, $p < 0.01$), anger ($t = 2.2$, $p < 0.03$), and sadness ($t = 2.4$, $p < 0.01$), and lower on content ($t = 2.2$, $p < 0.03$), and cautious–shy ($t = 3.9$, $p < 0.0001$) than the nonpregnant adolescents. The nonpregnant adolescents differed from the Reference

TABLE 7.1
Means and Standard Deviations

Comparisons	Reference Group N = 145 Mean SD	Pregnant Adolescents N = 80 Mean SD	Nonpregnant Adolescents N = 75 Mean SD	Significant t-tests
Joy	3.3 (1.7)	4.7 (2.0)	3.9 (1.4)	a, b, c
Interest	7.2 (3.4)	5.2 (3.5)	4.9 (3.0)	a, c
Content	2.8 (1.5)	1.8 (1.6)	2.4 (1.9)	a, b
Passive	1.1 (1.4)	1.3 (1.7)	1.3 (1.5)	
Surprise	1.7 (1.4)	2.8 (2.6)	2.8 (1.6)	a, c
Anger	1.9 (1.7)	2.9 (2.4)	2.2 (1.5)	a, b
Fear	1.9 (2.3)	2.3 (2.7)	2.7 (2.0)	c
Disgust	0.27 (.74)	0.18 (.82)	0.13 (.41)	
Distress	2.2 (1.9)	1.8 (20)	2.4 (1.8)	
Sad	3.8 (2.3)	4.9 (3.6)	3.6 (3.4)	a, b
Shy	2.5 (2.0)	0.93 (1.6)	2.0 (1.9)	a, b
Shame	0.13 (.41)	0.24 (1.1)	0.13 (.38)	

KS Test = $p < 0.001$ for overall group differences for 3 comparisons.
a = Reference vs. Pregnant Adolescent Groups.
b = Pregnant Adolescent vs. Nonpregnant Adolescent Groups.
c = Reference vs. Nonpregnant Adolescent Groups.

Sample on four emotions. The nonpregnant adolescents had a higher incidence of joy ($t = 3.1$, $p < 0.01$), surprise ($t = 5.6$, $p < 0.0001$), and fear ($t = 2.3$, $p < 0.01$), and a lower incidence of interest ($t = 5.0$, $p < 0.0001$) than the Reference Sample.

The emotions joy and sad are of particular interest. Usually, when the pregnant adolescents responded with high joy responses, they also responded with high sad responses. This bimodal response needs more careful investigation as it seems to occur repeatedly in higher risk groups (see chapter 8).

STUDY 2

In the second study, Pearson Product Moment correlations were used to determine relationships between the emotion responses on the IFP and prenatal interview variables, newborn feeding, six-month postpartum feeding, six-month play, and six-month depression and self-esteem scores. Many significant relationships were found (see Table 7.2); however, only the emotions with more than four significant relationships out of twenty-eight possible correlations will be discussed.

The emotion of joy showed a significant positive correlation with prenatal variables of personal experience ($r = 0.25, p < 0.04$), prenatal social worker's risk assessment ($r = 0.23, p < 0.05$), and newborn auditory frequency ($r = 0.28, p < 0.04$). A negative relationship was found with six-month feeding synchrony ($r = 0.30, p < 0.03$) and tactile stimulation ($r = -0.31, p < 0.04$). A negative relationship was found with appropriateness during play ($r = -0.37, p < 0.01$), supportiveness ($r = -0.41, p < 0.005$), and patience ($r = -0.46, p < 0.001$). In addition, a positive relationship was found between the emotion of joy and six-month reported self-esteem ($r = 0.36, p < 0.02$). A high score on self-esteem reflects low self-esteem and high scores on the prenatal variables reflect high risk. Thus, the higher the joy the mother saw in the pictures, the higher her risk for negative prenatal personal experiences, and the higher her risk as evaluated by the social worker. In addition, these young mothers talked less to their newborns during feeding and demonstrated less synchrony and touching while feeding their 6-month-old infants. The less appropriateness, supportiveness, and patience the mothers demonstrated during six-month play with their infants, the more often they reported lower self-esteem at the same time period.

The emotion of interest correlated positively with affectionate touching during newborn feeding ($r = -0.27, p < 0.05$), appropriateness ($r = 0.32, p < 0.02$), and patience ($r = 0.36, p < 0.02$) during six-month play, and negatively with six-month self-esteem ($r = -0.31, p <$

TABLE 7.2
Significant Pearson Product Moment Correlations

	Joy	Interest	Content	Anger	Cautious/Shy
Prenatal					
Accept Pregnancy			−0.30		
Personal Experiences	0.25				
Family Dynamics				−0.30	
Significant Other			−0.25		
Financial Resources				−0.26	
Social Work Assessment	0.23				
Emotional Support from FOC			−0.31	−0.36	
Abuse/Incest			−0.30		
Newborn Feeding					
Attentiveness					0.39
Auditory Quality	−0.28	0.27			0.31
Auditory Frequency					
Affectionate Touch				−0.29	0.30
6 mos. Feeding					
Vocalizations				0.38	
Synchrony	−0.30			−0.40	
Tactile	−0.31				
Responsiveness					0.40
6 mos. Play					
Appropriateness	−0.37	0.32			
Supportiveness	−0.41				
Patience	−0.46	0.36			
6 mos. Self-Esteem	0.36	−0.31			

0.04). The less interest the mothers saw in the pictures, the less affectionate they were during newborn feeding, the less appropriate and patient during six-month play, and the more at risk for low self-esteem.

The emotion, content, showed a significant negative correlation with four prenatal variables: acceptance of pregnancy ($r = -0.30$, $p < 0.01$); relation with father of child and his family ($r = -0.25$, $p < 0.04$); emotional support from father of the child ($r = -0.31$, $p < 0.01$). In other words, the less content the mother saw in the pictures, the more at risk she was for accepting her pregnancy, having a good relationship with the father of her child, and having an incestuous experience.

The emotion of anger showed significant negative correlations with three prenatal variables, family dynamics ($r = -0.30$, $p < 0.01$), financial resources ($r = -0.26$, $p < 0.03$), and experiences of childhood abuse ($r = -0.36$, $p < 0.003$). Anger correlated with one newborn variable, tactile stimulation of infant during feeding ($r = -0.29$, $p < 0.03$) and two six-month feeding variables, vocalization ($r = 0.38$, $p < 0.01$) and synchrony ($r = -0.40$, $p < 0.007$). In other words, the more anger responses, the less at risk the adolescent was with family dynamics, financial resources, and childhood abuse. The high occurrence of anger responses for the adolescent mothers was not associated with an unstable abusive family. However, the tendency for a mother to see more anger was associated with less affectionate behavior shown toward her baby during the newborn period, less synchrony, and more vocalizations during six-month feeding.

The emotion of cautious–shy was positively correlated with three newborn feeding variables; maternal attentiveness ($r = 0.39$, $p < 0.004$), auditory quality ($r = 0.31$, $p < 0.02$), auditory frequency ($r = 0.31$, $p < 0.03$), and one six-month feeding variable, maternal responsiveness (r

= 0.40, $p < 0.007$). In other words, the fewer cautious–shy responses the mother had, the less attentive she was and the less she talked to her newborn during feeding. She was also less responsive to her 6-month-old infant during feeding.

Discussion

At some level, one can make the assumption that parents' responses to facial expressions of infant emotions reflect the internal state of the adult. When viewing the IFP, adults responded that the infants experienced a variety of positive, negative, and mixed emotions. If the responses to the pictures are more projective, reflecting issues within the adult or parent, then it might be expected that a high-risk group would respond differently than a low-risk group. The results of the current investigation lend support to this assumption. Pregnant adolescents responded differently to the IFP than older parents. Interestingly, high-school students also responded differently to the pictures than both pregnant adolescents and older parents, perhaps indicating that age, or more likely developmental level, may play a role in how infants' facial expressions of emotions are viewed.

Both pregnant and nonpregnant adolescents responded with a significantly higher number of sad responses. In addition, the pregnant adolescents reported more joy responses. As mentioned, this bimodal distribution seems to occur more frequently in high-risk groups which may be a reflection of both some confusion and defensive denial about how babies may be feeling. If these mothers are struggling themselves, they may be more comfortable seeing the babies as happier on the one hand, while their responses reflect their sadness on the other. Interestingly, the pregnant adolescents also responded that they observed more anger than the other two groups, perhaps again reflecting some of their own internal conflicts.

The current results may point to an additional use of the IFP for early preventive intervention. Significant relationships were found between responses to the IFP, the prenatal interview, and feeding observations during the newborn period and feeding and play observations at six months. Thus, one might be alerted to parents who are at risk for problems in the parenting relationship before such problems occur and begin preventive intervention. For example, mothers who saw infants as showing much joy and also had a cluster of IFP associated with sadness and anger would likely be at high risk. Teenage mothers who reported high joy in the IFP tended to be at greater risk related to adverse life experiences, showed more problematic observations during the newborn feeding, were less attentive, talked less to their infants, and had low self-esteem. Moreover, they continued to look less at their infants at six months. The discrepancy between the positive emotion of joy that the mothers reported so often when viewing the IFP pictures and their attitudes and behaviors toward their own infants is suggestive of significant denial of negative feelings about the pregnancy and infant which might manifest themselves in both current and later problematic behaviors toward their infant. These mothers may be responding to the stress of early pregnancy with a more overt depressive reaction. It would be important to be sensitive to such mothers who might benefit from additional support during pregnancy and the perinatal period.

The results of the current study suggest important additional uses for the IFEEL Pictures with groups that are at high risk for having difficulties in parenting. The patterning of responses to the pictures has been shown empirically to differ for high- and low-risk groups which can be interpreted as reflecting risk factors in the parents.

Although additional replication studies with other high-risk groups would be informative, at this point it is possible to conclude that this method appears to be promising for differentiating risk factors. The IFP may provide another means for identifying parents and infants who might benefit from early preventive intervention efforts.

References

Butterfield, P. M., & Emde, R. N. (1986), Women "at risk" for parenting disorder perceive emotions in infant pictures differently. Paper presented at the World Association of Infant Psychiatry and Allied Disciplines, Stockholm, Sweden.

Hudson, W. W. (1982), *The Clinical Measurement Package: A Field Manual.* Homewood, IL: Dorsey.

Osofsky, J. D., Culp, A. M., & Eberhart-Wright, A. (1984), *Mother–Infant Feeding Scale.* Manual. Louisiana State University Medical Center, New Orleans.

———— Danzger, B. (1974), Relationships between neonatal characteristics and mother–infant interaction. *Develop. Psychol.,* 10:124–130.

———— Eberhart-Wright, A., Ware, L. M., & Hann, D. M. (1991), Children of adolescent mothers: Risk of psychopathology. Paper presented at the 37th International Psychoanalytic Association Meeting, Buenos Aires.

———— ———— ———— ———— (1992), Children of adolescent mothers: A group at risk for psychopathology. *Infant Mental Health J.,* 13:119–132.

Radloff, L. S. (1977), The CES-D Scale: A self-report depression scale for research in the general population. *Appl. Psychol. Measure.,* 1:385–401.

Vaughn, B. E., Taraldson, B., Crichton, L., & Egeland, B. (1980), Relationships and infant behavior during the first year of life. *Infant Behav. & Develop.,* 3:47–66.

8

Responses to IFEEL Pictures in Mothers at Risk for Child Maltreatment

Perry M. Butterfield

Do women who are emotionally preoccupied view pictures of infant facial expressions of emotion differently than women who are not experiencing emotional turmoil? The subjects selected initially to explore this question were a group of poverty level mothers who were participating in a prospective longitudinal study of women at potential risk for child maltreatment (RCM). This longitudinal intervention study was designed to provide these mothers with emotional support from experienced mothers in the same community, who had been successful in raising their children (Dawson, Robinson, and Johnson, 1982). As described in chapter 3, exploratory work with this sample revealed that a content analysis rather than an accuracy comparison with a group of fifty low-risk Denver women generated differences between the groups. The content

We gratefully acknowledge the Parent/Infant Project Investigation of Parent/Infant Support Through Lay Home Visitors. William J. Van Doorninck, Ph.D., Peter Dawson, M.D., M.P.H., Perry M. Butterfield, M.A., Helen Alexander, M.S.W., 1977–1979. Supported by Maternal Child Health Services (Social Security Act, Title V) Grant No. MC-R-080398.

analysis showed that more than half of the RCM mothers saw the early set of pictures differently from the comparison group (Butterfield, 1986). These findings indicated the need for comparative data with a normative sample of mothers. In addition, these findings influenced us to modify the picture set and the Lexicon (see chapters 4, 5, and 6).

The RCM sample has continued to provide a basis for comparison with early and late versions of our Reference Sample. Several analyses using the sample will be reported here: first, a description of the RCM mothers' emotion responses; second, a comparative analysis done after the development of the initial reference sample; third, some within-group analyses of the RCM sample; and, finally, a comparison of these results with the current reference sample and with other risk populations using the latest scoring programs.

Description of Pictures and Samples

In the original evaluation of the RCM mothers, thirty-five of the available seventy infant pictures were used. Twenty-two of these pictures have continued to be included in all modifications of the picture set (see appendix A-1) and are still contained in the IFEEL Pictures. These twenty-two pictures will be referred to as the Early IFEEL Pictures (EIFP) and are the ones used in all comparisons with the RCM sample and the Zahn-Waxler maternal depression group, described in chapter 9.

The initial reference sample included eighty-three mothers sampled from different groups in Denver and Topeka (see chapter 5). This sample was used for comparison purposes throughout the early development of the IFP. Two more groups of mothers from similar populations were added to complete the final reference sample, making a total of 145 subjects. There were no significant differences in the content analyses between the two samples. Early results, reported here, use the Reference 83 Sample; later results report comparisons with the final Reference 145 Sample.

Method

SUBJECTS

All of the women in three county maternity clinics in the Denver area, serving a poverty population in which there was a high incidence of abuse and neglect, were approached near their twenty-sixth week of pregnancy and were asked about participating in the longitudinal study. The RCM sample consisted of ninety-eight of these women who had been followed through their baby's fourteenth postnatal month. Mothers' mean age was twenty-two years, with approximately one-half of the sample being under twenty years of age. One third were never married. Yearly incomes were below $11,000, with a mean of $5500. Two-thirds of the mothers were enrolled when they were expecting their first child. Ethnic background included 74 percent Caucasian, 25 percent Mexican American, and 1 percent African American. The mean grade level in school was 11.2 years, and 44 percent of the mothers were working full- or part-time. Thirty-six percent felt that they had been abused as children and 41 percent were assessed as having a poor relationship with the baby's father.

PROCEDURE

All RCM mothers were evaluated as part of the longitudinal study prenatally, at birth, 1 month, 6 months, and 14 postnatal months. Multiple measures were used at each time point, the EIFP being administered at the fourteen-month visit.

The EIFP was used with the standard instructions, as suggested in chapter 4. The tester wrote the responses on the score sheet for the subject. The early pictures were on cards and were presented in random order.

Of the other measures done in the longitudinal project, only one, the one-month feeding observation, will be reported here. The Early Feeding Interaction Profile (Butterfield, 1978) combines both positive and negative ratings of early feeding behaviors into maternal and infant interaction profiles. The maternal profile scores factored into four distinct interaction styles, one predicted style (the "maternal" profile), and three deviant styles (the "depressed," the "intensive," and the "conflicted" profiles) (Dawson, Robinson, Butterfield, Van Doorninck, Gaensbauer, and Harmon, 1991).

Results

The results will present analyses done at different times during the ten-year development of the IFP.

THE RCM SAMPLE

The RCM mothers showed more joy, sadness, shame, and anger, and fewer interest and fear responses. In general, these mothers used few emotion categories to describe the pictures, commonly using one or two emotions in excess. For example, one mother cited eleven of the twenty-two pictures as joy, another perceived eight of the twenty-two as sad. However, these mothers used a wide range of emotion words within each category. They often chose extreme emotion words such as *despairing, furious, hysterical,* or *blameworthy* to describe the infant pictures. The RCM sample added many words to the Lexicon, particularly in the category "Other." Of specific interest is a group of descriptive words such as *cunning, devious,* and *sneaky,* which may be of clinical interest but are classed as ambiguous in emotional content. Noteworthy additions to the "Other" category by this sample were words such as *sexy* or *seductive* or functional words such as *nauseated* or *nursing.*

RCM VERSUS THE INITIAL REFERENCE SAMPLE

When the RCM mothers were compared with the initial Reference Sample of eighty-three mothers, the RCM mothers' responses were significantly different on seven of eleven emotion categories which were being used at that time. T-test comparisons of the mean number of responses per emotion revealed that the RCM mothers saw more sadness ($t = 3.57, p < 0.0001$), shame ($t = 3.20, p < 0.002$), anger ($t = 2.12, p < 0.03$), joy ($t = 4.77, p < 0.0001$), and surprise ($t = 3.26, p < 0.001$). They saw less interest ($t = -4.72, p < 0.0001$), and fear ($t = -2.69, p < 0.008$).

A profile of emotion content, using the reference sample as the norm, was developed for charting individual scores. Extreme responses for individuals were defined as any frequency of emotion code that was three or more standard deviations beyond the mean of the Reference Sample for that emotion. Forty-seven percent of the RCM mothers scored at the extreme level on one or more emotions. An interesting pattern which may have clinical relevance was the bimodal distribution of extremes with high negative responses and higher than normal positive responses. High joy coupled with high anger or sadness was the most prominent pattern occurring 20 percent of the time. Another pattern was the coupling of high surprise with high fear and anger. Such patterns were most often represented by one emotion at three standard deviations and one at two standard deviations from the Reference Sample means (see Figure 8.1). For the Reference Sample, the range of differences on any emotion did not exceed one standard deviation. For the RCM sample, therefore, a second response of two standard deviations or more was considered unusual or higher than normal (Emde, Butterfield, Osofsky, Gaddis, Ridgeway, Stern, Kaplan, and Zahn-Waxler, 1986).

WITHIN GROUP ANALYSES USING THE RCM SAMPLE

Analyses of concurrent variables from the high-risk longitudinal sample of RCM mothers were done to further our understanding of the relationship between the early pictures and the extremes of emotion defined by this group. Thirty percent of the RCM subjects were adolescent mothers. To identify the possibility of bias due to the teenage mothers in the sample, a within group comparison was done. The adolescent mothers showed less interest ($t = 2.56$, $p < 0.01$) and a trend toward more shame ($t = 1.87$, $p < 0.07$). Overall, the age factor did not contribute significantly to the uniqueness of the RCM sample. In subsequent samples (see Osofsky and Culp, chapter 7) age has been a differentiating factor. Within group comparisons such as memories of abuse as a child, race, or educational level also did not contribute to differentiated responses within the RCM group.

For purposes of other within group comparisons, the RCM mothers were divided into two groups, those who had responses to the EIFP similar to the Reference Sample and those who had extreme responses. Significant relationships were found between the RCM mothers who had extreme EIFP scores and dysfunctional ratings on the maternal feeding observations at one-month postpartum. Mothers with extreme shame responses to the EIFP were scored with the "intrusive" profile on the feeding scales ($X^2 = 7.48$, $p < 0.006$). Mothers with extreme sadness responses to the pictures were scored with the "depressed"

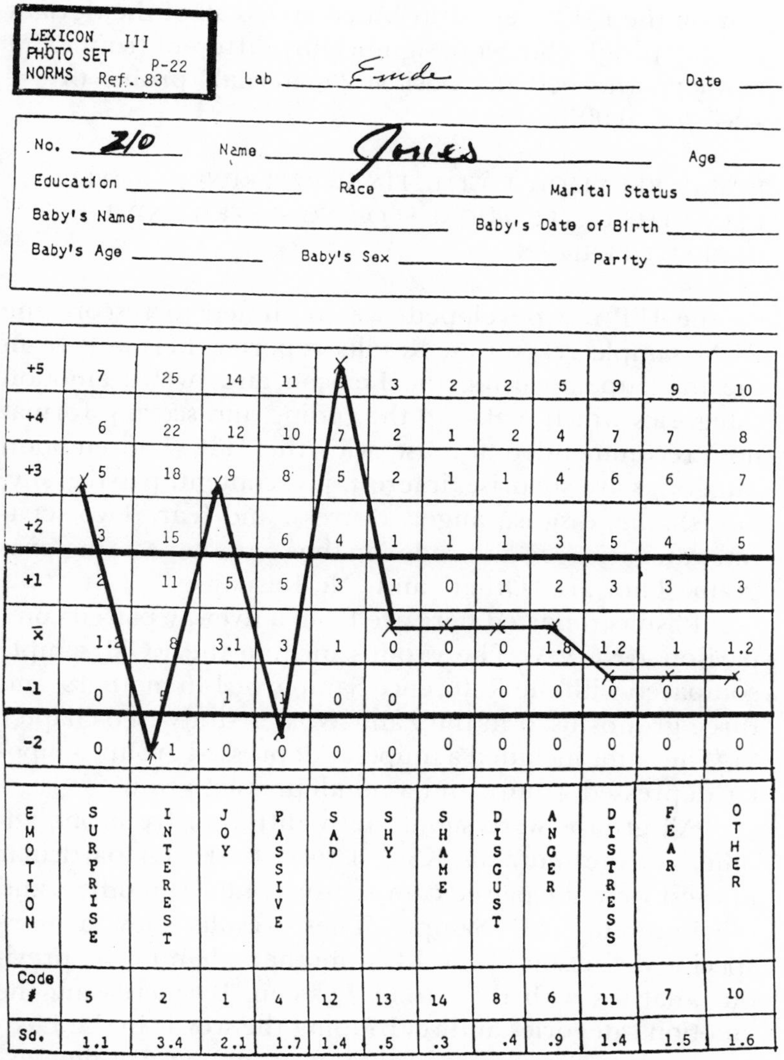

LEXICON III
PHOTO SET
NORMS Ref. 83 P-22

Lab Emde Date

No. 210 Name Jones Age

Education Race Marital Status

Baby's Name Baby's Date of Birth

Baby's Age Baby's Sex Parity

EMOTION	SURPRISE	INTEREST	JOY	PASSIVE	SAD	SHY	SHAME	DISGUST	ANGER	DISTRESS	FEAR	OTHER
+5	7	25	14	11	8	3	2	2	5	9	9	10
+4	6	22	12	10	7	2	1	2	4	7	7	8
+3	5	18	9	8	5	2	1	1	4	6	6	7
+2	3	15	[illegible]	6	4	1	1	1	3	5	4	5
+1	2	11	5	5	3	1	0	1	2	3	3	3
$\bar{x}$	1.2	8	3.1	3	1	0	0	0	1.8	1.2	1	1.2
-1	0	5	1	1	0	0	0	0	0	0	0	0
-2	0	1	0	0	0	0	0	0	0	0	0	0
Code #	5	2	1	4	12	13	14	8	6	11	7	10
Sd.	1.1	3.4	2.1	1.7	1.4	.5	.3	.4	.9	1.4	1.5	1.6

FIGURE 8.1
Subject Profile/IFEEL Pictures.

feeding profile ($X^2 = 401$, $p < 0.04$). Women who had low fear on the EIFP were distributed across all of the deviant feeding profiles but were significantly different from RCM mothers who had the positive "maternal" profile ($X^2 = 7.84$, $p < 0.005$).

RCM IN RELATION TO THE FINAL REFERENCE SAMPLE, USING THE CATEGORICAL SCORING SYSTEM AND THE CURRENT LEXICON

As the IFP test developed, we continued to rescore the RCM sample responses. Results reported here are from the final update using the Lexicon and twelve emotion categories which make up the coding and scoring format now recommended for use with the IFP. The emotion categories are surprise, interest, joy, content, passive, shy, sad, shame, disgust, anger, distress, and fear. Two separate categories are also coded in the computer scoring program: They are "Other" and "No Response."

Results reported here are from a fiveway paired comparison ANOVA. The groups include the RCM sample compared with the Reference Sample of 145 mothers, and three groups used in the Zahn-Waxler study (see chapter 9). The latter included a unipolar depressed group, a bipolar depressed group, and a nondepressed group.

All groups were significantly different from one another on the omnibus KS test ($p < 0.01$). Of particular interest were the paired comparisons of RCM mothers and the Reference 145 Sample. These results show a more specific definition of the RCM mothers than in the previous analyses with the earlier Lexicon. By increasing the emotion categories and regrouping the words in the Lexicon by their dimensional values (see chapter 4), some extremes were eliminated while strengthening others. As with the early analyses, RCM mothers were still higher on joy ($p < 0.01$), shame ($p < 0.001$), and other ($p < 0.0001$), and, in addition, saw less shyness ($p < 0.0001$), less interest ($p < 0.009$), and less fear ($p < 0.0008$). There was a trend toward their seeing less distress ($p < 0.06$). These comparisons did not reveal the extremes of anger and distress which were in the earlier analysis (see Figure 8.2).

The responses of the RCM mothers were also different from those of two depressed groups of mothers (see chapter 9) as shown by the paired comparisons ANOVA. When compared with either the bipolar or the unipolar samples, the RCM mothers saw more joy and shame, with less fear and shyness. The unipolar depressed mothers only showed significantly more distress than the RCM mothers and significantly less contentment than the bipolar sample (see Figure 8.3).

RCM USING THE DIMENSIONAL SCORING RESULTS

The five groups discussed above were all different from one another on the two dimensions of hedonic tone ($p < 0.001$) and arousal ($p < 0.005$). The paired comparisons of dimensions showed the RCM sample to be diferent from the final Reference Sample on hedonic tone ($F = 45.99$, $p < 0.0001$) and on arousal ($F = 9.49$, $p < 0.002$), with the RCM mean score for hedonic tone and for arousal level elevated on both dimensions. These scores are primarily influenced by the choice of words in a subject's responses. The RCM mothers chose words that were more positive in tone even in the negative emotion categories and more active in the context of excitement or arousal in contrast to the depressed groups that chose words which were more negative and low in arousal level.

Discussion

The EIFP task appears to tap different interpretations of emotions by high- and low-risk mothers. RCM mothers

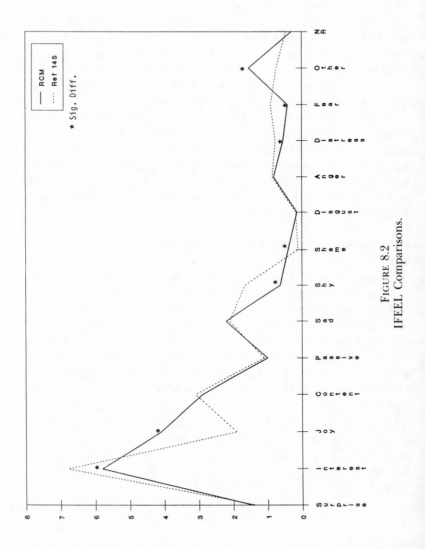

FIGURE 8.2
IFEEL Comparisons.

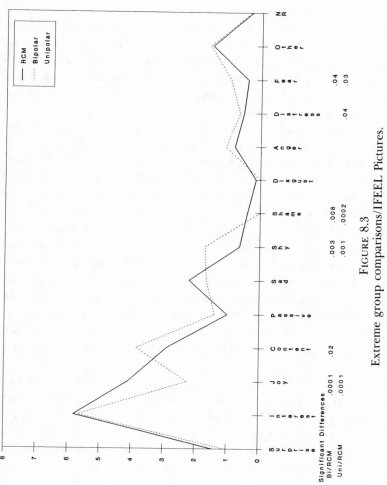

FIGURE 8.3
Extreme group comparisons/IFEEL Pictures.

tended to select fewer emotions per subject and to show more extremes in their choices. For example, not only might a typical RCM subject designate close to half of the twenty-two pictures as sad, but the selections of words used to describe the pictures tended to be descriptive. Such words as *despairing, alone, abandoned, heartbroken,* and *dead* were chosen in contrast to *sad, unhappy, weepy,* and *melancholy.* The pictures seemed to be tapping into something within the mother which overpowered the emotion in the baby's facial expression.

These mothers, like other groups of mothers at psychosocial risk (see chapter 7), more often showed a bimodal distribution including sadness or shame, coupled with an extreme amount of joy and/or surprise. Unlike the depressed samples of mothers who used low arousal response words for both positive and negative hedonic tone, RCM mothers used high arousal response words.

The post hoc comparisons of early feeding styles and extreme responses on the EIFP are tenuous. However, they are of interest in light of the subsequent study by Osofsky and Culp which also reported significant relationships between early feeding observations and extreme responses on the IFP, and Lodge who reported significant relationships between the IFP and other early behavioral measures (chapter 14).

The RCM mothers were a troubled group. For the most part, they were young, poorly educated, and struggling to survive. Many had a history of family violence and abandonment. The EIFP has continued to discriminate this group as different from the samples of low-risk mothers across the development of the reference samples and the Lexicon. The RCM group showed extremes of individual response patterns similar to other samples of mothers at psychosocial risk, but different from groups of depressed mothers.

The RCM mothers, as defined by the current IFP scoring system, show high attributions of shame with inappropriate perceptions of extreme joy, countered by low interest and little perceived caution, shyness, fear, or distress. The high number of "Other" responses for this group might also be said to indicate their disorganization. This profile presents an intriguing clinical view of the potential for child maltreatment.

These results suggest a potential differentiating role for the IFP to be investigated further with other clinical populations.

References

Butterfield, P. M. (1978), Early Feeding Interaction Profiles. Developed in conjunction with the Parent Infant Project. Scale. Typescript.

————— (1986), Women at risk for parenting disorders perceive emotion in infant pictures differently. Paper presented at International Conference on Infant Studies, Los Angeles, CA.

Dawson, P. M., Robinson, J. L., & Johnson, C. B. (1982), Informal social support as an invention. *Zero to Three*, 3/2:1–5.

————— ————— Butterfield, P. M., Van Doorninck, W. J., Gaensbauer, T. J., & Harmon, R. S. (1991), Supporting new parents through home visits: Effects on maternal/infant interaction. *Topics in Early Childhood Spec. Ed.*, 19/4:29–44.

Emde, R. N., Butterfield, P. M., Osofsky, J. D., Gaddis, E., Ridgeway, D., Stern, D. N., Kaplan, T., & Zahn-Waxler, C. (1986), Parental perceptions of infant emotions: A new instrument. Paper presented at the International Conference on Infant Studies, Los Angeles, CA.

9

Caregivers' Interpretations of Infant Emotions: A Comparison of Depressed and Well Mothers

Carolyn Zahn-Waxler and Elizabeth Wagner

Parents' relationships and interactions with their children undoubtedly are guided, in part, by more broadly based conceptions of children's capacities to experience, express, and regulate different emotions. Understanding of parent–child relationships, thus, would be advanced by knowledge of parents' views of children's emotions. Currently, little is known about factors that contribute to individual differences in parents' perceptions of affect in young children. One major source of influence undoubtedly includes the parents' histories of affective experiences with their own caregivers. This history of experience, in interaction with temperament, presumably results in particular emotion styles or traits that become elements of personality organization. These more enduring patterns, in turn, are

We wish to express our appreciation to the following individuals for their contributions to this project: Marian Radke-Yarrow, for valuable advice and for making the NIMH subject population available, Robert Emde and Perry Butterfield for facilitating data analysis, and Jean Mayo for preparation of the manuscript.

likely to influence how the emotions of others are perceived. If these perceptions contain significant distortions, there may be maladaptive consequences for parent–child interaction. One way to begin to explore such processes is to study caregivers with emotional problems, that is, those who are extreme in their own emotion expressions, and to compare them with psychologically well caregivers.

Until recently, methods have not been readily available to measure parents' perceptions of affect in children. The newly developed IFEEL Pictures (IFP) now provides such an opportunity. The IFP has been used with several risk populations, including disadvantaged and potentially abusive parents and adolescents (see chapters 7 and 8). Abusive parents have often been described as (1) having difficulty in regulating their own emotions, and (2) having distorted perceptions of their children's expression and regulation of affect. For example, they commonly perceive young children's negative emotions as being performed deliberately to disturb the parent; that is, as spiteful, malicious, and/or intentionally hostile. One source of these misattributions may derive from abusive parents' incorrect and confused conceptions about normal emotional development. Using the IFP, investigators have identified systematic differences in the ways in which potentially abusive and nonabusive parents differ in their interpretations of pictures of emotion expressions in babies (see chapter 8).

In this chapter, analysis of extreme groups is extended to another kind of risk population in which parental interpretations of children's emotions might be influenced, altered, and possibly distorted by the caregiver's affective state. Mothers with clinical depression (unipolar and bipolar) are compared with well mothers. Psychiatrically depressed individuals, by definition, experience more sadness and less pleasure than normal individuals (American Psychiatric Association, 1980). In addition to the dysphoria and anhedonia that characterize depression, other negative affective states are experienced as well. For example, Weissman and Paykel (1974) and Belle (1982) have found that depressed women as compared with nondepressed women show irritability, anxiety, and guilt, and these emotions are expressed in interactions with their children. For many depressed individuals, symptoms of affective disturbance are chronic and enduring. The question of interest here concerns whether the emotions of depressed caregivers influence how they view emotions in infants and young children. Do depressed mothers, for example, project or attribute their negative feelings and diminished positive affect to others? Do they overattribute some negative emotions, more than others, to young children? Or, are they unlikely to see negative emotions in children? The IFEEL picture deck provides a potentially useful tool for addressing such questions, because many of the infants' expressions in the pictures are ambiguous, muted, and/or complex blends of emotions. Hence, they are good stimulus materials for studying possible projections of emotions.

Method

SAMPLE

Ninety-eight mothers and their preschool-age children participated in the study. They came from families involved in a larger study of well and depressed parents.[1] The mothers had been screened with the use of the Schedule for Affective Disorders and Schizophrenia (SADS-L)

[1]The research reported in this chapter is part of a larger investigation: Longitudinal Study of Depressed and Normal Parents and Their Children, Protocol 79-M-123, National Institute of Mental Health, Intramural Research Program, Marian Radke-Yarrow, Principal Investigator. Portions of the research also were supported by the John D. and Catherine T. MacArthur Foundation Network on the Transition from Infancy to Early Childhood.

scored according to Research Diagnostic Criteria (RDC) (Spitzer and Endicott, 1978) and administered by a psychiatric nurse who had been trained to 100 percent reliability. In addition to the SADS-L interview, mothers filled out a mood inventory, the Profile of Mood States (POMS) (McNair, Lorr, and Droppleman, 1971). This provided an index of their current emotional state, sampled and summed across three occasions close in time to the other assessment procedures. Bipolar scales are used on the POMS to score the following dimensions of emotion: (1) agreeable–hostile; (2) elated–depressed; (3) energetic–tired; (4) clearheaded–confused; (5) composed–anxious; and (6) confident–unsure.

The families were from predominantly middle-class backgrounds, using the Hollingshead index. Forty-two mothers were diagnosis free; sixty-one had a diagnosis of major depression (36 with unipolar depression and 25 with bipolar depression). (Unipolar and bipolar groups mainly were combined for statistical analyses since preliminary analyses commonly indicated similar patterns of findings for the two groups.) There were twenty-two girls and twenty boys in the well group, and thirty-three girls and twenty-eight boys in the depressed group. Coders were kept unaware of the mothers' diagnostic status.

PROCEDURE

The IFEEL Pictures task was administered individually to mothers in a free period during their participation in the larger study protocol. They were given an early version of the IFP which included thirty-five pictures (see appendix A-1). In a later phase of test development by the research team that designed the instrument, the thirty-five-picture set was reduced to a twenty-two-picture set (EIFP). In statistical analyses, therefore, findings from our research sample are based on the twenty-two-picture set. Mothers followed the standard procedure of viewing the photographs in the deck, one by one, and describing the main emotion expressed in each picture. Analyses were based on the early lexicon (of emotion words) which was used to sort the words used by mothers into discrete emotion categories. The terms used to represent the discrete emotion categories included: joy, interest–excitement, surprise, fear–terror, anger–rage, distress, sadness, passive–sleepy, shame, guilt, shyness, disgust–contempt, and other. Frequency scores (the number of times each emotion term was used) were used in data analysis.

Results

DEPRESSED AND WELL MOTHERS' RESPONSES TO THE IFEEL PICTURES

Analyses of variance were conducted to examine whether depressed mothers differed from well mothers in their interpretations of infants' emotions. In addition to examining the diagnostic status of the mother, sex and age of the child were included as factors in the analyses. No effects were identified that could be attributable to sex and age of child. The means and standard deviations, comparing depressed (unipolar and bipolar depression groups combined) and well mothers are presented in Table 9.1. The subset of emotions that appeared most germane to the construct of depression were used in analysis. Analyses were restricted also in order to minimize repetitions of analyses using interdependent measures. There were very few significant correlations between (discrete) emotion categories of the IFP, suggesting that interdependence of measures was not a major problem.

TABLE 9.1

NIMH Depressed and Well Mothers' Perceptions of Infant
Emotions
(Lexicon III—22-Picture Set)

Emotions	22-Picture Set			
	Well Mothers		Depressed Mothers	
	X̄	S.D.	X̄	S.D.
Joy*	3.6	2.2	2.8	1.9
Interest	6.3	3.5	5.9	3.8
Sadness	1.8	1.3	1.6	2.2
Anger	.5	1.0	.7	.9
Fear*	.6	.9	1.3	1.4
Distress	1.1	1.1	1.0	1.0

*Depressed and well mothers differed significantly on their interpretation of this emotion.

There were some significant differences in the interpretation of emotions in infants in the two groups of mothers. Depressed mothers were more likely than well mothers to see expressions of fear and anxiety in the photographs ($F[1, 96] = 6.59, p < 0.025$). Moreover, *within* the group of depressed mothers, there was an association between fear and severity of depression (based on GAS scores from the psychiatric interview), $r[55] = 0.28, p < 0.05$. Well mothers were more likely than depressed mothers to perceive joy ($F[1, 96] = 4.36, p < 0.05$). Well and depressed mothers did not differ in their perceptions of sadness, the emotion conceptually most relevant to depression. For this emotion only, however, different *types* of depression appeared to have different effects. Bipolar mothers were somewhat less likely than unipolar and well mothers to report seeing sadness in the photographs of infants ($F[1, 96] = 3.31, p < 0.075$).

Sadness was the one emotion that showed significant heterogeneity of variance, Bartlett's Test ($F = 26.7$, $p < 0.0001$). The unipolar mothers showed much more variability (i.e., reporting either very little or a great deal of sadness) than mothers in the other two groups. This would suggest that depressed mothers appeared more polarized and extreme in their tendencies to view (or not view) infants as sad. One might hypothesize that two different defensive processes may color the depressed mothers' views of sadness in infants, denial and projection. In other words, some mothers try to prevent the emotion from coming into conscious awareness, while others, overwhelmed by sadness, see it everywhere.

SOCIOECONOMIC STATUS AND MOTHERS' RESPONSES TO THE IFEEL PICTURES

The higher the socioeconomic status of the mothers, the more likely they were to perceive interest (r [90] $= 0.37$, $p < 0.001$), and fear (r [90] $= 0.22$, $p < 0.05$) in the infants' photos, and the less likely they were to perceive sadness (r [90] $= -0.32$, $p < 0.005$). The patterns were the same for depressed and well mothers but were substantially greater in magnitude for the depressed mothers.

MOTHERS' SELF-REPORTED MOODS IN RELATION TO IFEEL PICTURES

Mothers' interpretations of infant emotions using the EIFP were examined in relation to their self-reported moods as assessed by the POMS. The number of significant correlations did not exceed that which would have been expected by chance. Current mood of mother, then, did not help to predict how she viewed emotions in infants.

Discussion

Depressed mothers' perceptions of infant emotions on the EIFP reflected, to a degree, the problematic emotions associated with depression. Sadness, anxiety, and lack of pleasure accompany depression. Depressed mothers correspondingly viewed the infants as more fearful and less joyous on the IFP than did well mothers. For sadness (the discrete emotion most closely associated with the dysphoric mood that accompanies depression), depressed mothers were either more likely or very unlikely to see sorrow in infants when compared with well mothers. Depressed mothers may either deny the presence of this emotion in young children or overattribute its occurrence in them. Children of depressed parents have, in fact, been found to be at increased risk for depression and other emotional problems (see review by Beardslee, Bemporad, Keller, and Klerman [1983]). As early as infancy, some offspring of depressed mothers show considerable negative affect (Tronick and Gianino, 1986). Moreover, their problems are generalized, that is to say, they are reflected in interactions not only with their own mothers, but with other adults as well (Field, Healy, Goldstein, Perry, Bendell, Shamberg, Zimmerman, and Kuhn, in press).

The present research design does not make it possible to determine the extent to which depressed mothers' atypical perceptions stem from their own emotional problems, from their experiences with particular emotional patterns of their own children, or from other relevant but as yet unidentified factors. Such issues need to be explored in future research, along with whether and how depressed mothers differ from other high-risk groups. There are some suggestions that depressed mothers appeared different as a group from mothers at risk for abuse and adolescent mothers. Depressed mothers do not show the bimodal high joy/high sad profiles that characterize these other risk groups and they also seem more likely to see fear (see chapters 7 and 8).

The group differences between depressed and well mothers using the EIFP are not strong in magnitude and are accounted for only by a subset of depressed mothers. It cannot be determined with the present study design why only some depressed mothers differ from the norm, or even whether atypical perceptions reflect greater or lesser accuracy. Some depressed mothers may be particularly *accurate* in their perceptions of emotions. Some investigations have documented high accuracy and lack of distortion (relative to controls) in depressed individuals' interpretations of negative or problematic events (Alloy and Abramson, 1979; Layne, 1983). What we do know is that depressed mothers differ in certain respects from well mothers and from other high-risk mothers in how they perceive infants' emotions. Because of these ambiguities, caution should be exercised in viewing the IFEEL Pictures as a screening device for identifying an at risk population of depressed women. The procedure may be more successful in identifying other at risk populations, and it may be interesting to speculate as to why this is the case. Our depressed sample differed from many of the other high-risk groups studied in this volume in that they were of much higher socioeconomic status. This protective factor may make support and help from others more readily available and decrease the overall environmental stress. Hence, these women may be buffered from the responsibilities, difficulties, and aversive aspects of child rearing that can overwhelm caregivers with emotional problems. The mothers, in turn, may be less vulnerable or susceptible to developing highly distorted perceptions of emotions in infants.

References

Alloy, L. B., & Abramson, L. Y. (1979), Judgment of contingency in depressed and non-depressed students: Sadder but wiser? *J. Experiment. Psychol.: Gen.*, 104:441–485.

American Psychiatric Association (1980), *Diagnostic and Statistical Manual of Mental Disorders*, 3rd ed. Washington, DC: American Psychiatric Press.

Beardslee, W. R., Bemporad, J., Keller, M. B., & Klerman, G. L. (1983), Children of parents with major affective disorder: A review. *Amer. J. Psychiatry*, 140:825–844.

Belle, D. (1982), *Lives in Stress: Women and Depression*. Beverly Hills, CA: Sage.

Field, T., Healy, B., Goldstein, S., Perry, S., Bendell, D., Shamberg, S., Zimmerman, E., & Kuhn, G. (in press), Infants of depressed mothers show "depressed" behavior even with non-depressed adults. *Child Develop*.

Layne, C. (1983), Painful truths about depressives' cognitions. *J. Clin. Psychol.*, 39:848–853.

McNair, D. M., Lorr, M., & Droppleman, L. F. (1971), *POMS—Profile of Mood States*. San Diego, CA: Educational and Industrial Testing Service.

Spitzer, R. L., & Endicott, J. (1978), *Schedule for Affective Disorders and Schizophrenia—Lifetime Version (SADS-L)*. New York: Biometrics Research Division, New York State Psychiatric Institute.

Tronick, E. Z., & Gianino, A. F. (1986), The transmission of maternal disturbance to the infant. In: *Maternal Depression and Infant Disturbance*, ed. E. Z. Tronick & T. M. Field. San Francisco: Jossey-Bass.

Weissman, M. M., & Paykel, E. S. (1974), *The Depressed Woman: A Study of Social Relationships*. Chicago: University of Chicago Press.

10

Perceptions of Infant Affect in Mothers of Prematures: The IFEEL Pictures Assessment

Nathan M. Szajnberg and Jarmila Skrinjaric

Birth is a celebration of life: premature birth can shatter that celebration. Although mothers may prepare psychologically for gestational catastrophes (Brazelton and Cramer, 1990), we are still learning about premature infants', mothers', and fathers' coping, adaptation, and adaptational failures. Parents may be facing an infant with medical complications or even the "normative" but different behavioral repertoire and state regulation of a premature baby (Field and Sostek, 1983). Do such complications alter the parents' affective state or the way they view affective signals from this infant?

One way to approach this question is to explore how parents of preterm infants differ in affective interpretation from other mothers. More specifically, how do mothers of premature infants perceive or interpret healthy, full-term infant affects? We used the IFEEL Pictures (IFP)

We would like to acknowledge the Betts Bradley for her dedication to this project and her invaluable assistance. We would also like to acknowledge the assistance of Michele Hudon and Ellen Babcock.

to investigate this question. Previous investigators have studied infant affect, identifying discrete categories including joy, surprise, anger, fear, sadness, disgust, and interest in the first year of life (Darwin, 1872; Ekman and Friesen, 1975; Izard, 1977). Developmental studies have identified additional categories by the second year of life (Emde, chapter 2). More recent work has described non-discrete, more continuous affects termed vitality affects, such as exuberance, phlegmaticism, and tension (Stern, 1985; Szajnberg, Skrinjaric, and Moore, 1989). Both discrete and vitality affects can be viewed dimensionally: intensity, pleasure, inner versus outer orientation. All of the studies mentioned above examined infants directly.

However, affect communication is an interpersonal construct, requiring emotional availability with the responsibility being assumed by the caregiver. The IFP assesses the caregiver's affective repertoire with affect inference being empathically based. Ekman and Friesen (1975) and Izard (1977) demonstrated that, across cultures, adults made similar inferences about emotions using prototypic adult facial patterns of discrete emotions. Our clinical experience, however, has suggested that a mother's recent life experience (having a premature infant) may influence her inferences about certain facial expressions. Our clinical experience is consistent with Emde's principle that emotions are an interpersonal construct: emotions are not necessarily isomorphic with particular facial expressions (Emde, chapter 1). Further, our impressions were consistent with the findings of others who have studied adolescent, abusive, or depressed mothers (see chapters 7, 8, and 9). In light of these issues, we initiated this descriptive study, examining premature mothers' interpretations of infant affect using the IFP. Because of differences in sample size and context between our mothers and the full-term Denver/Topeka reference sample, our work is exploratory.

Methods

SUBJECTS

Mothers were recruited from a perinatal high-risk unit at the University of Connecticut Health Center. Forty mothers of preterms were included if they had an average-for-gestational age premature infant (28–35 weeks) surviving at three to five days postpartum, without congenital anomalies. Adolescent mothers (less than 17 years old) were excluded. No mothers refused participation.

MEASURES

At three to five days postpartum, the following data were collected:

1. Infant's status, including birth weight, gestational age (Dubowitz, Dubowitz, and Goldberg, 1970), a morbidity score (Whitelaw, Minde, and Brown, 1983), and gender.
2. Maternal status, including age, race, parity, marital status, and socioeconomic status (SES) (Hollingshead and Redlich, 1968).
3. Mother's responses to the IFEEL Pictures.
4. Mother's responses to the Profile of Mood States (POMS) (McNair, 1971).

Results

The affect distribution for responses of mothers of preterms fell into two distinct subgroups. Subgrouping was based on a straightforward comparison with the full-term

Denver/Topeka reference sample. Sixteen mothers of preterms (40%) had the same affect distribution as the full-
term reference sample. These were termed the "nonextreme" subgroup. Twenty-four mothers (60%) showed affect attributions significantly different or "extreme" from
the first subgroup (and the reference sample). This second
subgroup skewed the distribution of the entire preterm
group.

Comparing the demographic distribution of the "extreme" (second subgroup) of mothers of preterms (n =
24) to the "nonextreme" subgroup (n = 16), the former
had less education ($\bar{X}ptEXT$ = 12.09 versus $\bar{X}pt$ $nonEXT$
= 13.69, p < 0.05). There were no differences on other
maternal variables (age, race, parity, marital status, and
employment, mother or father), nor infant variables (gender, gestational age, morbidity score). However, all five
mothers with twins were in the extreme subgroup. Mothers in the extreme group also had sicker and smaller infants, although this was a statistical trend that did not
achieve statistical significance.

Scores on POMS, a structured verbal measure of depression, did not correlate significantly with any of the
affects reported for the preterm study as measured by the
IFP.

An exploratory analysis was undertaken comparing
mothers of preterms from Connecticut with mothers in
the Reference Sample who had full-term infants 3 to 12
months of age. Again, because of context and sample size
differences, these results should be taken tentatively. The
mothers of preterms were assessed immediately postpartum; the full-term reference sample mothers were assessed
at varying time points throughout the first year postpartum. The mothers of preterms were less educated ($\bar{X}pt$ =
12.63, $\bar{X}ft$ = 14.19, p < 0.05) and younger ($\bar{X}pt$ = 25.9,
$\bar{X}ft$ = 27.7, p = < 0.07) and the fathers were lower wage-
earners ($\bar{X}pt$ = 1.93, $\bar{X}ft$ = 2.72, p < 0.05).

Statistically significant differences were noted on seven of the twelve categories of emotions (all $p < 0.05$). Mothers of preterms saw more sadness ($\bar{X}pt = 2.97$, vs. $\bar{X}ft = 1.83$), more surprise ($\bar{X}pt = 3.03$, vs. $\bar{X}ft = 1.64$), and more shyness ($\bar{X}pt = 1.39$ vs. $\bar{X}ft = 0.19$). They saw less distress ($\bar{X}pt = 3.36$ vs. $\bar{X}ft = 4.24$) less passivity–sleepiness ($\bar{X}pt = 1.74$ vs. $\bar{X}ft = 2.51$), less anger ($\bar{X}pt = 1.23$ vs. $\bar{X}ft = 1.94$), and less ambiguity "other" ($\bar{X}pt = 1.00$ vs. $\bar{X}ft = 2.15$).

Because of the demographic differences, an analysis of variance was performed to determine whether the main effects were robust. With the covariates of mother's education, father's employment, and mother's age, the main differences for affect did not change.

Discussion

Premature babies and their parents face multiple vicissitudes: the rupture of expecting a normal, healthy, full-term gestation; the anticipated complications of prematurity (different state regulation, prolonged nursery stay); difficult, even life-threatening medical complications; anxiety about the unknown sequelae of intracerebral bleeds; the mother's parenting experience; paternal and family support, as well as other vagaries. The IFP gives us a window into how the mother's (and in future studies, the father's) affective vocabulary is influenced by the experience of prematurity. This is the vocabulary that she will bring, most likely, to her new baby. This is the vocabulary her baby will use to construct its own affective repertoire that will color how it reads the world. Learning more about how mother's inferences about affect are influenced by prematurity will allow us to gain more understanding about the ways in which her premature baby's birth has affected her. This information gives mother (and us) the opportunity to help her adapt her affective repertoire so that it is more responsive to her baby's needs.

It appears that mothers of preterms as compared with mothers of full-terms attribute different emotions to standardized infant photographs. If supported by future research, such a finding would be consistent with other IFP work indicating differences in groups of high-risk mothers (depressed, adolescent, abusive, low SES). Our work suggests the influence of immediate life experience, in this case prematurity, on affect interpretation and empathy. Is the different attribution of affect adaptive or maladaptive? These possibilities are not necessarily mutually exclusive: for instance, a defense may have both adaptive and maladaptive characteristics. Sixty percent of our sample of mothers of prematures differed from the group of mothers of full-terms; 40 percent did not. Is one subgroup of premature mothers better adapted for their infants?

By way of "thought experiment," let us turn to one of our seven affects, shyness. We could hypothesize that a mother who read more shyness not only in the IFP, but also in her premature infant might approach him or her more cautiously. This response may be adaptive since some prematures respond better to a slower-paced approach in handling. On the other hand, another mother might read more shyness, yet feel that her baby should be "jazzed" out of this, resulting in infant aversion, even state disorganization, and possibly mother's feeling unsuccessful or rejected. To answer the question of the adaptive–maladaptive implications of a mother's IFP responses, we would need to know: What are the responses? How does she feel about them? Does she show this repertoire of affect responses to her infant? And, if so, how does *her* baby react?

Based on data from this exploratory study, it is not possible to answer the adaptive–maladaptive question.

But, some findings are suggestive. The mothers with less education and with sicker, smaller infants, tended to be in the "extreme" group. These characteristics put such mothers at higher risk for interactive difficulties. Thus, we might suspect that the extreme subgroup's differential affect attribution may be maladaptive. Further studies are needed to clarify these issues.

The lack of statistical correlation between IFP and POMS scores presents an intriguing methodological issue. Although mothers of prematures had elevated sadness scores on the IFP, this may not be the same phenomenon as "depression" scored on the POMS. The assessment techniques present different stimuli, and we would suggest that the IFP may be more evocative for a new mother than the more experience-distant list of words that comprise the POMS. In fact, the elevated sadness scores of the IFP may represent a different psychological experience than that represented on the POMS.

A central issue remains: What does a mother's interpretation of emotion as indicated by her responses to pictures have to do with infant interactions? When Fraiberg referred to "ghosts in the nursery," she suggested that memories and feelings may interfere with the mother reading her baby's needs (Fraiberg, 1969). Ainsworth, Blehar, Waters, and Wall (1978) discussed the relationship between contingent responsiveness and later attachment. Winnicott (1965) identified the psychopathological effect of a mother's intrusiveness that comes from her own needs rather than those of the infant. Stern, Sander, Kestenberg and others have studied the micromoments of empathic interaction or attunement that are necessary for good development (Sander, 1969; Kestenberg and Sossin, 1979; Stern and Kaplan, 1986; Szajnberg et al., 1989). More recently, Main has demonstrated how a mother's memories of childhood and attitudes toward her own attachment relations affect her interaction with her infant (Main, Kaplan, and Cassidy, 1986). Our exploratory work, if replicated, suggests that a mother's reading of emotion can be influenced by the contemporary experience of having a premature newborn.

Further Studies and Assessment Techniques

What influences responses to the IFP? Several possible factors may be interactive: parent's personality, exposure to the infant, infant characteristics, variations in birth experience, the anxiety of motherhood, and positive–negative feelings about the birth. Additional studies can tease these factors apart.

What is the meaning of the elevation or depression of specific affects as reported in the current one word IFP methodology? In chapter 12 we describe using the IFP as a projective test. Mothers told stories about each photograph after giving a one-word response. This approach helps expand the meaning of the single word responses. For, as Emde has described (chapter 1), affect interweaves with cognition and motivation. The projective technique can elucidate motivation.

Are these IFP findings baby specific? A discriminant validity study could help identify whether preterm mothers would respond differently to a set of nonbaby pictures.

Are these IFP findings based on the experience of giving birth to a preterm infant? Presenting the IFP to volunteer cuddlers versus preterm mothers per se would help us distinguish whether such brief exposure to a preterm influences affect attribution.

Finally, are "extreme" group reports on the IFP associated with disturbed mother–infant interaction? The IFP could be administered at birth with follow-up observations of interaction in order to address this issue.

In summary, our studies are suggestive. They need to be confirmed using a larger sample and compared with a geographically comparable group of mothers of full-terms interviewed immediately postpartum. If confirmed, our findings have significant implications for future studies that can establish the significance of differential affect attributions in preterm mothers and the impact upon their interaction with their infants.

References

Ainsworth, M. D. S., Blehar, M. C., Waters, E., & Wall, S. (1978), *Patterns of Attachment: A Psychological Study of the Strange Situation*. Hillsdale, NJ: Lawrence Erlbaum.

Brazelton, T. B., & Cramer, B. (1990), *The Earliest Relationship*. Reading, MA: Addison-Wesley Publishing.

Darwin, C. (1872), *The Expression of Emotions in Man and Animals*. Chicago: University of Chicago Press, 1965.

Dubowitz, L., Dubowitz, V., & Goldberg, C. (1970), Clinical assessment of gestational age in the newborn infant. *J. Pediatr.*, 77/1:1–10.

Ekman, P., & Friesen, W. (1975), *Unmasking the Face*. Englewood Cliffs, NJ: Prentice-Hall.

Field, T., & Sostek, A., eds. (1983), *Infants Born at Risk: Physiological, Perceptual, and Cognitive Processes*. New York: Grune & Stratton.

Fraiberg, S. (1969), Libidinal object constancy and mental representation. *The Psychoanalytic Study of the Child*, 24:9–47. New York: International Universities Press.

Hollingshead, A. B., & Redlich, F. (1968), Two factor index of social position. In: *A Decade Later: A Follow-up of Social Class and Mental Illness*, ed. J. K. Myers & L. L. Bean. New York: John Wiley & Sons.

Izard, C. (1977), *Human Emotions*. New York: Plenum.

Kestenberg, J., & Sossin, M. (1979), *Movement Notation*. New York: Dance Notation Bureau.

Main, M., Kaplan, N., & Cassidy, J. (1986), Security in infancy, childhood and adulthood: A move to the level of representation. In: *Monographs of the Society for Research in Child Development*, ed. I. Bretherton & E. Waters. 50(1-2, Serial No. 209), 66–104.

McNair, D. (1971), *Profile of Mood States-B*. San Diego, CA: Educational and Industrial Testing Service.

Sander, L. (1969), Regulation and organization in the early infant caretaker system. In: *Brain and Early Behavior*, ed. R. Robertson. London: Academic Press.

Stern, D. (1985), *The Interpersonal World of the Infant*. New York: Basic Books.

——— Kaplan, T. (1986), Perceptions of infant emotions: Parents of abused children and a modification of the technique for use with school-aged children. Paper presented at International Conference on Infant Studies, Los Angeles, CA.

Szajnberg, N. M., Skrinjaric, J., & Moore, A. (1989), Affect attunement, attachment, temperament and zygosity: A twin study. *J. Amer. Acad. Child & Adol. Psychiatry*, 28/2:249–253.

Whitelaw, A., Minde, K., & Brown, J. (1983), Effect of neonatal complications in the premature infant and early parent-infant interaction. *Develop. Med. & Child Neurol.*, 25:763–777.

Winnicott, D. W., ed. (1965), Psychoses and child care. In: *Through Paediatrics to Psycho-Analysis*. New York: Basic Books, pp. 219–228.

Part IV:

Related Techniques and Other Uses

11

IFEEL Stories: Pictures Used as Projective Story Stimuli

Joy D. Osofsky, Martin Drell, Della Hann

The IFEEL story technique makes use of a subset of IFEEL Pictures. It is modeled after the approach used with other projective techniques that require the respondent to tell a story about what is happening in a series of pictures. The purpose of using the pictures to tell stories is to assess some of the internalized thoughts and themes of mothers concerning babies in general and, more specifically, their understanding and feelings about infant emotions. The technique is designed to reflect the mother's experience of parenting and of being parented. As was discussed by Emde in chapter 2, we need assessment tools to help us understand difficulties and potential problems in the care-giver–infant regulatory system. We need to understand contributions from both the infant's and parent's side of the relationship. The IFEEL measure, especially when used with mothers and infants at risk, may contribute to a battery that would provide information about the negative emotions, pain, or even defensive reactions on the parent's side that may interfere with emotional availability. As such,

197

it may be helpful in learning more about the need for intervention.

In developing the IFEEL story technique, we found that a sequencing of pictures was especially evocative of thematic responses. We aimed at narrative responses instead of single word responses as in the IFEEL Pictures technique, and found, with our sample of young high-risk mothers, that this approach proved fruitful in portraying how these women viewed their emotional world and that of their infants. While mothers did not respond in general to the IFEEL pictures in terms of the infants having feelings, they often focused more on negative than positive emotions (e.g., with themes of anger and distress). In addition, their story productions sometimes reflected a sparse, limited world with few themes and little hope of success. These responses were consistent with our observations of mother–infant interaction and they seemed to indicate the way such mothers experience their own lives with their children (Hann, Osofsky, and Carter, 1989). We will now describe the method and our findings in more detail.

Method

Stimulus sets of pictures were assembled from the IFEEL Pictures Booklet. Each set contained pictures of the same baby displaying a variety of emotions as a stimulus for story-telling by mothers. Sequences within a set included a range of expressions with a shift from either a positive or negative emotion to its opposite, and with a middle photo being either an affect blend or one displaying an ambiguous emotion. To gather preliminary data for the IFEEL story technique, four separate sets of three sequenced photos were included. Picture trials were presented to the individual subjects in a standard fashion with the instructions: "Here are some pictures of babies. Please tell us a story about these pictures." If the mothers asked questions about the pictures, we emphasized that there were no right or wrong answers and encouraged them to tell a story.

In order to develop a coding scheme for the story responses, the responses were recorded verbatim and presented blind to one of the authors (MJD) for preliminary analysis.

SUBJECTS

The subjects were part of an ongoing longitudinal study of adolescent mothers and their infants identified during the prenatal period and followed until the infants were 4½ years of age. The four sets of IFEEL stories technique were administered to forty adolescent mothers when their infants were 36 months of age. This sample was chosen for pilot work because these young mothers and their infants were at risk for having developmental and adaptive problems and difficulties in the caregiver–infant relationship. In addition, as part of the longitudinal study, there was a large amount of additional data available for comparative purposes. The adolescent mother sample has been described in detail in chapter 7. Briefly, the mothers were under 18 years, unmarried, and of lower socioeconomic status. Their families were marked by instability, with living situations and social support varying throughout the course of the study.

ILLUSTRATIONS OF RESPONSES BY THE SAMPLE

Before discussing the ways that we have proceeded to develop an understanding of the IFEEL story technique, we will present six sets of illustrative responses to one of these picture sequences. The following exemplifies a sequence of three pictures showing the same baby with first a positive emotion, then a blend, and finally a negative emotion.

1. K.B. (16 years old)—She started to do something she shouldn't do. Somebody tries to talk to her and tell her she shouldn't do it. She did it anyway and got a spanking.
2. J.T. (15 years old)—He's playing. His Mom told him he had to take a nap and he was crying.
3. M.B. (17 years old)—I know this is my Mommy. She's wanting me to go to a stranger. I'm in the stranger's arms and I don't like it.
4. V.S. (15 years old)—Reaches to Mom.
   Gets picked up and bounced.
   When gets to the top gets scared.
5. T.S. (16 years old)—Very sad—"I just want to cry."
6. A.W. (16 years old)—Getting ready to go somewhere with Mom and Dad. Wondering what someone is trying to do. They made her mad. She's totally upset. Tears in her eyes.

In these stories, a variety of emotions are used by the young women to describe the babies' feelings, including sad, mad, scared, guilty, and, less often, happy and playing. Despite the variety of their responses, negative themes tend to predominate with babies more often described as distressed, mad, scared, or making trouble. As mentioned above, these responses to the pictures occur commonly in the themes offered by adolescent mothers as well as in the behaviors observed when they interact with their infants during play or a snack time.

For the preliminary organization of the material, we focused on a number of issues that came up repeatedly. Based on those issues, we derived a set of orienting questions that were modified as subsequent sequences were analyzed. The questions listed below present the structure that we developed to understand the responses to the

IFEEL stories. The stories were then coded according to these areas:

1. What is the gender of the infant described in the story?
2. Are there any identifying words or statements concerning the age of the infant in the story?
3. What is the infant in the story doing?
4. In relation to affect, is there evidence of an internal or external locus of control?
5. Are there other persons in the story? If so, are they identified? What, if anything, are they doing, especially related to affects? Are the people described as causing something to happen or as soothing?
6. Are there inanimate objects in the story? If so, are they identified? What, if anything, are these objects described as doing that is especially related to affects? Are the inanimate objects described as causing something to happen or soothing?
7. What are the themes in the stories? Are there recurring themes linked by mothers to affect states in the pictured infants?
8. What positive and negative affects are identified?
9. Are each of the pictures in the sequence represented in the story?

Preliminary Findings

Several strong impressions have emerged from our preliminary analyses. First, adolescent mothers responded to the pictures of the infants in terms of their having feelings. However, the stories that the young mothers told tended to be rather sparse. When they described affects, the young mothers tended to focus more on negative ones such as anger and distress. Second, the young mothers tended not to specify the people in their stories. Except for "mothers," the world was described in terms of generic adults labeled as "someone," "somebodies," and "strangers." Fathers were seldom mentioned. Third, there seemed to be a "finite" number of narrative themes used by this group, the most prominent being the frustration of infants at the hands of adults who do not help them in overcoming obstacles or in mastering problems. Were these repetitive narrative themes of frustration a reflection of a young mother's experience of the world in general or of life with baby in particular? Additional sources of information from interviews and from observations lend validity to these speculations. Mothers reported instability in their lives and a lack of supportive people on whom they could rely. In addition we frequently observed negative and sometimes frustrating interactions between mothers and their infants.

Although we do not have a control or comparison group for this preliminary phase of our work, samples of three responses from pilot work with a low-risk sample are listed below. The responses were elicited from the same sequence of pictures that was used with the adolescent mothers. We recognize that there are educational, age, and language differences between the groups being compared, but we believe it informative to include responses generated by a variety of individuals. In our systematic comparisons, we will match risk group variables as much as possible in order to have confidence that we are measuring differences in affective responses rather than potential socioeconomic differences.

1. D.B. (34 year old, female, Ph.D., single)—He is doing something that he is not supposed to be doing, maybe with the stereo. Then he gets hurt somehow or breaks something and starts crying

and his mother comes and picks him up and tells him it is all right to make him feel better. But he looks like he doesn't believe her, and that he is still going to be in trouble.

2. A.B. (37 year old, college educated, mother of 3)
   a. Arms out—reaching out for somebody—tear in eye.
   b. Eyes big—being held by Mom—I believe you but not really surprised—eyebrows raised.
   c. Big tears, big cry—Mom has left.

3. K.O. (14 years old, female, single)—Getting in trouble—looks at Mom and Dad. They told him what he did, starts crying because he knows he is in trouble.

The responses of the low-risk sample of ten persons were coded according to the questions listed above. Initial findings indicate that this group provided a wider range of responses than occurred with the young mothers. The stories tended to be more complex, and more subtle variations in affect were apparent. Affects were more often specifically labeled. The infants described in these stories tended to have more of an internal locus of control and more frequently were described as responsible for contributing to their own negative affect states. In addition, negative affects were usually not seen as caused by frustrating adults. Adults were more frequently specifically identified and there were more fathers in the stories. Adults were more often depicted as helpers.

New sets of responses with different populations are currently being collected. These will be used to refine the IFEEL story technique coding system that, to date, has focused on the questions listed earlier. After additional comparative data are collected the coding system will then be standardized by rating additional groups.

Implications

The IFEEL story technique appears promising in our quest for furthering knowledge about individual differences in parents' ideas and expectations about the affective themes of infants. It will be important to determine whether these theories and expectations vary across populations. If this is the case, subsequent findings may prove to have clinical usefulness. The IFEEL story technique might become a useful adjunctive technique if used with other measures of infant development and developmental psychopathology to highlight potential difficulties in the mother–infant relationship. As further assessments are done with different populations, questions about the influence of development, maturation, sex, mental status, life experiences, and culture on responses to this measure can be determined. The technique may have promise in clarifying potential cross-generational problems between the mother–caregiver and her infant; for example, if the mother–caregiver responds in a repetitive way or with statements that seem unrelated to the emotion that the infant in the picture is displaying, it may be an indication of conflict or a defensive reaction. As we test the technique further, it would be interesting to obtain the responses of grandparents to the pictures and compare them with those of their daughters and sons. We may be able to tap narrative themes and expectations.

In conclusion, based on our early work with this method, the IFEEL story technique appears promising in eliciting both productive narrative themes and striking individual differences. Others may want to use the technique for exploratory research. Our group plans future studies with high-risk populations, including teenage mothers, mothers of infants at high risk for developmental psychopathology, and homeless mothers and children under current study. We believe that this technique may be particularly promising in conjunction with other measures to learn more about individual difference aspects of the mother–infant relationship.

Reference

Hann, D. M., Osofsky, J. D., & Carter, S. L. (1989), A comparison of affects between infants of adolescent and older mothers. Poster presented at Biennial Meeting of the Society for Research in Child Development, Kansas City.

12

The IFEEL Pictures as a Projective Instrument: Pre- and Full-Term Mothers

Nathan M. Szajnberg

What does it mean when mothers of premature infants categorize IFEEL Pictures differently than mothers of full-terms? Is there more personal meaning to mothers' responses than a single affect word response captures? To answer these questions, we designed a second study, using the IFEEL Pictures like a projective stimulus such as Murray's (1938) Thematic Apperception Test (TAT). Our hypothesis was that mothers of preterms and full-terms would differ on a dimensional basis (see chapter 1).

The TAT is a standardized set of black-and-white silhouettes to which the viewer is asked to respond by telling a story about each card. Because of our observations that mothers of premature babies responded evocatively to the IFP, we thought that the IFP might be functioning like a projective test.

Method

There were two steps to this study of responses of mothers of pre- and full-term infants. First, twenty mothers of premature babies were recruited using the same inclusion–exclusion criteria as in our first study (see chapter 10). Mothers were asked to give a single word response to the IFEEL Pictures (IFP). While the experimenter scored these in the twelve affect categories of the Lexicon, mothers were asked to complete the Profile of Mood States (POMS) (McNair, Lorr, and Droppelman, 1971).

After the mother completed the POMS, the pictures that fell into extreme affect categories (> 2 standard deviations from the Reference Sample) were identified. There was an average of 8.75 extreme affect responses per mother making a total of 175 extreme responses for twenty mothers. The mothers were then asked to review each ("extreme") picture which had been pulled from her responses. She was reminded of her affect word and was asked to tell a story about how the child came to feel this way. When she appeared to be finished, she was asked if there was anything else she wanted to say. After the mother said she was done, the same procedure was followed with the next picture.

Twenty mothers of full-term infants were recruited. They responded to the entire IFP. After they completed the POMS, mothers of full-terms were prompted with their affect word to tell a story in response to the preterm mothers' "extreme" set of photographs. The seven baby pictures selected were those which accounted for most of the premature mothers' extreme responses (>2 standard deviations from the norms). The seven pictures were numbers 105, 107, 109, 116, 120, 123, and 125. The stories told by the two sets of mothers were read and categorized into two sets of rationally derived categories: tension filled and nontension filled (positive, negative, and neutral). Each story would be classified into one of four subcategories: tension filled, positive, negative, or neutral.

The categories were defined as follows. Tension-filled stories leave the listener and the narrator hanging. Like the opening lines of a good short story, or opening shot in a movie, the listener's attention is raised, but the story is not resolved. Positive, negative, or neutral stories resolve. Positive stories are pleasurable or hopeful. Negative stories have an uncomfortable tone—sad, angry, disgusting. Neutral stories are simply that, neutral.

These categories were experimentally confirmed by three judges who were not aware of the purpose of the study. Judges practiced with hypothetical modal stories for each category, then categorized mothers' actual stories (interrater reliability = 83%).

Results

Mothers responded with stories to the pictures as they would have with a TAT: some hesitated, then launched into a short tale with much feeling; others did not hesitate. For many, there appeared to be a cathartic quality to the story-telling.

The mothers of preterm infants told 175 stories; four stories were not audible on the audiotape, therefore, 171 were rated.

Three pictures (125, 105, and 107) accounted for the majority of preterm mothers' extreme responses.

The mothers of full-terms were given seven pictures and therefore each told seven stories (there were no refusals). However, there was audiotape malfunction for two mothers, leaving eighteen mothers for story rating (126 stories).

There was a statistically significant difference in story categorization between mothers of full-terms and mothers of preterms $(X^2 = 44.7, p < 0.001)$.

Mothers of full-terms told more negative and neutral and far fewer tension-filled stories than mothers of preterms. Interestingly, although both groups told few positive stories in response to these pictures, mothers of preterms told three times more positive stories than mothers

TABLE 12.1
Story Categorization: Full-Term Versus Preterm Mothers

	Story Category	Tension Filled	Negative	Neutral	Positive	Total
Full-Term	# Stories	18	63	40	5	n = 126
(n = 18)	% Stories	14.4	44.6	32.0	4.0	= 100%
Pre-Term	# Stories	75	39	36	21	n = 171
(n = 20)	% Stories	44.0	23.0	21.0	12.0	= 100%

of full-terms (preterm = 12.0% positive; full-term = 4.0%).

THE PROFILE OF MOOD STATES (POMS)

For mothers of preterms, the relationship between sad affect categorization on the IFP and the POMS score was not statistically significant. The lack of relationship may be due to the fact that these two measures evoke different responses.

Comparing mothers of full-terms with mothers of preterms on the POMS, there was a trend toward full-terms having higher scores than preterms (preterm POMS $x = 31.7$; full-term POMS $x = 47.5$; $p < 0.10$).

STORY TYPES

The actual stories illustrate the flavor of mothers' responses as well as the distinctiveness of the categories. The reader may wish to look at the IFP Booklet as he or she reads the stories, or refer to pictures 106, 108, and 116 in chapter 4. Full-term mothers told stories about the seven pictures noted above (105, 107, 109, 116, 120, 123, 125).

However, the reader may notice that other pictures are listed. These were from some preterm mothers, as we did not tell them which pictures they should tell stories about. As noted in the methods section, for preterm mothers we elicited stories with those pictures to which each mother provided an "extreme" response.

Tension-filled Stories. Mother W. looked at picture 105 saying that the baby looked "enthralled." She gave this story.

"His eyes are opened so wide. He's got such a look, it is almost like the Poltergeist picture. 'They're here' and something has really got his attention. He is just overwhelmed with it."

When we asked what happened next, she said she didn't know.

(105: This child has its fist covering its mouth with a quiet pensive look, eyes focused on the observer. The face is dimly, indirectly lit.)

Mrs. F. looking at picture 108 said that the baby was "surprised." She gave this story.

"Well, it's like being at the Catskill Game Farm (zoo). Well, like when I brought my 3-year-old out to the Catskill Game Farm he looked like that when the goat came up to sniff him." [Her son said] "Will he bite me or kiss me?" (What happened?) "That's it."

(108: This child is open-eyed, with slight gaze aversion and mouth slightly agape. There is something between a pensive and a surprised quality. The face is well lit.)

Mrs. K. said of picture 114, "Very surprised, shocked." Her story was: "I don't know what he could be shocked about though. I don't know. I can't explain this one. I don't know." (Can you tell us a story?) "He could be like an animal or some babies look like that when they see a dog or something, you know, and they are just trying to figure out what it is and they fall in love with him so it could be an animal, something new, that they have never seen before."

(114: This appears to be the same child as in 108. It is wide-eyed, with slight left esotropia, but eyes focused on the observer, mouth slightly agape. There is a quiet, attentive appearance. The face is well lit, although from the side.)

Negative Stories. Mrs. L. looked at picture 116 and said "Sad." Her story was: "Looks like a girl. She looks very sad. She looks like maybe something is going on in the family. Like an argument around her. She looks unhappy about it."

(116: This child has a dreamy quality, eyes focused beyond and to the right, lips closed and possibly slightly pursed. There is a pensive, perhaps sad quality.)

Mrs. M., looking at picture 126, said "Lonely." "He looks very unsure of himself, like he wants to be picked up and he's not going to be. He looks very alone and scared."

(126: An unusual photographic angle. Child appears to be on its back, looking upward, almost toward the crown of its head. One hand is fisted. Eyes open, inner brow is arched upwards, mouth agape.)

Mrs. H., looking at picture 117, said "Sad." Her story was "She is crying because above is something she wanted and couldn't have it because it is something she shouldn't play with."

(117: This child is clearly distressed, crying, eyes screwed shut, mouth open, brows furrowed.)

Neutral Stories. Mrs. K., looking at picture 105, said "Sleepy." Her story was: "He is sucking his finger, it looks like he laid down to fall asleep."

(See above for 105 description.)

Mrs. W., looking at picture 121, said "Curious. Like he's somewhere new and he's just gotten something new that caught his attention. He is really interested in it. It looks like he's almost going to go over and investigate himself."

(121: A quiet, pensive quality to this child who is looking to the right and beyond, eyes open, lips closed. Perhaps a slight down-turn at the mouth angles. Highly lit from the right.)

Positive Stories. Mrs. P. said of picture 104, "Happy. Maybe someone is playing with her. Maybe someone is giving her a bottle and she is happy."

(104: A quiet, happy tone with child looking to the left, as if focusing on someone [or something]. Smiling, lips slightly open.)

Mrs. B., looking at picture 105, said "Content. It looks like he is probably watching something that he would probably want to do. He's just happy watching it. [What kind of things?] I don't know. Maybe somebody's bouncing a ball or something and he's just watching it all."

(See above for 105 description.)

Mrs. W., looking at picture 126, said "Excited. It's a little boy. It looks like they have something hanging over his head, maybe a hot air balloon or a mobile and he is just *enthralled* with all the colors and excitement that is going on above him."

(See above for 126 description.)

Mrs. J., looking at 106, said "Happy. She looks like she's with somebody she knows real well too and she has all her needs taken care of. She doesn't have anything to worry about either."

(106: An impish quality to its open-mouth grin. This child focuses on the observer.)

Discussion

This preliminary study provides information about the IFP as a story-telling stimulus. First, we found that the pictures were powerful evocative stimuli, eliciting both mother's affect perceptions, and stories about each picture. Second, the stories differentiated mothers of full-terms from preterms, with mothers of full-terms seeing and telling more negative and neutral stories and mothers of preterms seeing and telling mostly tension-filled stories. Although both groups told few positive stories, mothers of preterms gave three times as many such tales. Finally, on the Profile of Mood States (POMS), there was a statistical trend toward sadder moods for preterm mothers, although there was no correlation between the preterms' POMS and sad affect scores on the IFP.

The results might suggest that because mothers of preterms told tension-filled stories about the IFEEL Pictures, mothers of preterms may be expressing more tension about the birth of their infant. This finding follows our clinical impressions. Mothers of preterms are faced with the tense atmosphere of a baby born too soon, possibly ill or at-risk; these are mothers uncertain about the future. The threefold predominance (compared to mothers of full-terms) of positive stories (12% versus 4%) may represent the hopefulness of the mothers of preterms, a hypomanic defense against depression, or denial (i.e., a more primitive defense than hypomania).

Mothers of full-terms told mostly negative (44.6%) or neutral (32%) stories. This finding is tempered by the study's design: We preselected the seven target pictures as those which mothers of preterms had categorized as extreme. We used this method in order to learn how mothers of full-terms reacted to the same pictures. A different design, such as asking stories on all thirty pictures, might give different results, but would be asking a different question.

Three pictures (125, 105, and 107) accounted for many of our preterm mothers' extreme responses. The reader may note that these pictures share a tentative, pensive, quiet, and perhaps slightly sad tone. These pictures show complex emotions and emotion blends, not the clearcut (Darwinian) basic affects (Darwin, 1872). It appears to us that these complex ambiguous photographs are more likely to elicit a subjective response from a mother. These responses may also tell us more about what the mother is bringing to the stimulus photograph and, possibly, to her birth experience and infant.

There is personal meaning behind the mother's projected affect responses. She can make use of the baby pictures to articulate a frame of mind that is influenced by the nature of her recent motherhood (prematurely or not). The evocative, cathartic nature of mother's responses contrast with the more recalcitrant, even opaque responses from mothers when one uses a more typical clinical (that is, verbally based) interview. The photographs seemed to facilitate mothers' articulation of feelings.

The result of the POMS comparing mothers of fullterms and preterms is in the hypothesized direction: Preterm mothers are more likely to feel saddened by this predicament. However, when looking within the group of mothers of preterms, there was no correlation between POMS and sad responses to the IFP. We conjecture that the photographic stimulus of the IFP may evoke different (and we believe more powerful and sincere) feelings than the word stimuli of the POMS.

The findings of this study suggest that the IFP may be a useful clinical and clinical-research instrument to initiate an assessment of how mothers, particularly mothers of preterms, are feeling about the birth experience. Future research directions might be to study overall trends across story categories (sense of mastery; sense of hopefulness), as well as the story patterns of mothers at risk.

However, the author would like to say a few words about the process of interviewing preterm and full-term mothers with the IFP, using a story-telling technique. The psychoanalytic literature is coming alive to the therapeutic nature of telling a meaningful narrative (Cohler, 1992). In addition, Fraiberg (1980) has taught us that interviewing a mother when her infant is present may evoke much more personal material than interviewing the mother alone. The story-telling approach appears to touch upon both of these areas of work, bringing together a personal narrative around the central axis of mother's birthing. We hope that others will explore how gratifying and enlightening it is to offer a mother such an opportunity to explore her reactions to the vicissitudes of giving birth.

References

Cohler, B. (1992), Psychoanalysis and the classroom: Intent and meaning in learning and teaching. In: *Educating the Emotions: Bruno Bettelheim and Psychoanalysis*, ed. N. Szajnberg. New York: Plenum.

Darwin, C. (1872), *The Expression of Emotion in Man and Animals*. Chicago: University of Chicago Press, 1965.

Fraiberg, S. (1980), *Clinical Studies in Infant Mental Health: The First Year of Life*. New York: Basic Books.

McNair, D. M., Lorr, M., & Droppleman, L. F. (1971), *Profile of Mood States*. San Diego, CA: Educational & Industrial Testing.

Murray, H. A. (1938), *Exploration in Personality*. Oxford, U.K.: Oxford University Press.

13

Pictures of Infants' Emotions: A Task for Assessing Mothers' and Young Children's Verbal Communications about Affect

Carolyn Zahn-Waxler, Doreen Ridgeway, Susanne Denham, Barbara Usher, Pamela M. Cole

Almost as soon as children begin to use language they talk about feelings, first their own and shortly thereafter, the emotions of others. During the preschool years these communications increase with age in both frequency and complexity. During the second and third years of life, children also begin (1) to discuss past and future emotions and (2) to talk appropriately about antecedents, causes, and consequences of emotional states (see review by Bretherton, Fritz, Zahn-Waxler, and Ridgeway [1986]). These communications serve adaptive purposes, since language is a primary means by which humans can inform others about their inner lives. Young children can use language to express awareness of others' physical and emotional

We wish to express our appreciation to the following individuals for their contributions to this project: Marian Radke-Yarrow, for valuable advice and for making the subject population available; Elizabeth Wagner, Wendy Habelow, and Kathleen Free, for coding and analysis of data, Carroll Izard for making the infant photographs available; and Jean Mayo for preparation of the manuscript.

needs, as well as their own prosocial intentions (Zahn-Wax-ler, Radke-Yarrow, and King, 1979). Some research indi-cates a relation between early abilities to talk about feelings and expressions of social competence (e.g., Denham, 1986). It is advantageous for humans to be able to commu-nicate from very early on about matters that govern their behavior, and language ability is critical in human interac-tions. Important components of these communications in-clude communication of intentions, goals, and feeling states (Johnson-Laird, 1983).

Little is known about why children differ from an early age in the frequency and quality of their verbal com-munications about emotions. While differences in temper-ament and cognitive capabilities may play a role, parental communication patterns also may influence when and how children talk about affective states and experiences. A few studies have begun to examine, in healthy, low-risk popu-lations, how mothers talk to their children about feelings (Grief, Alverez, and Tonis, 1984). Mothers are found to differ in the frequency and quality of emotion language used with their children. There are indications, as well, of connections between maternal and child communication patterns in this domain. For example, in a naturalistic study, Dunn, Bretherton, and Munn (1987) report associa-tions between mothers' and children's use of feeling state utterances, for children in the second year of life. In other words, the more mothers talk about emotions, the more their children do so as well.

This chapter focuses on caregivers' communications about infants' emotions during interactions with their own young children, using a structured procedure to elicit emotion language. Photographs of infants expressing emotions are viewed and discussed by mothers with their children. The procedure also provides an opportunity to examine the emotion language of young children, as well as correspondences between mother and child communication patterns. One purpose of the research is to determine whether findings from existing research are replicated when the new procedure is used. The second goal is to extend analysis of individual differences to a population in which there is known emotional disturbance; more specifically, where the caregiver has a diagnosed affective disorder. Are the adaptive functions of emotion language altered or compromised early in development when verbal communications about feelings are mainly with a caregiver whose own emotions are deregulated?

The emotions of individuals with depression may differ in several ways from those of persons who do not have an affective disorder (e.g., less pleasure and interest; more sadness, guilt, anxiety, and irritability). The negative emotions of depressed individuals are often expressed verbally in the form of complaints, dissatisfaction, and a pessimistic focus on the dismal aspects of life. In interpersonal situations with adults, depressed individuals communicate self-devaluation, sadness, and helplessness (Hokanson, Sacco, Blumberg, and Landrum, 1980); and their conversations are more frequently self-focused and negatively toned (Jacobson and Anderson, 1982). Their children also may be exposed to high levels of negative emotion language and little discussion of positive emotions. Depressed and well mothers' emotion language is examined here, both in relation to the age and gender of their children. Two- and 3-year-old children are studied because this is the period in development when emotion language emerges, increases in frequency, and begins to take different forms. Hence, this may mark a time of particular vulnerability and risk for the child of an emotionally distressed caregiver, if that child is learning how to talk about feelings from that parent. Sex differences are also important as depression is two to three times more common in females than males and there is evidence for intergenerational transmission (see review by Nolen-Hoeksema [1987]). One way of exploring possible psychosocial patterns of transmission is to examine differences between mother–son and mother–daughter communication styles. Variations in frequency, accuracy, and types of verbal communications about emotions are considered.

Method

SAMPLE

One hundred and three mothers and their children participated in the study. They came from families involved in a larger study of well and depressed parents.[1] The mothers had been screened within two to three months of the laboratory visit with the use of the Schedule for Affective Disorders and Schizophrenia (SADS-L) scored according to Research Diagnostic Criteria (RDC) (Spitzer and Endicott, 1978), and administered by a psychiatric nurse who had been trained to 100 percent reliability. In addition to the SADS-L interview, the majority of mothers filled out the POMS mood inventory (Profile of Mood States; McNair, Lorr, and Droppleman, 1971). This provided an index of mothers' current emotional states, sampled and summed across three occasions that coincided with the laboratory assessments. Mothers diagnosed with depression also reported more feelings of depression on the POMS than did well mothers ($t[87] = 3.71$, $p < 0.001$).

The families were from predominantly middle-class backgrounds, using the Hollingshead index. The children

[1]The research reported in this chapter is part of a larger investigation: Longitudinal Study of Depressed and Normal Parents and Their Children, Protocol 79-M-123, National Institute of Mental Health, Intramural Research Program. Marian Radke-Yarrow, Principal Investigator. Portions of the research were supported by the John D. and Catherine T. MacArthur Foundation Network on the Transition from Infancy to Early Childhood.

ranged in age from 2 to 4 years. A cross-sectional research design was used to examine (1) age differences in children's emotion language and (2) mothers' emotion language with younger and older children. There were seventy-one 2-year-old children and thirty-two 3-year-old children studied. Forty-two mothers were classified as well; sixty-one had a diagnosis of major depression (36 with unipolar depression and 25 with bipolar depression). Unipolar and bipolar groups were combined for analyses since preliminary analyses indicated similar patterns of findings for the two groups. There were twenty-two girls and twenty boys in the well group, and thirty-three girls and twenty-eight boys in the depressed group. Coders were uninformed about the mothers' diagnostic status.

Mothers' and children's emotion language was assessed using the Parent–Child Affect Communication Task (PACT), during one of the sessions of the larger study. For this task, the mother and child were seated in a comfortable chair or sofa and given a set of eight photographs of infant emotions. The mother was asked to go through the pictures one by one with her child, after the experimenter left the room. The instructions were deliberately general in order to maximize individual differences in the mothers' communications about emotions. The observation period was ten minutes in length, though some mothers and children terminated it early. The entire sequence was videotaped. In addition, verbal transcripts of mother and child language were made for coding purposes.

Two different sets of photographs have been developed for this task. One set (Ridgeway, 1987) includes eight emotional expressions of infants selected from a set of thirty from the IFEEL Pictures. These pictures included 106 (joy), 104 (joy), 101 (joy–interest), 122 (sleepy), 112 (interest–anger), 103 (interest–distress), 119 (distress–

anger), and 127 (surprise–fear). Another set of photographs, the set used here, includes photographs of facial
emotion expressions obtained from Izard. They were
based on his coding of discrete expressions of surprise,
joy, interest, sadness, anger, disgust, contempt, and fear
in infants (Izard, Huebner, Risser, McGinnes, and Dougherty, 1980). A scoring system was developed by Ridgeway
and Zahn-Waxler (1986) to assess emotion language during parent–child interaction. The codes were used to categorize separately both mothers' and children's responses.
Raters read and coded transcripts of the verbal dialogues.
The transcripts identified only whether the speaker was
mother or child and which picture was discussed. Repetitions of the other's emotion words were categorized separately and not used in statistical analyses. (Thus, analyses
were always based on initiations of emotion language.)

1. *Emotion words* (i.e., words that refer to discrete emotions as well as behavioral expressions of emotion):
   a. Positive terms (e.g., happy, love)
   b. Negative terms (e.g., sad, mad, cries)
   c. Evaluative terms (e.g., good, bad)
(internal state language was also coded [e.g., hungry,
thirsty] but it occurred rarely.)
2. *Referent* (i.e., whether the speaker is referring to
   feelings of self or other [a potential measure of
   egocentrism or decentration])
3. *Causes of emotion.* Four types of causal statements
   were coded:
   a. Statements of cause and consequence that refer
      to others only (e.g., "Baby's angry because his
      mama's not there"; "She's crying because she
      hurt herself.")
   b. Cause and consequence statements that refer to
      self only (e.g., "I cried when I fell down.")

    c. Other causes emotion in self (e.g., "When you kiss me, I feel better.")

    d. Self causes emotion in other (e.g., "I hit Joey and you got mad.")

The great majority of causal utterances were those that referred to others only (category a), probably because the procedures were focused on eliciting discussion of others' (i.e., the infants') emotions. The remaining categories of causal utterances were coded too infrequently for statistical analysis.

4. *Functions of utterances containing emotion words*

    a. *Commenting.* Noting someone's feeling without further explanation or clarification (e.g., "Look this baby is crying"; "There was a real sad one"; "A cheerful baby")

    b. *Explaining/clarifying.* Explaining the causes and consequences of feeling states, asking questions about feelings, or rectifying misunderstandings (e.g., "She's happy because her mom came back"; "He's sad because he has no one to play with"; "She's not mad, she's hurt"; "Do you think the doctor is doing anything to make the baby cry?")

    c. *Attempts to guide behavior* (e.g., "She'll feel better now that her mommy's back"; "Let's see if we can find a happy baby"; "Don't hit the baby [picture]")

    d. *Socialization of emotion*

       i. Confirmation ("It's okay to feel mad"; "He's happy, well that's good")

       ii. Disconfirmation (e.g., "We don't like sad faces"; "The baby shouldn't be crying")

       iii. Denial (e.g., "The baby's not crying") (for photograph of crying infant)

(Categories c and d occurred too infrequently for statistical analysis.)

5. *Accuracy of emotion term*

Accuracy was based on a rating of the emotion-descriptive terms uttered by each individual for each picture (Cole, 1988). Terms describing emotional experience (sad, happy) or emotional expression (laughing, crying) formed the basis of the rating. Repetitions of the other's terms were not included. The criteria for accuracy were based on Izard's research on infant display of discrete emotion (Izard et al., 1980). A four-point rating scale was developed:

-1 = inaccurate (e.g., asking if the smiling baby was sad without ever self-correcting or accepting the correct response of the other);

0 = no emotion terms provided (e.g., describing baby as little or pretty);

$+1$ = accurate but not specific to the discrete emotion (e.g., "This baby's not crying"), for interest photo; "This baby is interested," for surprise photo; "This baby is upset," for anger photo; "This baby is unhappy," for disgust photo;

$+2$ = accurate, precise description of the specific emotion, e.g., "This baby is smiling/glad/happy/laughing" for joy photo; "This baby is sad/crying/unhappy" for sadness photo; "This baby is scared/afraid/worried" for fear photo.

Interrater reliabilities for emotion language and accuracy codes were based on two raters' coding of emotion language and accuracy items. Twenty percent of the cases were sampled and percentages of agreement were calculated. Two different pairs of raters were used for emotion language codes and accuracy ratings. The majority of percentages of agreement ranged from 90 to 100 percent; occasionally they were between 80 and 90 percent.

Results

Verbal transcripts from three dyads are provided in appendix B. They illustrate qualitative as well as quantitative differences that exist in dyadic communication patterns. For dyad 1, the pictures become a vehicle for discussing emotional issues and concerns in their relationship, and comments about the infants in the pictures seem extraneous, irrelevant, and often inappropriate. The language of the mother in dyad 2 is very constricted and unelaborated. The mother in dyad 3 provides richly elaborated, developmentally sensitive discussions about emotions that encourage, but do not require, the child to talk about feelings.

GROUP DIFFERENCES IN MOTHERS' AND CHILDREN'S
RESPONSES ON PARENT–CHILD AFFECTIVE
COMMUNICATIONS TASK (PACT)

Analyses of variance were conducted to examine whether depressed and well mothers differed in how they talked to their children about emotions. Age and sex of the child were also included as factors to examine whether mothers spoke differently about emotions to their boys and girls and to their 2- and 3-year-old children. Parallel analyses of variance were conducted to examine patterns of emotion language in the children. The means and standard deviations for emotion language measures are presented in Tables 13.1 and 13.2. Analyses of total numbers of words used by mothers and children indicated that depressed and well mothers did not differ in their overall verbal production as indexed by the total number of words in the transcripts (x = 151.7 for depressed mothers and x =

TABLE 13.1
Mothers' Communications about Emotions

| | Well Mothers of | | | | Depressed Mothers of | | | |
| | 2-year-olds | | 3-year-olds | | 2-year-olds | | 3-eyar-olds | |
	$\bar{x}$	SD	$\bar{x}$	SD	$\bar{x}$	SD	$\bar{x}$	SD
Emotion Terms								
Positive	2.8	3.4	6.9	6.8	2.2	2.8	3.4	4.7
Negative	3.7	4.2	4.6	4.4	3.1	3.6	4.9	4.4
Evaluative Emotion Terms	0.4	0.7	1.3	2.2	0.9	1.9	1.2	1.9
Functions of Emotions								
Comments (positive)	0.8	1.3	0.3	0.5	0.5	0.8	0.7	1.4
Comments (negative)	0.5	1.0	0.1	0.3	0.9	1.2	0.8	1.3
Explanations (positive)	2.1	2.8	6.9	6.4	2.1	2.8	3.0	4.1
Explanations (negative)	3.5	4.3	5.0	5.1	2.7	3.7	4.4	4.6
Accuracy of Emotion Language								
Positive emotions	1.1	1.6	2.1	1.4	0.8	1.2	1.5	1.8
Negative emotions	1.8	2.4	3.3	3.3	2.0	2.2	2.4	2.2

164.0 for well mothers, $t < 1$), nor did their children's verbal output differ ($x = 49.6$ for children of depressed mothers and $x = 44.2$ for children of well mothers, $t < 1$). There was a great deal of variability on this measure for both groups.

AGE DIFFERENCES

Mothers spoke differently to 2- versus 3-year-old children about emotions and the younger versus older children spoke differently about feelings as well. For example, mothers of 3-year-old children were more likely to talk both about positive emotions ($F[1,102] = 7.17, p < 0.01$) and negative emotions ($F[1,102] = 2.87, 0.05 < p < 0.10$) than mothers of 2-year-olds. Mothers of 3-year-olds also more frequently provided explanations or reasons for the emotions expressed, especially positive emotions ([1,102]

TABLE 13.2
Children's Communications about Emotions

| | Children of Well Mothers | | | | Children of Depressed Mothers | | | |
| | 2-year-olds | | 3-year-olds | | 2-year-olds | | 3-year-olds | |
	$\bar{x}$	SD	$\bar{x}$	SD	$\bar{x}$	SD	$\bar{x}$	SD
Emotion Terms								
Positive	1.1	1.7	2.3	2.1	0.7	1.1	1.5	1.8
Negative	2.6	2.4	3.7	2.7	2.3	2.0	3.8	3.8
Evaluative Emotion Terms	0.2	0.6	0.1	0.3	0.3	1.0	0.4	0.6
Functions of Emotions								
Comments (positive)	1.1	1.6	1.9	2.1	0.8	1.5	0.8	0.9
Comments (negative)	1.9	2.3	2.7	2.4	1.5	1.8	2.5	2.3
Explanations (positive)	0.2	0.7	0.6	0.7	0.1	0.4	1.1	1.3
Explanations (negative)	0.9	1.6	0.9	0.8	0.9	1.4	1.8	3.5
Accuracy of Emotion Language								
Positive emotions	0.8	1.4	1.1	1.4	0.3	1.0	1.5	1.9
Negative emotions	1.9	2.2	1.6	2.4	1.9	2.0	2.9	2.1

$= 8.64, p < 0.005$) ($F[1,102] = 3.11, 0.05 < p < 0.10$ for negative emotions). Similarly, 3-year-old children differed from 2-year-old children on many of the same dimensions of emotion language. Older children more often than younger children used positive emotion terms ($F[1,102] = 9.06, p < 0.005$) and negative emotion terms ($F[1,102] = 5.75, p < 0.05$). Older children also gave more explanations for emotions, mainly for positive emotions ($F[1,102] = 18.69, p < 0.001$). Accuracy scores tended to increase with age for both mothers and children, reflecting increases in the frequency of use of emotion language, as well as in accuracy.

MATERNAL DEPRESSION

Maternal diagnosis qualifies in important ways the findings on age differences in emotion language. The increase with age in mother's use of explanations for positive emotions occurred for children of well, but not depressed, mothers, $F[1,102] = 6.00, p < 0.025$, for the interaction of maternal diagnosis and age of child (see Table 13.1). In contrast, simple, unelaborated comments on negative emotions were almost twice as likely to come from depressed than well mothers, $F[1,102] = 4.62, p < 0.05$, regardless of age. The findings for the children did not parallel those of the mothers. There were no differences in the accuracy scores of depressed and well mothers, or in the accuracy scores of their children.

SEX OF CHILD

Mothers talked more frequently with their girls than with their boys, about emotions, especially the negative emotions, and particularly at the "older" ages (3 years). This effect was seen in a significant interaction of age and sex of child for negative terms $(F[1,102] = 5.68, p < 0.025)$ ($\bar{x} = 3.2$ and $\bar{x} = 6.7$ for mothers of 2- and 3-year-old girls, respectively; $\bar{x} = 3.6$ and $\bar{x} = 2.8$ for mothers of 2- and 3-year-old boys, respectively). Regarding children's emotion language, the increase with age in negative emotion words tended to be more characteristic of girls than boys, $F[1,102] = 3.25, p < 0.075$ ($\bar{x} = 2.4$ and $\bar{x} = 4.8$ for 2- and 3-year-old girls, respectively; $\bar{x} = 2.4$ and $\bar{x} = 2.7$ for 2- and 3-year-old boys, respectively). Girls also talked about positive emotions more than boys, $F[1,102] = 5.38$, $p < 0.05$ ($\bar{x} = 1.4$ for girls and $\bar{x} = 0.7$ for boys).

CORRELATIONS BETWEEN MOTHERS' AND CHILDREN'S EMOTION LANGUAGE

There were many significant associations between how mothers and their children talk about emotions: $r[101] =$

0.60, $p < 0.001$ for positive emotion terms; $r[101] = 0.55$, $p < 0.001$ for negative emotion terms; $r[101] = 0.38$, $p < 0.001$ for evaluative terms; $r[101] = 0.39$, $p < 0.001$ for explanations or reasons for positive emotions; $r[101] = 0.43$, $p < 0.001$, for explanations or reasons for negative emotions. When correlations were computed separately for mothers and children with children's age controlled, the patterns still held. Correlations were similar in magnitude when conducted separately for well and depressed samples. Analyses were based on initiations of emotion language terms and not repetitions of the others' communications. Hence, significant correlations between mothers' and children's language are not necessarily predetermined by the construction and nature of the task. Moreover, in a recent study using the same procedures and pictures with somewhat older preschool children and their mothers (Denham and Rouse, 1989), the correlations between mothers' and children's emotion language scores do not reach statistical significance.

REPLICATION STUDY

The Parent–Child Affect Communication task, again using the Izard pictures, was administered to a second sample of fifty mothers and their 2-year-old children (Usher, Ridgeway, Barrett, Nitz, and Wagner, 1988). This was a volunteer sample who participated in a study of early emotional development at the National Institute of Mental Health, hence providing an opportunity to assess emotion language as well. Mothers were unscreened with respect to psychopathology. They were similar in demographic characteristics to the original sample. Consistent with the original sample, there were a number of significant correlations between mothers' and children's communications about emotions; $r(48) = 0.52$, $p < 0.001$, for positive emotion terms; $r(48) = 0.58$, $p < 0.001$, for negative emotion terms; $r(48) = 0.65$, $p < 0.001$, for evaluative terms; $r(48)$ = 0.58, $p < 0.001$, for explanations about positive emotions; and $r(48) = 0.40$, $p < 0.005$, for explanations about negative emotions.

Discussion

Pictures of infant emotions were used to elicit dialogues between mothers and their young children. Descriptive findings from these short narratives about emotions and affective themes corroborate other studies on the early emergence of emotion language in children. They indicate as well that children's early patterns of expression are closely linked to maternal communications about emotions. The mothers who (1) talked about emotions; (2) provided causes and explanations for emotions; and/or (3) used evaluative (sometimes judgmental) terms to characterize individuals—had children who did so as well. This was the case whether mothers were well or depressed.

Group differences between depressed and well mothers in their patterns of communication about emotions were identified. Psychiatrically normal mothers were more likely than depressed caregivers to provide their children with reasons or causes of emotions, especially positive emotions. In contrast, depressed mothers, more than well mothers, emphasized negative emotions in unelaborated communications about these emotions. Moreover, maternal behavior in the two groups appeared to be differentially influenced by the child's developmental level. Well, but not depressed, mothers were more likely to provide explanations or consider the causes of emotions with older than with younger children. Well mothers may be more attuned to the cognitive and social–emotional capabilities of their children, and hence provide more developmentally appropriate communications.

We were interested in whether depressed mothers were more (or less) veridical in their interpretations of emotions than well mothers. The emphasis placed by depressed mothers on negative emotions may have reflected either distortion or exaggeration, or accurate appraisals. Other studies suggest that the heightened focus of depressed individuals on negative events and problems actually may reflect accurate assessments of situations, whereas nondepressed persons may be overly optimistic and biased against seeing problems that exist (Alloy and Abramson, 1979; Layne, 1983). Here, depressed and well mothers were equally *accurate* in their descriptions of emotions, but apparently concentrated on different pictures. Depressed mothers emphasized negative emotions (e.g., photos of anger and sadness) while well mothers focused on the pictures of positive affect (e.g., joy and interest) and sought out explanations for why the infants were experiencing positive affect. The majority of photographs conveyed negative emotions. Well mothers may make active, not necessarily conscious, attempts to draw their children's attention away from others' negative states. Future research on this issue might profitably use the IFEEL Pictures which contain a higher proportion of positively valanced photographs of emotion and fewer "peak" expressions of negative emotion.

The patterns of emotion language of children of depressed versus well mothers did not parallel those of the mothers. Effects of depression on children's emotion language may become more evident over time, as their communication patterns become more established and consolidated. The relationships between mothers' and children's communications are consistent with, but do not necessarily confirm, a socialization model; that is, the possibility that young children's emotion language is influenced by their mothers' verbal communication patterns. Other types of research designs and observation contexts would help to more fully address hypotheses regarding causal mechanisms; for example, observing mothers' communication patterns with other children, and children's patterns with other mothers.

Sex differences also were evident, both in terms of how mothers talk to their boys and girls about emotions, and also in the use of emotion language by the two sexes. Mothers talked more about emotions, especially negative ones (e.g., sadness and distress) with their girls than their boys. And girls talked more about emotions, both negative and positive feelings, than boys. Dunn et al. (1987) studied 18- and 24-month-old children and found that mothers of 18-month-old girls initiated more conversations about feeling states than mothers of boys. There were no sex differences in the children at 18 months, but by 24 months girls referred to feeling states more often than boys. There is a large literature (see reviews by Frodi, Macaulay, and Thome [1977]; Hall [1978]; Brody [1985]; Zahn-Waxler, Cole, and Barrett [in press]) indicating that females show greater interpersonal sensitivity than males; for example, they are more accurate in their interpretatons of others' emotions and psychological defenses and they report more empathic feelings as well. The research on emotion language in very young children just described suggests both (1) that girls receive early training in the expression of characteristics that many would view as "appropriate" to their sex role, (2) that girls are receptive to the messages.

The procedure developed here to elicit emotion language places main emphasis on discussion of others' emotional expressions and experiences. In contrast, Fivush (1989) has used a procedure to elicit mother–child communication about the young child's *own* emotions. Fivush found that with daughters, mothers focused more on the emotional state itself rather than the causes and consequences. Moreover, mothers of daughters, more than mothers of sons, focused on positive emotions and tended not to attribute negative emotions, especially anger, to their daughters. It would be interesting to determine whether these patterns become exaggerated or altered in other ways when the mother has an affective disorder. For example, depressed women (for whom problems in expressing anger and disagreement are common) may avoid acknowledging the anger of their daughters, and at the same time dwell on the problems of others. This may be one mechanism by which females learn to suppress hostility and conflict while simultaneously feeling obligated to focus on the needs of others (Zahn-Waxler, Cole, and Barrett, in press). There are corresponding implications for the development of internalizing problems, such as depression, in female offspring.

It cannot be determined from the present research design whether mothers mainly are socializing different patterns of emotion language or responding to existing differences between boys and girls (and younger and older children). Longitudinal multimethod research designs are needed to trace transactions between mother and child, in order to identify interactive patterns and causal processes. The longitudinal research of Dunn et al. (1987) provides a valuable model for examining direction of influence. In their work sex differences in children's emotion language emerged only *after* a differential history of exposure to mothers' emotion language (which was directed more toward girls than boys).

We have examined mainly quantitative dimensions of emotion language, but there are important qualitative differences as well. Some dyads' verbal communications are synchronous, regulated, appropriate and sensitive to the partner's signals. In other dyads, the patterns seem more inappropriate, idiosyncratic, and imbalanced. Some mothers appear to avoid talking about what is most salient in

the picture (i.e., emotion) and rather focus on more extraneous issues (e.g., the "infant's" name, gender, attrac-
tiveness). Some mothers intrude and override their children's efforts to communicate about emotions. Others
demonstrate exquisite sensitivity in knowing when to lead,
when to follow, how much information to convey, how
to provide corrective feedback when the child incorrectly
labels an emotion, and how to guide the child into developing his/her own hypotheses about the underlying causes
of different feeling states. These qualitative dimensions
merit further examination.

Adaptations of procedures like the Parent–Child Affect Communication Task, employing both the IFEEL and
the Izard pictures, might be used to facilitate mother–child
communication for mothers who do not speak often or
readily to their children about feelings. The IFP would
allow greater exploration of positive emotions and subtle,
blended emotions. Because children develop a language
of emotions in the first years of life, they are ready early to
receive simple communications about feelings, and could
potentially benefit from the information provided. Children's repertoire of emotion language provides them with
a mechanism for understanding their own and other's feelings, both of which are important dimensions of social
competence and development of self. It may be possible
to teach mothers to provide accurate labels and reasonable
explanations for emotions to their children. Different risk
groups, and even well mothers who have difficulty talking
about feelings, might profit from such training experiences.

References

Alloy, L. B., & Abramson, L. Y. (1979), Judgment of contingency
    in depressed and non-depressed students: Sadder but
    wiser? *J. Experiment. Psychol.: Gen.*, 104:441–485.

Bretherton, I., Fritz, J., Zahn-Waxler, C., & Ridgeway, D. (1986), The acquisition and development of emotion language: A functionalist perspective. *Child Develop.*, 57:529–548.

Brody, L. R. (1985), Gender differences in emotional development: A review of theories and research. *J. Pers.*, 53/ 2:102–149.

Cole, P. (1988), Emotion Language Accuracy Coding System. Typescript.

Denham, S. (1986), Social cognition, prosocial behavior, and emotion in preschoolers: Contextual validation. *Child Develop.*, 57:194–201.

——— Rouse, M. C. (1989), Baby looks very sad: Discussions about emotions between mother and preschooler. Poster presented at American Psychological Association, New Orleans, LA.

Dunn, J., Bretherton, I., & Munn, P. (1987), Conversations about feeling states between mothers and their young children. *Develop. Psychol.*, 23:132–139.

Fivush, R. (1989), Exploring sex differences in the emotional content of mother–child communications about the past. *Sex Roles*, 20/11,12:675–691.

Frodi, A., Macaulay, J., & Thome, P. R. (1977), Are women always less aggressive than men? A review of the experimental literature. *Psychol. Bull.*, 84/4:634–660.

Grief, E., Alverez, M., & Tonis, M. (1984), Parents teaching of emotions to preschool children. Paper presented at Eastern Psychological Association, Baltimore, MD.

Hall, J. A. (1978), Gender differences in decoding non-verbal cues. *Psychol. Bull.*, 85/4:845–857.

Hokanson, J. E., Sacco, W. P., Blumberg, S. R., & Landrum, G. C. (1980), Interpersonal behavior of depressed individuals in a mixed-motive game. *J. Abnorm. Psychol.*, 89:320–332.

Izard, C. E., Huebner, R. R., Risser, D., McGinnes, G. C., & Dougherty, L. M. (1980), The young infant's ability to produce discrete emotion expressions. *Develop. Psychol.*, 16/ 2:132–140.

Jacobson, N., & Anderson, E. (1982), Interpersonal skill and depression in college students: An analysis of the timing of self-disclosures. *Behav. Ther.*, 13:271–282.

Johnson-Laird, P. N. (1983), *Mental Models: Towards a Cognitive Science of Language, Inference, and Consciousness.* Cambridge, MA: Harvard University Press.

Layne, C. (1983), Painful truths about depressives' cognitions. *J. Clin. Psychol.*, 39:848–853.

McNair, D. M., Lorr, M., & Droppleman, L. F. (1971), *POMS—Profile of Mood States.* San Diego, CA: Educational & Industrial Testing Service.

Nolen-Hoeksema, S. (1987), Sex differences in unipolar depression: Evidence and theory. *Psychol. Bull.*, 101/2:257–282.

Ridgeway, D. (1987), The relationship between communication and attachment security. Paper presented at the Society for Research in Child Development, Baltimore, MD.

———— Zahn-Waxler, C. (1986), *Parent-Child Communication Task Coding Manual.* Typescript.

Spitzer, R. L., & Endicott, J. (1978), *Schedule for Affective Disorders and Schizophrenia—Lifetime Version (SADS-L).* New York: Biometrics Research Division, New York State Psychiatric Institute.

Usher, B., Ridgeway, D., Barrett, K., Nitz, K., & Wagner, E. (1988), Maternal correlates of children in communications about emotions. Paper presented at International Conference on Infant Studies. Washington, DC.

Zahn-Waxler, C., Cole, P., & Barrett, K. (in press), Guilt and empathy: Sex differences and implications for the development of depression. In: *Emotion Regulation and Dysregulation*, ed. K. Dodge & J. Garber. New York: Cambridge University Press.

———— Radke-Yarrow, M., & King, R. (1979), Child rearing and children's prosocial initiations toward victims of distress. *Child Develop.*, 50:319–330.

14

Prenatal and Postnatal Maternal Perception of Infant Emotions and Quality of Mother–Infant Interaction

Ann Lodge, Lynn C. Blackwood, Jr., Ellen Kveton,
Margaret McDowell, Alan Rountree

The quality of maternal empathy, attitudes, and expectations is of critical importance for identification of maternal and other risk factors that may distort or threaten the developing relationship of mother and baby. At birth the parent is required to adapt these prenatal expectations to the actual characteristics of the infant. Sometimes this task may require considerable perceptual, cognitive, and emotional adjustment, particularly in high-risk birth situations or in the case of considerable discrepancy between prenatal expectations and mother's experience of the infant following birth.

The work of Ainsworth and her colleagues has demonstrated relationships between quality of maternal caregiving and subsequent infant–mother attachment patterns (Ainsworth, Blehar, Waters, and Wall, 1978). A major prospective study by Egeland, Breitenbucher, and Rosenberg (1980) examined the relationship between maternal personality variables prenatally and subsequent child abuse

237

and neglect. Maltreating mothers were characterized as higher in anxiety, defensiveness, and rigidity, showing a tendency to react to frustration in an aggressive, hostile manner (Egeland et al., 1980).

The appropriateness and sensitivity of maternal reaction to infant facial cues appears to be a critical factor affecting maternal behavior toward her infant, especially during the early months when vocal and motoric communication is relatively less developed. An important source of inappropriate responses or affective misattunement (Stern, 1985) in the infant–parent relationship may stem from parental misinterpretation of the infant's emotional state based upon facial cues. The quality of maternal monitoring as well as emotional availability and responsiveness to nonverbal affective signaling may be expected to have an important impact upon the infant's social and emotional development (Emde, 1984). The infant is largely dependent upon his or her mother or caregiver for interpersonal cues and environmental structuring to assist in containing and modulating emotional experience, particularly when it may be associated with stress and discomfort.

Interpreting from a projective perspective, the perceptual styles associated with different maternal personality characteristics may be expected to influence responses to the IFEEL Pictures (IFP) which involves identification of emotional states by responding to photographs of infant facial expressions. This study explored relationships between IFP responses obtained prenatally and postnatally and other postnatal measures of the quality of parent–infant interaction during a brief unstructured play situation. The latter yielded ratings according to the Crittenden (1983) Child–Adult Relationship Experimental Index (CARE-Index) which has been found useful in discriminating among parents with a history of abusive, neglectful, or adequate caregiving (Crittenden, 1981, 1983, in press).

The present study was part of a larger longitudinal study concerned with prediction and preventive intervention in abuse and neglect (Blackwood, Lodge, McDowell, Rountree, and Sheehan, 1986). The study involved the relationships between prenatal maternal personality characteristics and attitudes and subsequent patterns of mother–infant interaction, attachment, and child development. The IFP was one of several instruments administered in order to examine maternal perceptions of infant cues and emotional state and their possible impact upon the subsequent evolution of the mother–infant relationship.

Methodology

The study participants were volunteers drawn from the obstetrical clinics of three hospitals in the Hampton Roads, Virginia, area. One hundred fifty-six pregnant women agreed to participate in the research, representing about 70 percent of those who were asked. Thirty percent of the 156 subjects were recruited in the second trimester of pregnancy and 70 percent in the third trimester. All participants were expecting their first children.

The participants were interviewed four times over the course of the study; once prenatally, twice during their infants' first year, and again when their infants were between the ages of 14 and 20 months. The IFP was administered at the prenatal interview and at each of the two visits made during the infant's first year. At each of the three postnatal visits, the mother was asked to "play with your baby as you would at home" and mother–infant play was videotaped. These five-minute play episodes were scored by two raters who had never met any of the mothers, using Crittenden's CARE-Index (Crittenden, 1983). This instrument assesses the mother's sensitivity to her infant's cues as well as the infant's responsiveness to the mother's behavior on seven dimensions: facial expression, vocal expression, body contact and position, expression of affection, control of activity, pacing of turns, and choice of activity. Mothers are rated according to the number of sensitive behaviors (i.e., appropriate and contingent upon baby's cues), controlling behaviors (i.e., covertly or overtly hostile, intrusive, or interfering behaviors), and unresponsive behaviors (i.e., passive and uninvolved, ignoring).

There was considerable attrition in the study sample. Ninety-five mothers (60.9% of the population interviewed prenatally) brought their infants (97 infants, including two sets of twins) to the Infant Development Center for one follow-up visit during the first postnatal year. Of these 95 mothers, 58 returned to the Center for a second visit during their infants' first year. Fifty-nine mothers brought their infants for a third visit during their infants' second year. As a result of time limitations and/or technical difficulties, not all mothers were videotaped or administered the IFP at all Center visits. Ninety-one mothers were videotaped at the first visit, fifty-seven at the second visit, and forty-seven at the third visit. At the first visit, eighty-seven mothers were both videotaped and administered the IFP. Fifty-two of these mothers were both videotaped at the second visit and administered the IFP. Forty-four mothers who completed the IFP at the first visit, and twenty-nine mothers who completed the IFP at the second visit, also were videotaped when their infants were between the ages of 14 and 20 months.

In analyzing the demographic characteristics of the study population recruited prenatally ($n = 156$) and those who came to the Center at least once postnatally ($n = 95$), some differences were found. Women who were employed full-time prenatally were somewhat less likely to come to the Center. Women wih some college and women who were married and living in a nuclear household were more likely to come to the Center. Women who were judged to have extremely low levels of social support (i.e., unmarried, low income, living alone or with nonrelatives, having no relationship with the baby's father, and little family support) did not come to the Center. Poor perinatal and social outcomes were concentrated in this latter group of women.

Mean infant age was 4.6 months at the first visit, 8.1 months at the second visit, and 16.7 months at the third visit.

Results

TEST–RETEST STABILITY OF RESPONSES TO THE IFEEL PICTURES

Table 14.1 shows the responses by category of emotion received at the three interviews when the IFP was administered. (Because the categories shy, shame, and disgust averaged less than one response, they have been eliminated from statistical analyses.) Paired t-tests reveal no significant changes in the number of responses in any category except Fear which decreased significantly from the prenatal interview to the first postnatal interview. Table 14.2 shows the significant positive test–retest correlations within each emotion category. The values indicate substantial significant stability for most categories from the prenatal period through the first year of life (see Table 14.2).

QUALITY OF MOTHER–INFANT PLAY

With the exception of maternal age (inverse association of age with controlling behaviors at the first visit only), no demographic variables correlated significantly with the quality of maternal behavior during play with her infant.

TABLE 14.1
Responses to IFEEL Pictures Administered Prenatally and
Twice During First Year Postnatally

	Prenatal Visit (N = 156)		1st Visit (N = 87)		2nd Visit (N = 52)	
	Mean	Standard Deviation	Mean	Standard Deviation	Mean	Standard Deviation
Sleepy	2.2	1.7	2.4	2.0	2.3	2.0
Interest	6.7	3.8	6.9	3.8	6.7	3.2
Joy	5.5	2.9	5.9	3.0	6.0	2.8
Surprise	2.4	2.2	2.0	1.8	2.0	2.0
Distress	3.9	3.0	3.9	2.2	4.2	2.5
Anger	2.0	2.1	2.0	1.7	2.3	2.2
Sad	3.6	3.1	3.2	2.5	3.0	2.6
Fear	1.4	1.7	0.9	1.2	0.9	2.3
Other	1.5	2.0	2.3	2.5	2.3	2.6
Number of Categories	7.6	1.4	7.6	1.3	7.5	1.2

Maternal responses to the IFP, however, were correlated with the quality of maternal interactive behaviors, as shown in Table 14.3. A number of categories of responses given during the prenatal period were associated with maternal interactive behaviors at all three postnatal visits. Moreover, some significant correlations did not appear until the visit during the infants' second year of life. Although the levels of correlation tend to be low and are limited to 15 percent of tests being significant, the pattern of results seems useful to summarize.

PRENATAL RESPONSES

The number of prenatal responses in the categories of sleepy, interest, and joy, as well as the total number of categories within which mothers' responses fell, were significantly associated with maternal behaviors during at least two Center visits. Sleepy responses were positively

TABLE 14.2

Correlations Over Time of Responses Within Each Category on
IFEEL Pictures Administered Once Prenatally and Twice
Within the First Postnatal Year

	Prenatal Responses by Responses at First Visit (N = 92)	Prenatal Responses by Responses at Second Visit (N = 52)	First Visit by Second Visit (N = 52)
Sleepy	0.51**	0.37**	0.43**
Interest	0.65**	0.54**	0.65**
Joy	0.55**	0.34**	0.56**
Surprise	0.48**	0.70**	0.66**
Distress	0.51**	0.45**	0.51**
Anger	0.39**	0.66**	0.47**
Sad	0.46**	0.46**	0.43**
Fear	0.57**	0.65**	0.42**
Shy	0.21*	−0.05	−0.02
Shame	0.16	−0.08	0.44**
Disgust	0.11	−0.08	−0.10
Other	0.22*	0.23*	0.53**
Range	0.54**	0.56**	0.37*

$*p = 0.05.$
$**p = 0.01.$

correlated with maternal sensitive behaviors and negatively correlated with maternal unresponsive behaviors at
both the first visit and the third visit. Prenatal interest
responses were positively associated with sensitive behaviors at the second and third visits, and were negatively
correlated with controlling behaviors at the second visit
and unresponsive behaviors at the third visit. Prenatal joy
responses, however, were negatively associated with sensitive maternal behaviors. This finding probably is explained
in part by the larger number of emotion categories used
by more sensitive mothers. It appears that more sensitive
mothers were more likely than other mothers to recognize

TABLE 14.3

Correlations Between Responses to the IFP (Prenatal and Postnatal) Prenatally and Sensitive, Controlling, and Unresponsive Maternal Behaviors During Play

	First Visit			Second Visit			Third Visit		
	Sens.	Con.	Unres.	Sens.	Con.	Unres.	Sens.	Con.	Unres.
Prenatal									
(Number)	(N = 91)			(N = 57)			(N = 47)		
Sleepy	0.20*	ns	−0.19*	ns	ns	ns	0.28*	ns	−0.21
Interest	ns	ns	ns	0.24*	−0.26*	ns	0.27*	ns	−0.24*
Joy	−0.17*	ns	ns	ns	ns	ns	−0.23*	ns	ns
Surprise	ns	ns	ns	ns	ns	ns	ns	ns	0.30*
Distress	ns	ns	ns	ns	ns	ns	ns	ns	ns
Anger	ns	ns	ns	ns	ns	ns	ns	ns	ns
Sad	ns	ns	ns	ns	ns	ns	−0.30*	ns	0.24*
Fear	ns	ns	ns	ns	ns	ns	ns	0.23*	ns
Shy	ns	ns	ns	ns	ns	ns	ns	ns	ns
Shame	ns	ns	ns	ns	ns	ns	0.36**	ns	ns
Disgust	ns	ns	ns	ns	ns	ns	ns	ns	ns
First Visit									
(Number)	(N = 87)			(N = 55)			(N = 44)		
Sleepy	0.19*	ns	ns	ns	ns	ns	ns	ns	ns
Interest	ns	ns	ns	0.21*	−0.32**	ns	ns	ns	ns
Joy	ns	ns	0.23*	ns	ns	ns	ns	ns	ns
Surprise	ns	ns	ns	ns	0.23*	−0.21	ns	ns	ns
Distress	ns	ns	ns	ns	ns	ns	ns	ns	ns
Anger	ns	ns	−0.21*	ns	ns	ns	ns	ns	ns
Sad	ns	ns	ns	ns	ns	ns	ns	−0.24*	0.23
Fear	ns	ns	ns	−0.22*	0.25*	ns	ns	ns	ns
Shy	ns	ns	ns	−0.23*	0.27*	ns	ns	ns	ns
Shame	ns	ns	ns	ns	ns	ns	ns	ns	ns
Disgust	ns	ns	ns	ns	ns	0.34**	ns	ns	ns
Second Visit									
(Number)				(N = 52)			(N = 29)		
Sleepy				ns	ns	ns	ns	ns	ns
Interest				ns	−0.30*	ns	ns	ns	ns
Joy				ns	ns	ns	ns	ns	ns
Surprise				ns	0.29*	ns	ns	ns	ns
Distress				ns	ns	ns	0.51**	−0.41**	ns
Anger				ns	ns	−0.30*	ns	ns	ns
Sad				−0.31*	0.27*	ns	−0.30*	0.32*	ns
Fear				ns	ns	ns	ns	0.34*	ns
Shy				ns	0.25*	ns	ns	ns	ns
Shame				ns	ns	ns	ns	ns	ns
Disgust				ns	ns	ns	0.31*	ns	−0.38*

* = $p = 0.05$ ** = $p = 0.01$

a wider range of infant emotion states, and less likely to view infant expressions as reflecting joy. By the middle of the second year of life, prenatal responses in the categories of sad, fear, and shame correlated with maternal interactive behavior. Sad responses correlated positively with unresponsive behaviors and negatively with sensitive behaviors. Fear responses correlated positively with controlling behaviors, and shame responses correlated positively with sensitive behaviors.

FIRST VISIT RESPONSES

A somewhat different pattern of association of responses with maternal interactive behaviors appeared when the IFEEL Pictures were administered at the first Center visit several months after the birth of the infant. A significant correlation between sleepy responses and sensitive behaviors was observed at the first visit, which was the only significant relationship with sensitive behaviors at that time. There were no associations between responses given at the first visit and controlling behaviors observed at that time. Unresponsive behaviors at the first visit, however, were positively correlated with the number of joy responses and inversely correlated with the number of anger responses. Responses on IFP given at the first Center visit, while unrelated to maternal interactive behaviors observed at that time, proved to be associated with expectable behaviors observed at later visits. The number of responses in the interest category given at the first postnatal visit correlated significantly with behaviors observed approximately four months later at the second visit; as might be expected, there was positive association with sensitive behaviors and a negative association with controlling behaviors. Surprise responses at the first visit were positively correlated with controlling behaviors and inversely correlated with unresponsive behaviors at the second visit. Other categories of

IFP emotions yielded associations that might be considered expectable. Both fear and shy responses given at the first visit were inversely associated with sensitive behaviors and positively associated with controlling behaviors at the second visit; disgust responses at the first visit were positively associated with unresponsive behaviors at the second visit and sad responses given at the first visit were inversely correlated with controlling behaviors and positively correlated with unresponsive behaviors at the third visit.

SECOND VISIT RESPONSES

Interest responses given at the second Center visit were inversely correlated with controlling behaviors at that time, as were interest responses given prenatally and at the first Center visit. Also consistent with the pattern of association between responses given at the first visit and maternal behaviors at the second visit is the finding that surprise and shy responses given at the second visit were positively correlated with controlling behaviors observed at the second visit. At the second visit, sad responses were observed to be positively correlated with controlling behaviors. In contrast, sensitive behaviors at the second visit were inversely correlated with sad responses. This association between sad responses given at the second visit and maternal behaviors was observed again when mothers returned during their infant's second year (third visit), with an inverse association with sensitive behaviors and a positive association with controlling behaviors. Unresponsive behaviors at the second visit were inversely correlated with anger responses.

The pattern of correlations between IFP responses given at the second visit and maternal behaviors observed at the third visit shows some similarities with relationships noted above. In addition to the similar inverse association of sad responses with sensitive behaviors, fear responses given both prenatally and at the second visit were positively correlated with controlling behaviors. Distress responses and disgust responses given at the second visit were positively correlated with sensitive behaviors at the third visit. Distress was inversely associated with controlling behaviors, and disgust was inversely associated with unresponsive behaviors.

Discussion

The findings from this study suggest relationships among variables that are in need of further exploration. Other developmental research has indicated that both mother's experience and expectations during pregnancy and the initial mother–infant bonding period contribute significantly to the lasting matrix of attachment. Therefore, changes in maternal perceptions and attitudes toward her infant during both the prenatal and postnatal periods may be particularly important in predicting patterns of mothering. Tronick and Gianino (1986) have described the coordinated exchange of emotional messages in terms of a mutual regulation model. Their data demonstrate a relationship between maternal affective display and infant behavior as well as the impact of the infant's emotional signals upon the mother.

The current findings may lend support to the hypothesis that maternal perceptions of infant emotional states can be determined unconsciously by the role the infant is anticipated to play in meeting mother's needs. Thus, a mother who is in need of nurturance and affection from her baby may tend to emphasize developmentally advanced emotional states and a high degree of active involvement (engagement cues) such as "interest" as opposed to those which reflect dependency needs. Similarly, emotions associated with disengagement cues such as sleepiness, boredom, or turning away may signal unacceptable rejection. Ironically, mothers with little energy or nurturance to give their infants may emphasize self-sufficient states of joy and happiness in their perception of infant state indicating possible defensiveness that relieves them of responsibility for contributing appropriately to such states.

Kveton (1989) examined quality of infant–parent attachment at 17 months with a sample from this study population as related to attitudes measured by the Bavolek (1984) Adult–Adolescent Parenting Inventory (AAPI). Her findings indicated that the mothers of infants who developed an insecure attachment were significantly more likely than mothers of secure infants to evidence strong belief in the use of physical punishment. It is interesting that the present results demonstrated fear responses given prenatally and at the second visit showed a positive correlation with controlling behaviors, while distress showed an inverse correlation at the third (16–17-month) visit. These data may suggest that when the infant–parent relationship is perceived in conflictual terms beginning in the prenatal period, it may be associated with subsequent disturbance in interaction and attachment.

The new mother is confronted with the task of interpreting and responding to her infant's needs on the basis of facial cues, cries, vocalizations, and other expressive behaviors. This can be a challenge to a highly trained and sophisticated observer and may be overwhelming for a young inexperienced mother. Infants vary in the clarity of cues (Barnard and Eyers, 1979) as well as other temperamental characteristics (Brazelton, Koslowski, and Main, 1974; Carey and McDevitt, 1978). Mothers respond to the demands of this situation based upon their own personality and temperament as well as their ability to learn from the interactions with their infant. The projective perspective would suggest that such adaptability will be influenced by the mother's current emotional state and needs.

Many theorists (e.g., Ainsworth, Crittenden) empha-size that the mother's personality characteristics, need state, and related expectations will exert the predominant influence upon the quality of mother–infant interaction and attachment despite infant variability. However, Brazelton and his colleagues have presented convincing evidence concerning the important role that infant charac-teristics may play in determining the nature of infant–par-ent interaction (Brazelton et al., 1974). The findings of Broussard and Hartner (1971) have suggested that mater-nal perception of her neonate may represent a mixture of accurate awareness as well as projective elements which may encourage a self-fulfilling prophecy.

The results of the present study suggest that an im-portant determinant of maternal receptiveness to infant emotional states as revealed by facial cues and capacity for appropriate interpretation may be reflected in their responses to the IFP. These data suggest further that the appropriateness of maternal emotional responsiveness in-dicated by this measure is a significant predictor of the sensitivity displayed in interaction with her infant. The change over time in maternal perception of infant emo-tional states, which we found with less sensitive mothers, represents another area in need of further investigation.

References

Ainsworth, M., Blehar, M., Waters, E., & Wall, S. (1978), *Patterns of Attachment: A Psychological Study of the Strange Situation.* Hillsdale, NJ: Lawrence Erlbaum.

Barnard, K. E., & Eyers, S. J. (1979), *Child Health Assessment, Part 2: The First Year of Life* (DHEW Publication No. HRA 79-25). Hyattsville, MD: U.S. Dept. of Health, Education and Welfare, Public Health Services, HRA, Bureau of Health Manpower, Division of Nursing.

Bavolek, S. J. (1984), *Handbook for the Adult–Adolescent Parenting Inventory (AAPI)*. Eau Clair, WI: Family Development Resources.

Blackwood, Jr., L. C., Lodge, A., McDowell, M., Rountree, A., & Sheehan, D. (1986), *Early Intervention with Parents of Infants at Risk for Abuse and Neglect*. Final report. Washington, DC: Office of Human Development Services.

Brazelton, T. B., Koslowski, B., & Main, M. (1974), The origins of reciprocity: The early mother–infant interaction. In: *The Effect of the Infant on Its Caregiver*, ed. M. Lewis & L. Rosenblum. New York: John Wiley.

Broussard, E. R., & Hartner, M. S. (1971), Further considerations regarding maternal perceptions of the first born. In: *The Exceptional Infant*. Vol. 2, ed. J. Hellmuth. New York: Brunner/Mazel.

Carey, W. B., & McDevitt, S. C. (1978), Revision of Infant Temporal Questionnaire. *Pediatrics*, 61:735–739.

Crittenden, P. M. (1981), Abusing, neglecting, problematic, and adequate dyads: Differentiating by patterns of interaction. *Merrill-Palmer Quart.*, 27:1–18.

——— (1983), *Mother and Infant Patterns of Interaction: Developmental Relationships*. Doctoral dissertation, University of Virginia, Charlottesville, VA.

——— (in press), Family and dyadic patterns of functioning in maltreating families. In: *Early Prediction and Prevention of Child Abuse*, ed. K. Browne, C. Davies, & P. Stratton. Chichester, U.K.: John Wiley.

Egeland, B., Breitenbucher, M., & Rosenberg, D. (1980), Prospective study of the significance of life stress in the etiology of child abuse. *J. Consult. & Clin. Psychol.*, 48:195–205.

Emde, R. N. (1984), The affective self: Continuities and transformations from infancy. In: *Frontiers of Infant Psychiatry*, Vol. 2, ed. J. D. Call, E. Galenson, & R. L. Tyson. New York: Basic Books.

Kveton, E. M. (1989), *The Quality of Infant–Parent Attachment at 17 Months as Related to the Quality of Parent–Infant Interaction and Prenatal Parenting Attitudes*. Doctoral dissertation. Virginia Consortium for Professional Psychology.

Stern, D. (1985), *The Interpersonal World of the Infant.* New York: Basic Books.

Tronick, E. Z., & Gianino, A. F. (1986), The transmission of maternal disturbance to the infant. In: *Maternal Depression and Infant Disturbance*, ed. E. Z. Tronick & T. M. Field. San Francisco: Jossey-Bass.

Part V:
Looking Ahead

15

Research and Clinical Implications

Joy D. Osofsky and Robert N. Emde

The beginning of our book set forth the rationale for the IFEEL Pictures as a research tool for exploring the ways in which parents and others interpret infant emotions. Perhaps, we reasoned, since emotions are so important for caregiving communication, a standard set of infant pictures, along with expectable caregiving responses, would be useful for researchers interested in exploring variations in caregiving. Perhaps such a technique would also be useful in clinical settings where early identification of caregiving problems could lead to increased understanding and appropriate intervention. Our book has reviewed the conceptual and empirical background for the IFEEL Pictures, the practical and descriptive features of the instrument, and its psychometric properties. Studies reporting the use of the technique for group comparisons (e.g., mothers at risk for problems in parenting) were followed by studies that used the pictures in other than standard ways in order to enhance clinical information-gathering and individual assessment. It is important to reiterate our caution, however. Although the IFEEL Pictures generate responses that may point to interesting processes and

255

their deviations, the technique has not yet been standardized for individual differences research or for individual
assessment.

In this, our final chapter, we will extend our horizons.
First, we will consider the use of the IFEEL Pictures in
different settings from those of our reference sample and
in other cultures. Preliminary findings in these areas provide additional incentives for research. Second, we will
consider the use of the IFEEL Pictures in clinical research.
A variety of approaches will be summarized that offer
promise for identifying and exploring early problems in
caregiving. Finally, future prospects for the IFEEL Pictures will be discussed in the light of work with the measure to date and our speculations.

Use of the IFEEL Pictures in Other Cultures and Settings

Exploratory studies in non-English-speaking countries are
being carried out in Argentina, France, Israel, Japan, and
Sweden. An obvious modification for all such studies involves the use of emotion words in the relevant language
of the population under study rather than in English. In
some of these studies, a forced choice response format,
involving the major labels of the emotion categories (e.g.,
anger, fear, sadness, joy, surprise, interest, disgust, shame,
guilt), has been introduced. A more elaborate variation,
employed by our Japanese colleagues, has involved the
creation of a totally new lexicon according to emotion categories using the verbal responses of the non-English language and local cultural differences. Researchers in Japan
have also developed a new version of the IFEEL Pictures,
using Japanese babies (see appendix C-1); others have
used our original IFEEL Pictures, or adapted them somewhat for their population.

Studies in different countries offer particular opportunities for exploring the usefulness of the IFEEL Pictures

in a variety of contexts. One would expect that varying values and belief systems would influence responses, particularly if a free response approach for labeling emotions is used. Moreover, one would expect that combining data across cultures would provide greater opportunities for testing associations of individual responses with other measured variables; for example, those of disordered relationships or of individual psychopathology. Where such associations are context-bound, they would not be consistent across cultures and would direct the researcher's attention to particular aspects of meaning within that culture.

A cautionary guideline needs to be noted in spite of the above-noted opportunities. If the investigator has any reason to believe that context is substantially different from that of our United States reference sample (see chapter 4), care should be exercised in interpreting individual differences based on reference sample comparisons. A reference sample from the local region may be needed for comparison purposes in such instances. An example of a finding that highlighted the need for this cautionary note came to our attention just before going to press. It occurred within the United States and was mentioned in chapter 5. Data collected from regional samples of southern black respondents (both middle-class and poverty samples) were substantially different from our reference sample, which included primarily midwestern white respondents. Further testing, interview, and correlational studies with other samples and measures will be needed to interpret such differences and, in any event, individual differences would need to be gauged against a reference sample in the same regional context with similar demographic characteristics.

We now turn to some preliminary reports from countries other than the United States. The reader will note that both contextual factors and different elaborations of emotions in other countries have led to changes in the way the IFEEL Pictures are used. Over time, we will be able to gain more understanding of how these changes may influence the interpretation of data.

One of the interesting variations in the use of the measure has emerged from work in Japan (see appendix C-1 for a more detailed description of the Japanese project). As our colleagues in Japan (Inoue, Hamada, Fukatsu, Takiguchi, and Okonogi) began to work with the Lexicon for the IFEEL Pictures that we originally developed in the United States, they found that some categories of emotion, important for understanding Japanese socialization, were not included. More research was then done in order to define these categories, and new pictures were taken of Japanese babies in order to make the Japanese version of the IFP, the Japanese IFEEL Pictures (JIFP), more compatible with the cultural perspective in that country. From a vast sample of pictures of 12-month-old babies, they have selected a set of thirty pictures that emphasizes blends of emotions and is, in some ways, parallel to the deck used in the United States. Many categories of emotion have been introduced in Japan, including a number having to do with social relatedness, *amae*, and attention-seeking. We await further results of their research with much interest.

Sweden has provided another cultural context for exploring the use of the IFP. De Chateau and Garberg (1986) varied the standard set used in the United States by replacing five pictures of a black baby with five Caucasian pictures from the original United States pool of photographs; this change was necessary because there were so few black families in Sweden. The modified set of IFEEL Pictures was then administered in a standard fashion. Responses from ten multiparous middle-class women were classified according to twelve categories of emotions.* One category

---

*The coding lexicon for the Swedish study was one used before the final scheme presented in other chapters of the book was adopted. The scheme in-

of response that seemed especially interesting was a low arousal, neutral to positive category of emotion which combined the emotion designations of passive and content. This category of emotion in the Swedish study seemed overrepresented, occurring as 17 percent of all responses, with three individuals scoring four standard deviations above the mean established for the United States reference sample. Results from this preliminary pilot study did not show differences with respect to other categories of emotion. A striking difference in the administration of the scale was noted, however. Whereas United States women typically take twenty to thirty minutes to complete the test, Swedish women took twice as much time. Factors that may contribute to the difference in response time (e.g., comparing seasonal differences between winter administration and summer administration) may be pursued in a later study. An implication of this work also is that, under some circumstances, it may be advisable to limit the time available.

Argentina provides yet another cultural setting for exploring the usefulness of the IFP. Verthelyi (1986) studied two groups of thirty pregnant women, one group of unmarried adolescents between 13 and 18 years of age, and another group of married adults between 19 and 35 years of age. The adolescent mothers were of lower socioeconomic status. The IFEEL Pictures were administered in the same way as in the United States with responses scored according to a translation of the English language Lexicon. The Argentine subjects had no difficulty responding to the task, and no new expressions had to be added in the course of administration. Interestingly, no apparent differences were detected between groups in the

---

cluded joy, surprise, interest, anger, fear, sadness, disgust, shy, shame, distress, passive, and other. This lexicon differed from our current one in ways that are described in chapter 4.

recognition and use of the emotional expressions in Argentina. Preliminary findings also showed that adolescent mothers gave fewer responses to the IFEEL Pictures than did adult low-risk mothers; adolescents tended to give more neutral responses when they found it difficult to provide an emotion label. Thus, when comparing individual assessments in Argentina with the United States reference sample, the responses of adolescent mothers in Argentina showed even fewer deviations from United States values than did Argentine adults. The interpretation was that the adolescents were more restricted, less free with their feelings, and less mature.

We believe that the preliminary cross-cultural studies done with the IFP are promising for a number of reasons. First, they indicate that the IFP have cross-cultural validity if the population being sampled is similar to the reference sample in the United States and context is taken into account. Under these conditions, similar responses appear to be elicited. Thus, interpreting pictures of infant facial expressions may have considerable generality. At the same time, these studies, particularly in Japan, have emphasized the importance of both context and cultural factors in eliciting responses to the IFP.

The cross-cultural discussion introduces an important aspect of the IFP measure that needs to be highlighted. This concerns the use of our reference comparison sample. The investigator–clinician should realize that, even for English-speaking countries, the reference sample cannot be considered normative in the sense of being a standardized representative sample from a known larger population. Rather, it is a sizable convenience sample of low-risk mothers that can be used for "reference" with respect to new data, providing one is aware of the nature and limitations of the original sample (see chapters 4 and 5). We recommend that our reference group comparison be thought of as one among many possible comparison groups, and that one or more relevant control groups within the population being examined also be used. For studies of individual differences, expanded sampling may also be necessary, with the investigator using the reference comparison sample as only one source of orientation.

The dimensional scoring system has been of interest in cross-cultural investigations. When the IFP are mapped by the subject, according to hedonic tone and arousal level, results become language free, thus reducing one measure of variability (see appendix A-4, coding sheet). The results can be compared across samples using the dimensional norms from the reference sample. This scoring method is currently being considered for use in France and Italy.

We will now discuss some thoughts about future research involving group comparisons, individual differences, and validation. We will then turn our attention to clinical application.

Research Needs and Opportunities

RECOMMENDED METHODS TO BE USED WITH THE IFEEL PICTURES

A computer program is available to automate the scoring of the IFP. Included in the program is the ability to compare groups of subjects with regard to both discrete emotions distribution and dimensional coding. Both the Kolmogorov-Smirov test for comparing the distribution of responses over emotion codes and t-test procedures for comparing mean level of responses are available as options in the IFP program. More detailed information on the use of the program and statistical techniques are available in Kean and Appelbaum (1990).

GROUP COMPARISON AND INDIVIDUAL DIFFERENCE STUDIES

Group comparison studies offer considerable research opportunities. Studies in this volume provide an early wave of this type of research that raises a number of interesting questions. The IFP measure as a projective technique allows parents to respond in terms of their internal states. Correspondingly, indications from the initial studies in this volume are promising for further research with groups at high risk for parenting problems. Research comparing high- and low-risk groups on the IFP, including mothers who are young, poor, depressed, and child abusers, showed different patterning of parental responses (see chapters 7, 8, 10, 13, 14). Several groups at risk for problems in parenting, including adolescent mothers and child abusing mothers, displayed a similar bimodal pattern of responses including high joy and high sad responses. We believe that this bimodal distribution may be a reflection of both confusion and defensive denial about how babies may be feeling. In a sample of depressed mothers, the bimodal profile of high joy/high sad which occurred in the other risk groups was not seen. Rather, depressed mothers emphasized negative emotions more and showed a great deal of variability in their perceptions of sadness, either reporting very little or a great deal (see chapter 9). This latter response suggests that defensiveness might be influencing their responses through either denial or projection. Further, several studies in this volume (see chapters 7, 8, 14) indicate that discrepancies in expectations and attitudes about pregnancy and parenting may be associated with patterns of IFP responses.

Early studies have also indicated the potential usefulness of the IFP measure in distinguishing among groups of parents whose infants display different characteristics. Szajnberg's study (see chapter 10), although exploratory, suggested that some mothers of premature infants may have different patterns of responses. It might be expected that studies of infants with different early temperamental characteristics (irritability, activity, inhibition, for example) could help us learn more about infants and parents in potentially high-risk situations. Studies of changing responses over time in both infants and parents with differing characteristics may lead to a greater understanding of interactional influences in the caregiver–child relationship.

These issues lead us to a consideration of individual differences. The studies reported in this volume are exploratory and suggestive (see chapters 10, 14). More detailed analyses of individual response patterns will be important if the IFP measure is to be used in the future for screening purposes. Through such research, it may be possible to define patterns of individual responses that are predictive of later problematic outcomes. If this proves to be so, the IFP may become helpful to clinicians who are working with infants and families.

VALIDATION STUDIES

We now come to the need for more validation studies. Research probing the meaning of the IFP measure has only started. Based on the studies reported in this volume, we know that the IFP can be used to distinguish between groups at high and low risk for parenting problems, and that it may begin to be used in individual difference research. But there are a host of other important questions. How does the IFP technique relate to other measures of parenting function and competence? One approach to the question would be to do comparative studies with both paper-and-pencil and projective measures that assess feelings specific to parenting. One study of this type is underway by Ann Lodge and her collaborators (1990) relating the IFP measure to the Thematic Apperception Test (TAT). Other approaches to answering the question of validation would include relating the IFP measure to perinatal assessments of parental attitudes and expectations, including an evaluation of the risk status of the infant. Standard paper-and-pencil measures such as those of self-esteem and depression might be included in studies for comparison with IFP results. Some initial studies of this type have been done (see chapters 7, 9, 14) and appear promising in that interesting relationships have been found between the IFP and other self-report measures of parenting.

Another area for validation research concerns real-life interactions. How does the IFP measure relate to behavioral observations of parents interacting with their children? The answer to this question is crucial for research that may develop the IFP for predictive purposes. We know from chapters 5 and 14 that the IFP measure exhibits both stability and change across time in mothers' responses as their children grow older. Preliminary research relating the IFP to behavioral observations is reported in chapters 4, 7, and 14. More research is needed in this area.

Use of the IFEEL Pictures in Clinical Research and Application

Specific clinical applications of the IFEEL Pictures have yet to be developed. This is not surprising considering that data is still needed concerning population norms and established links to clinical problems. But early work with the measure in several areas appears promising. We will discuss a number of forms of administration that may be used in exploratory clinical work. We will then indicate some possible additional settings and adaptations for the use of the IFEEL Pictures.

IFEEL PICTURES AND STANDARD INDIVIDUAL ADMINISTRATION

The form that has been used most frequently has been the individual picture-by-picture administration of the IFP with the respondent being asked to describe with one word what the infant is feeling. This administration was used to study the distribution of responses out of which the Reference Sample was established. The group and individual profiles of responses that have been developed based on this standard administration provided the first stimulus to our thinking that high-risk groups might exhibit different profiles than the standard Reference Sample. Although we have not studied individual profiles in a systematic way, this direction may be a promising one for future work.

IFEEL STORIES

A second way of using the IFEEL Pictures was modeled after the approach used with several other projective techniques where the respondent is asked to tell a story about what is happening in a series of pictures (see chapter 11). Utilizing this method, four sets have been developed including three pictures in each set. The emotional expressions depicted in two of the sets progress from positive to negative and, in the other two sets, from negative to positive. The sets also include ambiguous facial expressions of emotions. The responses to this measure seem to reflect the mother's experience of parenting as well as her response to the specific pictures in a similar fashion to other projective techniques. In the pilot work with this technique, repetitive themes have occurred which may have important clinical implications. Further, for areas that are particularly conflictual, mothers may have more difficulty telling stories which may be especially revealing. We feel that the IFEEL Stories hold considerable promise for elucidating problems with parenting in risk groups. A drawback to the method is that it may be experienced as more difficult and, hence, be less revealing when individuals are not as verbal. In such cases, a combination of methods, including some described below, may be useful.

CO-CONSTRUCTION OF STORIES

Co-construction of stories involves a semistructured administration of sets of the pictures (see chapter 13). Two methods are possible with this approach: (1) The interviewer may start a story and ask the mother to continue and complete it; or (2) the mother and child can be asked to construct a story together about a set of pictures. With the first approach, the interviewer can maintain some systematic control over the direction of the story which then varies according to the individual's ideas or projections. This technique is similar to some that are used as part of psychiatric evaluations and treatment (e.g., Winnicott's "squiggle technique" [1989]). In the second case, how the story is developed can reveal much about the mother–child relationship and style of interaction, as well as important content for the dyad. This approach can be used in a more or less structured way depending upon the goals of the interviewer.

IFEEL PICTURES INCORPORATED IN A PSYCHIATRIC INTERVIEW

Another clinically oriented method using the IFEEL pictures has been developed by Szajnberg (see chapter 12).

After the standard administration of the IFP test, the interviewer presents to the mother again those pictures that elicited extreme emotion. The pictures are used as part of a psychiatric interview to uncover more of the mother's conflictual feelings about parenting and her infant. The IFEEL Pictures serve as a means of focusing on the mother's internalized conflicts that may not be readily accessible. While this method has been used for assessment purposes, it could be adapted for use by the clinician in treating parents and children.

These alternative methods of administering the IFEEL Pictures add to its potential usefulness as a clinical tool. Projective techniques, in general, offer additional information to the clinician focusing on internalized conflicts that may not be easily identifiable. The IFEEL Pictures may uncover material specific to parenting and/or aid the clinician in more quickly identifying "risk factors" and understanding issues that interfere with the mother's ability to parent her infant (Fraiberg and Shapiro, 1975).

ADDITIONAL SETTINGS AND ADAPTATIONS OF THE IFEEL PICTURES

Pending additional research, the IFEEL Pictures and variations of the measure may be appropriate to use in a variety of educational and clinical settings. The settings might include clinics and offices, child guidance centers, and other settings where individuals at high risk for parenting problems might be seen. Since the instrument has not yet been established for screening or clinical use, however, we would not recommend its applied use other than for exploration.

Future Prospects

The IFEEL Pictures were introduced by emphasizing their promise in exploring parental interpretations of infant emotions. We will now discuss some remaining issues and speculate about future uses of the measure.

The meaningfulness of the IFP technique may lie in the extent to which it indexes the emotional availability system in early caregiving. Emotional availability is a dyadic construct that refers to the infant's ability to signal emotional needs and the caregiver's capacity to accurately interpret and communicate accessibility in meeting these needs. For the infant, the emotional availability of the parent will influence the amount of exploration and interpersonal security that is shown. Thus, it may be expected that emotional availability would be associated with sensitivity on the parent's side and security on the infant's side (Ainsworth, Blehar, Waters, and Wall, 1978; Emde, 1980; Sorce and Emde, 1981; Osofsky, 1992). The recognition and understanding of positive and negative emotions are extremely important for emotional availability. Experiencing excessive distress or few positive emotions can interfere with the emotional availability of the parent. In studies with high-risk groups (Emde, Gaensbauer, and Harmon, 1981; Sroufe, 1983; Osofsky and Eberhart-Wright, 1988; Hann, Robinson, Osofsky, and Little, submitted; Osofsky, Eberhart-Wright, Ware, and Hann, 1991, 1992), the quality, range, and amount of negative and positive emotions have been used as indicators of the emotional availability of a parent. In some high-risk samples, more negative, mixed, and inappropriate emotions are expressed by mothers along with fewer positive emotions. In other samples, there is a restricted range of emotional expression. The studies reported in this volume have shown a number of atypical patterns of maternal response to the IFP set that are associated with risk. These include not only an increase in a variety of negative emotions but also some patterns in which high joy co-occurs with negative responses (see chapters 7 and 8). When subjects have excess responses in some categories of emotion, they usually have fewer responses in the interest and content categories. Future research should continue to assess atypical IFP patterns in relation to patterns of parent–infant interaction that are known to place the dyad at high risk for problematic outcomes.

The relationships of the IFEEL Pictures to individual measures such as parental anxiety, stress, depression, support, self-esteem, feelings about the pregnancy and parenting, and aspects of the marital relationship should also be pursued in future research. It may be that parents displaying certain patterns of responses are more likely to have difficulties in parenting and that the IFP may offer an additional early indicator of problems.

To date, the IFEEL Pictures have been used primarily for research purposes. Because responses do seem to differentiate parents at high risk for parenting problems from the standard reference sample, however, the possibility for using the measure for screening purposes seems promising. By understanding potential deficiencies in the infant's environment, including parental misconceptions, expectations, and attitudes that differ from the norm, it may be possible to offer mothers and their infants early preventive intervention that might alleviate stress and potential problems. Thus, it is conceivable that the IFP measure could be used for alerting purposes in designing early preventive interventions and could then be used later to evaluate change resulting from such interventions. One would anticipate that after therapeutic intervention, the pattern of parental interpretations of infant emotions on the IFEEL Pictures would be more similar to the standard reference sample.

The early enthusiasm of our colleagues for the IFP has encouraged its continuing use by both researchers and clinicians. The appeal of the baby pictures added to our incentives. We can only hope that this early interest on the part of investigators will lead us to a greater understanding of how parents interpret infant emotions. Correspondingly, we hope that we can add to our knowledge about development and our ability to enhance caregiver–infant relationships.

References

Ainsworth, M. D. S., Blehar, M. C., Waters, E., & Wall, S. (1978), *Patterns of Attachment: A Psychological Study of the Strange Situation.* Hillsdale, NJ: Lawrence Erlbaum.

Butterfield, P. M. (1986), Women "at risk" for parenting disorders perceive emotions in infant pictures differently. Poster presentation to Third World Congress of the World Association of Infant Psychiatry and Allied Disciplines, Stockholm, Sweden.

De Chateau, P., & Garberg, A. (1986), *IFEEL Picture Test: A Pilot Study in Sweden.* Typescript, Karolinska Institute, Stockholm.

Emde, R. N. (1980), Emotional availability: A reciprocal reward system for infants and parents with implications for prevention of psychosocial disorders. In: *Parent–Infant Relationships,* ed. P. M. Taylor. Orlando, FL: Grune & Stratton, pp. 87–115.

———— Gaensbauer, T., & Harmon, R. (1981), Using our emotions: Some principles for appraising emotional development and intervention. In: *Developmental Disabilities in Preschool Children,* ed. M. Lewis & L. Taft. New York: S. P. Medical & Scientific Books, pp. 409–424.

Fraiberg, S., & Shapiro, V. (1975), Ghosts in the nursery: A psychoanalytic approach to the problems of impaired infant–mother relationships. *J. Amer. Acad. Child Psychiatry,* 14:387–421.

Hann, D. M., Robinson, J. L., Osofsky, J. D., & Little, C. (submitted), *Emotional Availability in Two Caregiving Environments: Low Risk Adult Mothers and Socially-At-Risk Adolescent Mothers.*

Kean, G., & Appelbaum, M. (1990), *Using the IFEEL: A Scoring and Statistical Analysis Program.* Quantitative Systems Laboratory Report, No. 1. Vanderbilt University, Nashville, TN.

Osofsky, J. D. (1992), Affective development and early relationships: Clinical implications. In: *Psychoanalysis and Psychology,* ed. J. W. Barron, M. N. Eagle, & D. L. Wolitzky. Washington, DC: American Psychological Association, pp. 233–244.

———— Eberhart-Wright, A. (1988), Affective exchanges between high risk mothers and infants. *Internat. J. Psycho-Anal.,* 69:221–231.

———— ———— Ware, L. M., & Hann, D. M. (1991), Children of adolescent mothers: Risk of psychopathology. Paper presented at the 37th International Psychoanalytic Association Meeting, Buenos Aires.

———— ———— ———— ———— (1992), Children of adolescent mothers: A group at risk for psychopathology. *Infant Mental Health J.,* 13:119–132.

Sorce, J. F., & Emde, R. N. (1981), Mother's presence is not enough: The effect of emotional availability on infant exploration. *Develop. Psychol.,* 17/6:737–745.

Sroufe, L. A. (1983), Infant–caregiver attachment and patterns of adaptation in preschool: The roots of maladaptation and competence. In: *Minnesota Symposium on Child Psychology,* Vol. 16, ed. M. Perlmutter. Hillsdale, NJ: Lawrence Erlbaum.

Verthelyi, R. (1986), Adolescent and adult mothers' responses to the IFEEL Pictures in Argentina. Typescript.

Winnicott, D. W. (1989), The squiggle game. In: *Psychoanalytic Explorations: D. W. Winnicott,* ed. C. Winnicott, R. Shepherd, & M. Davis. Cambridge, MA: Harvard University Press, pp. 299–317.

Appendix A

Appendix A includes material which clarifies or exemplifies the history and use of the IFEEL Pictures as described in chapters 3 and 4. In this appendix, you will find a table which defines the evolution of the Picture Sets described throughout the book, a history of the collaboration, examples of our two subject response forms, and examples of the IFEEL Pictures Lexicon used for scoring the data. Also included in the Appendix is information about how to obtain a computer program for scoring and analysis of the IFEEL data.

Appendix A-1

Photograph Sets in the Evolution of the IFEEL Pictures
(numbers identify individual pictures)

Photo Set A-70	B-38	C-40	Ref. 145 E-40	P-22	G-30	IFP*
Chapter 3, 4	3, 8	9	4	8, 9	7, 10, 14	
Photos	Photos	Photos	1	1	1	102
1-70	1-35	1-35	2	2	2	101
	of A-70	of A-70	5	5	5	103
Reported	Plus	Plus	6	6	6	104
in Emde	3 B & W	Photos	7	7	···	···
et al.,	Photos	Listed	8	8	···	···
1985	from	Below	9	9	9	105
	Izard		10	10	···	···
			11	11	11	107
			12	12	12	108
			···	···	···	···
			···	···	···	···
			···	···	···	···
			17	17	17	109
			···	···	···	···
			19	19	19	121
			20	20	20	110
			21	21	···	···
			22	22	22	112

Photo Set			Ref. 145			
A-70	B-38	C-40	E-40	P-22	G-30	IFP*
Chapter						
3, 4	3, 8	9	4	8, 9	7, 10, 14	
			23	23	···	···
			26	26	···	···
			27	27	27	113
			···	···	···	···
			···	···	···	···
			30	30	30	114
			31	31	31	115
			32	32	32	116
			34	34	34	118
		36	36	···	36	119
		41	41	···	41	120
		···	43	···	43	122
		···	45	···	···	···
		48	48	···	48	123
		···	50	···	···	···
		59	59	···	···	···
		···	61	···	61	125
		···	62	···	62	126
		64	64	···	64	127
			65	···	65	128
			67	···	···	···
			201	···	201	129
			303	···	303	106
			305	···	305	111
			306	···	306	117
			307	···	307	124
			308	···	308	130

*All pictures on the same row are the same pictures. The change of numbers from G-30 to IFP was done for convenience and clarity.

Appendix A-2
Listing of Recent Collaborative Efforts

1978–1981. Collaboration with the University of Delaware, Carroll Izard and Laboratory. IFEEL Pictures set A-70. Chapters 2 and 3.

> Emde, R. N., Izard, C., Huebner, R., Sorce, J. F., & Klinnert, M. D. (1985), Adult judgments of infant emotions: Replication studies within and across laboratories. *Inf. Behav. & Develop.*, 8/1:79–88.

1980. NIMH Collaboration. IFEEL Pictures, set C-40. Marian Radke-Yarrow, Carolyn Zahn-Waxler, and Ronald Iannotti; chapter 9.

1981. Cornell Collaboration. IFEEL Pictures, set D-40 sent to Daniel Stern, Terrel Kaplan, and Sandra Kaplan for use with assessment of abused mothers and children.

1981. Topeka Collaboration begins. IFEEL Pictures, set D-40 to Joy Osofsky and Anne Culp. Modification of this set begins collaboratively. Leading to Reference Sample development and statistical validation of current IFP.

1983. University of Pittsburgh. IFEEL Pictures, set D-40 sent to Paul Taylor.

1984. L. C. Blackwood, Ann Lodge. IFEEL Pictures, set G-30. Clinical intervention study of maternal emotional responsiveness; chapter 10.

1984. Colorado State University. IFEEL Pictures, set E-30. Doreen Ridgeway. Dimensional vs. discrete scoring of the IFEEL Pictures; chapter 6.

1985. Menninger Foundation. Joy Osofsky and Anne Culp. A study of Adolescent Parents. IFEEL Pictures, set E-30; chapter 7.

1985. Lawrence, Kansas, Rex Culp. Study of test-retest situations using IFEEL Pictures, three-six-nine months; chapter 5.

1986. University of Connecticut, Nathan Szajnberg —Mothers of premature babies—in clinical interviews and follow up situations; chapters 10 and 12.

1986. Peter de Chateau, Karolinska Institute, Sweden, IFP with Swedish mothers—picture set modified. Typescript.

1986. Renata Verthelyi, Universidad Belgrano, Buenos Aires, Argentina. Adolescent and adult mothers' responses to IFP in Argentina. Typescript.

1987. Toronto, Canada, Hospital for Sick Children. Miri Halperin-Elian. 150 normal mothers. Controls for twin study, Set G-30.

1987. University of North Carolina, Chapel Hill. Mark Appelbaum. Statistical considerations of the IFEEL evaluation.

1988. Keigo Okonogi, Keio University, Tokyo, Japan, development of Japanese IFEEL Pictures and comparison studies with IFP. Publication in Japanese.

Some Continued Research Underway Using IFP.

Alain Lazartigues—Paris, France
Flavia Costa—Brazil
Keryl Egan—Sydney, Australia
Karin Grossman—Regensburg, Germany
Martha Cox—Child & Family Study, Morgantown, NC
Ann Easterbrooks—Tufts University, Medford, MA
Arietta Slade—City College, New York
Charles Zeanah—Bradley Hospital, Providence, RI

Appendix A-3

Individual Response Sheet: IFEEL Picture Set

Age: _____   Race: _____   Subject #: _____

Education: _____   Marital Status: _____   # of Children: _____

Sex of Children: ____ ____ ____   Age of Children: ____ ____ ____

Is mother currently employed: _____   Type of employment: _____

Type of employment (father): _____   Total family annual income:

Type of child care, if any: _____   ____ $10,000

Hours of child care per week: _____   ____ $11,000 - $25,000

____ $26,000 - $40,000

____ $41,000 and above

101. _____	116. _____
102. _____	117. _____
103. _____	118. _____
104. _____	119. _____
105. _____	120. _____
106. _____	121. _____
107. _____	122. _____
108. _____	123. _____
109. _____	124. _____
110. _____	125. _____
111. _____	126. _____
112. _____	127. _____
113. _____	128. _____
114. _____	129. _____
115. _____	130. _____

8/88
PMB

Appendix A-4
Dimensional Code Sheet

Below is a copy of the Affect Grid you have just read about. Now you are ready
to use the grid to describe each picture in the picture booklet. Write in the
space at the bottom of each grid the picture number and the word which describes
the strongest and clearest feeling the baby in the picture is expressing. Then,
put an "X" on the Grid where you believe this word or feeling state belongs.

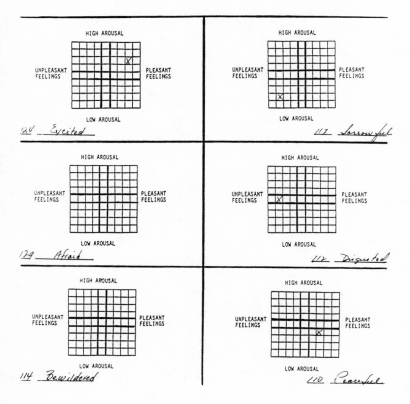

124 _Excited_

112 _Sorrowful_

129 _Afraid_

112 _Disgusted_

114 _Bewildered_

110 _Peaceful_

Appendix A-5
Scoring the IFEEL Pictures

The IFEEL Pictures are scored from a Lexicon of emotion words used and mapped by mothers to describe the baby pictures. It is enclosed with the IFEEL manual. The Lexicon provides a code score for words grouped by emotion category and also gives coordinate scores, arousal and hedonic tone, for word placement on the emotion map. Examples of some of the emotion categories are included in the following pages.

A computer-scoring program designed for standard IBM-compatible DOS or MacIntosh systems is available. The program is entitled "The IFEEL Computer Scoring Program" and was prepared by Mark Appelbaum and Gregory Kean. It assigns both categorical and dimensional scores as the word is typed and will calculate group Means and Standard Deviations. The program also calculates t-test values, comparing your data with the Reference Sample. This program may be purchased by writing to Mark Appelbaum, Ph.D., George Peabody College for Teachers, Department of Psychology and Human Development, Vanderbilt University, Box 512, Nashville, TN 37203.

THE IFEEL PICTURES LEXICON
Examples below represent emotions from each of the
quadrants on the Dimensional Emotions Map

High Arousal; Positive Hedonic Tone

Joy
Emotion C

Enthusiastic	7.6	8.1
Excited	7.4	8.4
Exhilarated	7.4	8.3
Feeling good	8.1	6.8
Feeling important	7.4	6.7
Fine	7.7	6.8
Flirting/flirtatious	6.9	7.3
Friendly	7.6	6.8
Fulfill/ed/ment	8.2	6.5
Fun	7.7	6.7
Giggly	7.8	7.7
Glad/ness	8.3	7.1
Glee/ful	7.9	7.4
Happy	8.4	7.5

Low Arousal; Positive Hedonic Tone

Content
Emotion D

Accepting	7.2	5.3
Agreeable	6.8	5.3
Appeased	6.8	4.0
Asleep	8.0	1.4
At ease	6.1	3.9
At peace	7.9	3.5
Bliss	7.5	5.4
Calm	6.9	3.2
Casual	6.9	4.7
Comfortable	7.7	3.8
Complacent	7.7	5.1
Consoled	6.1	3.9
Content/ed	7.3	4.2
Daydreaming	7.2	3.8
Docile	6.8	2.6

Low Arousal; Negative Hedonic Tone		
	Sad	
	Emotion F	
Abandoned/ment	1.5	2.5
About to cry	2.1	4.5
Agony	1.5	3.8
Alone	3.3	4.3
Brokenhearted	1.9	4.5
Crushed	2.3	4.4
Dejected/ion	2.3	3.4
Depressed/sion	2.1	2.2
Deserted	1.5	2.5
Desolate/tion	2.2	3.1
Despair	2.3	4.4
Devastated	1.5	3.8
Discouraged	2.2	4.0
Disheartened	2.5	3.7
Down	2.3	2.5

High Arousal; Negative Hedonic Tone		
	Fear	
	Emotion L	
Afraid	1.9	7.5
Alarm/ed	3.2	7.5
Anxious/anxiety	3.0	7.5
Apprehensive/ion	3.5	6.6
Avoiding/ance	3.2	6.0
Distrusting	1.9	6.8
Dread	1.8	6.0
Edgy	2.7	7.2
Escape/ing	4.6	7.3
Fear/ful	2.6	7.9
Freaked out	3.2	7.5
Fright/ened	2.0	8.0
Horror/horrified	1.7	8.5
Intimidated/ion	1.9	6.1
Leery	2.8	5.8

Appendix B

This appendix contains examples of the verbal transcripts resulting from the picture story task described in chapter 13. These transcripts illustrate differences in depressed and nondepressed mothers' affective communications with their children when talking about selected pictures of infant facial expressions of emotion.

Appendix B-1

Dyad 1

M: Here's a baby. Look at that baby.
  C: Ah, I like that one.
M: Yeah, there's the newborn's teeth.
    And that's #2.
  C: That baby, do you like that baby?
  C: Yeah. Oh.
M: That's baby #3.
  C: Oh.
M: What's wrong with this baby?
  C: She's crying.
M: Aw. That's baby #4.
  C: You wish I were a baby and I laughed like it.
M: Oh I love you just the way you are.
    Once you were a baby and you laughed and cried.
    See this baby.
  C: Yeah.
    Did you, you did make me cry?
M: #5.
    Did I make you cry?
    No I never tried to make you cry.
  C: What did I, what happened?
M: What happened to you when you would cry?
    I guess sometimes you would be hungry or sad.
    Or you'd have wet pants or you'd get a tummy ache.
  C: What a stuckache?
    I say stuckache. When I'm a baby.

M: A stuckache.

  C: A stuckache.

M: What's that book?

  C: . . .

M: She'll be back.

    Look at this baby book.

    That's your favorite kind.

    Chocolate baby.

  C: No it's not.

M: Here's #6.

    That baby's got hair this morning.

  C: #7.

M: There's #7.

    What's this one going to be then?

Appendix B-2

Dyad 2

M: Look at these pictures. Come on up. Let's go see. Look
at that.
This is baby 1. There's baby 1. Do you see baby? Look
at baby (C leaves room) Here's baby #2. What's
the baby doing? What's the baby doing?

C: Open the mouth.

M: (laughs) Open the mouth.

C: Open the mouth!

M: Yeah. Here's baby #3.

C: That's baby.

M: That's a baby. Oh, Here's baby #4.

C: Baby cry.

M: Yea.

C: Baby really sad.

M: Oh, I know it. We don't like to see that. Oh, there's
baby #5.

C: Cry.

M: Yea.

C: Cry.

M: Well, sort of. Baby #6.

C: Baby number.

M: There's baby #7.

C: Yea.

M: Baby #8.

C: Cry.

M: Yea.

C: It's boy. It's a boy.
M: It's a boy and look at that.

Appendix B-3

Dyad 3

M: Look at this baby.
Does this look a bit like Christopher?
Look like this baby.
  C: Does it.
M: I think it does.
Now what's the baby doing?
  C: I don't know.
M: Well he's looking at something.
Got his eyes on something, looking at something.
  C: His house.
M: He's looking at what?
  C: His house.
M: His house. He's looking at the top of his house.
  C: Top of his house.
M: He's looking up at the top of his house, I see.
This is baby #2.
  C: Is that Anthony's baby?
M: It's not Anthony's baby but it looks a bit like Anthony's
       baby, doesn't it?
  C: Who's he looking to?
M: Who's he looking at?
He's looking at you.
I think he was looking at the camera, wasn't he?
Who took the photo, do you think?
  C: I don't know.
M: Maybe it was his mommy.

What's this baby doing?

C: He's looking at me.

M: He's looking at you. Is he a cheerful baby or a sad
       baby?

C: Cheerful baby.

M: He's cheerful, yes?
     What's he smiling at?

C: Me, me.

M: He's smiling at you.

C: Yeah.

M: That's nice.
     What's this baby.

C: I don't know.

M: This is baby three.

C: I wanna go home . . . nap.

M: What's that baby doing?

C: I don't know.

M: You don't know. It's just another baby.
     That baby has a lot of hair I think. Doesn't it?
     It's got more hair than the other baby.
     I think that's an older baby.

C: Think it.

M: This is baby #4.

Appendix B-4

Dyad 3 (Continued)

C: He looks a little bit sad.

M: He does.
Poor baby.
This is baby #5.
How does he look . . . to you?

C: Terrible.

M: He looks terrible.
Poor baby, he's so upset.

C: Who made him upset?

M: Who made him upset?

C: Yeah.

M: Who do you think did that?

C: I don't know.

M: You don't know. I think it was maybe his brother.
Maybe his brother did that, do you think?

C: I don't know.

M: Do you think his brother took a toy away from him?
Made him upset.

C: Yeah.

M: Or maybe he's hungry.

C: Yeah.

M: Babies sometimes cry when they are hungry.

C: No. This one looks happy.

M: This one looks happy.
Let me look at his number. He's baby #6.
And he looks happy. He's got a smile on.

C: What's he?

M: Here's baby seven.

C: Seven.

M: Is he happy?

C: Yeah.

M: He's happy. Well, that's good.
Baby #8.

C: Two babies.
xxx in front of them, right mom?

M: No. I think they must be chairs.
I think he's sitting on a chair.
See back there.

C: I want a happy baby.

Appendix C:
The Japanese IFEEL Pictures

Kako Inoue, Yoko Hamada, Chikako Fukatsu,
Toshiko Takiguchi, Keigo Okonogi

This appendix contains a brief report on work done with the IFP in Japan. It describes the development of the Japanese IFEEL Pictures and subsequent studies using one or both picture sets.

The infant's emotional development depends on how the mother or caregiver reads the emotional signals that the baby sends, how she processes them in her own intrapsychic world, and how she conveys the result to her infant. In order to do this, she must recognize her infant's emotions, adjust accordingly, and react appropriately.

In order to determine whether or how mothers attune themselves affectively and make themselves emotionally available, the IFEEL Pictures technique was developed to measure a mother's ability to read the expressions of infants. Based on this technique, the present study was designed to develop a new set of pictures aimed toward Japanese people, particularly mothers, which will be called the Japanese IFEEL Pictures (JIFP).

Support for this research comes from the Yasuda Life Welfare Foundation 1988–1990 to Kako Inoue, and from The Foundation for the Development and Promotion of Psychoanalysis 1988–1989 to Yoko Hamada and Keigo Okonogi.

299

We believe that empirical research regarding the ability of mothers to read or empathize with an infant's emotional signals is necessary if we are to help support healthy mother–child relationships and sustain the healthy development of children.

Evaluation of the IFEEL Pictures in Japan

The IFEEL Pictures (IFP United States version) were administered to Japanese subjects in December 1987. The IFP were made into slides and presented to a total of 540 unmarried women and pregnant women, who were asked to write down the emotions that they recognized using a free response method.

The responses of thirty of the subjects were selected at random and classified by the KJ method. The KJ method (Kawakita, 1987) consisted of integrating the various ideas during a brainstorming session. The free responses were grouped into separate concepts with each concept forming the basis for a new category system. Although this system has many points in common with the category system developed for use in this book (see chapters 4 and 5) it also presents a number of unique characteristics. For instance, the Japanese category system includes "refusal" in the "fear" category and includes a new category, "withdrawn."

The results of this primary study were presented at the Pacific Rim Congress of the World Association of Infant Psychiatry and Allied Disciplines held in Hawaii April 1988.

While proceeding with the study described above, we realized that it was vital that the respondents have a sense of kinship with the photographic stimuli. Unless the photographic stimuli were familiar to the respondents, their

Requests for information should be sent to: Kako Inoue, % Keigo Okonogi, Department of Neuropsychiatry, Keio University, School of Medicine, Shinanomachi, Tokyo, Japan.

answers might be purely conjectural and hence show less of a personal "pull." Because the IFP presents American infants as models, it held little familiarity for many Japanese respondents; therefore, we felt it was necessary to reconstitute the IFP with Japanese infants as models.

Development of the Japanese IFEEL Picture Test

PURPOSE

We began developing the Japanese IFEEL Picture technique in May 1988 on the basis of the above considerations. Although this picture set is based on the American IFP, its photographic stimuli and category system were developed independently.

Our purpose was to empirically corroborate that this technique can help demonstrate individual differences in the way mothers, women in general, and men read infants' emotional signals. In addition, we aimed to provide a tool for exploring cultural differences for reading signals. The first steps of our research therefore involved the selection of photographic stimuli, the gathering of a large amount of data, and standardization of the set.

The process of developing the JIFP followed the protocol described below.

DESCRIPTION OF SELECTION OF PICTURES

Twenty-five 12-month-old infants were selected and their parents were asked if their infants' pictures could be used for the JIFP guidelines. Three professional photographers photographed the infants in their homes. They were given the following instructions: (1) take the infant's portrait in its natural daily environment; (2) include the infant's various expressions; (3) avoid including objects or other people. Approximately 3500 pictures were taken. Twenty representative cuts of each of the twenty-five infants were printed. Five researchers on our team spent fifteen hours over seven days choosing approximately one hundred of these pictures for use in the test, according to the following criteria: (1) photographic quality (focus); (2) frontal shot or at most 45-degree profile; (3) the exclusion of mother's face, toys, or other objects; (4) in case of successive pictures of the same infant's expression, the shot with the best photographic quality was chosen; (5) when necessary, pictures were touched up to erase unwanted surroundings.

The selected pictures were grouped by the KJ method described above on the basis of the category systems which we had established for the American version of the IFEEL Pictures.

Four days after the selection of the pictures, the same group members narrowed the number of pictures down to sixty-eight. Another six were added in which the background had been blotted out, to evaluate the effect of the background, thus bringing the total to seventy-four.

These seventy-four pictures were shown to fifty-two adult subjects, fifteen men and thirty-seven women, who were physicians, clinical psychologists, nursery staff, and psychology students. Their ages ranged from 22 to 57 with the majority in their twenties and thirties. They were asked to describe the expressions they read in the pictures using a free response method.

After all of the responses had been gathered, four researchers classified these responses by the KJ method and prepared a new category system (Table C.1). This category system is comprised of twenty-seven categories and is more detailed than the system that had been formerly established for the IFEEL Pictures. The new system includes such categories as "boredom," "perseverance," "loneliness," "serenity," "object seeking" (*amae*), which were not part of our first category system.

Four researchers then coded the responses of the fifty-two subjects according to this new category system. The

TABLE C.1
Category System

1. Bubbling Joy	Happy, enjoying itself, laughing
2. Shyness	Shy, bashful, in fear of stranger
3. Fatigue	Tired, disappointed, depressed, looking blank, day dreaming
4. Thinking	Thinking, meditative, reflective
5. Anger	Feeling disagreeable, angry, rejection, feeling vexed, protest, feeling distaste, being shocked, feeling rebellious, irritated
6. Loneliness, sadness	Sad, feeling miserable, despondent, fragile
7. Sleep	Sleepy, sleeping
8. Anxiety	Anxious, cautious, what to do, tense, indecisive, in trouble, worried
9. Frustration	Frustrated, protesting, displeased, sulky, peevish, unconsolable, perverse
10. Self-assertiveness	Looking nonchalant, superior, selfish, self-assertion, egotistical, proud, satisfied
11. Fear	Fearful, scared
12. Suspicion	What's happened? What's up? That's funny.
13. Surprise	Surprised
14. Attention	Looking interested, concentrating, watchful, curious, expectant, finding something interesting
15. Object seeking	"Amae," affectionate, seeking object
16. Cry	Crying, wanting to cry, on the verge of crying
17. Pain	In pain, displeased, uncomfortable, in a bad mood, it's tough going in discomfort
18. Desire	Wanting, wanting to eat, longing for, hunger
19. No emotion	
20. Others	
21. Serenity	Feeling relaxed, calm, tranquil, peaceful, serene, satisfied, untroubled

Table C.1 *(Continued)*
Category System

22. Seeking attention	Amiable and charming, cute, frolicsome, amused
23. Envy	Envious, jealous
24. Boredom	Bored, disinterested
25. Perseverance	Persevering
26. Will	Strong-willed, tough-minded, hanging-in-there, enthusiastic, ready for challenge
27. Solitude, withdrawal	Alone, solitary, lonely, introverted, withdrawn

results from the fifty-two subjects were then pooled and a principal components analysis was done using the seventy-four photographic stimuli as items and the twenty-seven categories as samples. The results of the analysis gave an eigenvalue of 18.58 for the first principal component, 13.27 for the second, 9.97 for the third, and a cumulative contribution ratio of 53.4 percent down to the third principal component.

Four researchers then made the final selection of the photographic stimuli. They were guided according to the following criteria: (1) selection of representative pictures in view of the configuration of the principal component analysis; (2) photographic quality (focus); (3) diversity in the degree of ambiguity (pictures in which feelings could be easily recognized were included as well as those for which feelings were difficult to judge); (4) scattering of the response categories; (5) equal representation of the children used as models; (6) selection of pictures in which the percentage of categorized responses were close to the responses given to each picture of the IFEEL Pictures (chapters 4 and 5).

The above procedure led to the final selection of thirty pictures for use in the Japanese IFEEL Pictures.

PRELIMINARY STUDIES

In order to test the validity and reliability of the JIFP, we conducted the following experiment.

A total of 167 students (ages 19 to 20) at a women's junior college in Tokyo were involved in a series of experiments in April 1988. We compared their responses to the IFP and to the JIFP. To avoid the bias due to the order of the presentation, half of the 167 subjects were given the JIFP first and the IFP second and the order for the other half was reversed. The photographs of each test had been made into slides for projection, and subjects used free responses to describe what kind of emotions or feelings were appropriate for each picture. One hundred fifty-one of the students were retested using the JIFP one month later. All responses to the JIFP and the IFP were categorized twice by two independent raters into the 27 categories (Table C.1) previously developed.

COMPARISON OF THE IFEEL PICTURES AND JAPANESE PICTURE SET

To examine the correspondence between the two tests, in each of the twenty-seven categories, we analyzed the correlation and the mean difference among the two sets (Table C.2).

There was a significant correlation at the $p < 0.01$ level between the frequencies of using each category in the IFP and the JIFP. From these results, one can conclude that the two picture sets are measuring the same psychological aspects.

Interestingly, there were differences in respondents' attributions for the twenty-seven categories in the two picture sets. The Japanese pictures had significantly more bubbling joy, shyness, anger, sleep, self-assertiveness, object seeking (*amae*), no emotion, seeking attention, envy,

TABLE C.2
Correlations and Differences in Frequencies of Using Each
Category in Response to JIFP/IFP Photo Sets

Category	IFP/JIFP	Mean	S.D.	Corr. Coeff.	T value	
1	IFP	2.12	1.11	0.545**	−10.91**	J>I
	JIFP	3.45	1.88			
2	IFP	0.31	0.57	0.410**	−5.41**	J>I
	JIFP	0.65	0.87			
3	IFP	0.82	1.05	0.341**	−1.35	
	JIFP	0.94	1.03			
4	IFP	0.40	0.91	0.606**	2.11*	I>J
	JIFP	0.27	0.79			
5	IFP	2.45	1.69	0.460**	−1.03	J>I
	JIFP	2.60	1.77			
6	IFP	2.69	1.92	0.649**	8.85**	I>J
	JIFP	1.60	1.57			
7	IFP	0.57	0.79	0.390**	−16.76**	J>I
	JIFP	2.07	1.22			
8	IFP	2.54	1.75	0.501**	7.10**	I>J
	JIFP	1.49	1.25			
9	IFP	1.87	1.47	0.436**	−1.85	
	JIFP	2.10	1.58			
10	IFP	0.47	0.81	0.425**	−4.97**	J>I
	JIFP	0.85	1.03			
11	IFP	1.29	1.19	0.464**	9.02**	I>J
	JIFP	0.54	0.77			
12	IFP	2.14	2.04	0.631**	3.30**	I>J
	JIFP	1.75	1.64			
13	IFP	2.47	1.41	0.301**	11.46	I>J
	JIFP	1.19	1.09			
14	IFP	3.67	2.41	0.588**	7.08**	I>J
	JIFP	2.57	1.96			

TABLE C.2

Correlations and Differences in Frequencies of Using Each
Category in Response to JIFP/IFP Photo Sets

Category	IFP/JIFP	Mean	S.D.	Corr. Coeff.	T value	
15	IFP	0.50	0.89	0.424**	−3.07**	J>I
	JIFP	0.73	0.93			
16	IFP	0.25	0.77	0.663**	1.19	
	JIFP	0.20	0.56			
17	IFP	0.89	1.13	0.545**	0.37	
	JIFP	0.86	1.07			
18	IFP	0.49	0.88	0.359	1.36	
	JIFP	0.40	0.65			
19	IFP	1.56	2.14	0.711**	−3.37	J>I
	JIFP	2.04	2.66			
21	IFP	1.33	1.20	0.379**	−1.78	
	JIFP	1.73	1.48			
22	IFP	0.07	0.35	0.286**	−2.64	J>I
	JIFP	0.16	0.41			
23	IFP	0.22	0.46	0.391**	−2.98**	J>I
	JIFP	0.36	0.62			
24	IFP	0.54	0.93	0.387**	−2.17**	J>I
	JIFP	0.72	1.00			
25	IFP	0.18	0.48	0.284**	−4.14**	J>I
	JIFP	0.39	0.57			
26	IFP	0.10	0.53	0.200**	−3.39**	J>I
	JIFP	0.23	0.48			
27	IFP	0.07	0.25	0.280**	0.83	
	JIFP	0.05	0.21			

N = 169.
**P > 0.01.
 *P > 0.05.

boredom, perseverance, and will. The IFP had more thinking, loneliness, sadness, anxiety, fear, suspicion, surprise, and attention.

TEST–RETEST RELIABILITY

To test the reliability of the JIFP, this technique was administered twice, one month apart. The results indicated that there were significant correlations between test–retest administrations for all twenty-seven categories, with correlation coefficients ranging from 0.21 to 0.63 ($p < 0.01$ in all instances).

Ongoing Studies and Future Studies

In future studies we are broadening the range of subjects to include men, including fathers and fathers to be, mothers, pregnant women, adolescents. We are also including clinical cases such as mothers with postpartum depression, neglecting mothers, and abusing mothers. Moreover, Yoko Hamada has administered the IFP to schizophrenic mothers and normal mothers as the subject of her thesis for a medical doctorate.

In the future, we plan to administer the JIFP to a non-Japanese population in order to examine the cross-cultural differences and similarities. Further research will also include refinement of our category system. Finally, we plan to apply the JIFP to a wide range of samples in order to provide data for standardization.

Reference

Kawakita, J. (1987), *Conceptualization*. Tokyo: Chuukoushinsho (in Japanese).

Name Index

309

Subject Index

315